HUMANS, MACHINES, AND DATA

HUMANS, MACHINES, AND DATA

Future Trends in Warfare

BRENT M. EASTWOOD

Published by EBookPbook
Printed in the United States of America

ISBN: 9798721855269 (paperback)

TABLE OF CONTENTS

INTRODUCTION

War is a human endeavor. It is also a sociological struggle. It can be studied in a manner that considers sociopolitical change, as the sociologist Morris Janowitz reminded us in his analysis of war and peace that he wrote in 1975. This was during one of the most tumultuous times in American history – when Saigon fell, and the country was torn apart by war guilt. Since Vietnam, there have been numerous iterations of social change, reform, and technology in warfare, many of them grounded in the sociology of the military. For example, the advent of the volunteer force rather than dependence on the draft changed the social organization of the military, but that happened decades ago. Thus, my book is a much-needed update on the sociology of war – a literature that has been neglected for years. The last definitive work, "Sinisa Malesevic's *The Sociology of War and Violence,* was published in 2010, in which Malesevic wrote about the "sociology of new warfare," among other types of sociopolitical analysis of war and organized violence.[1]

My book is also about the future and it posits that future war is more human than the imminent predictions of the rising supremacy of machines and data. This book analyzes technology, whether it be drones, robotics, the cyber domain, information war, or artificial intelligence. It envisions a battlefield filled with technological wonders that will

[1] Malesevic, Sinisa. 2010. *The Sociology of War and Violence.* Cambridge: University Printing House.

transform conflict as we know it. In this book I argue that the sociology of war drives technology and technology drives the sociology of war.

This book has three target audiences. Academics are one audience since I make the argument that war is a sociological struggle, and sociology may not be top of mind to many readers. Academic social scientists are well-versed in the discipline and will recognize the finer points. Those who are warfare experts and military practitioners will find ample reading about numerous facets of future warfare. Those who are general interest readers who love the examination of the future are targeted too since I include many aspects of future war that will appeal to a broader audience. If you like futuristic studies, this book is for you. You will be amazed by the future technologies I describe. No other book on future warfare paints on such a broad, comprehensive canvas.

I would ask readers from the general public to be patient as I examine sociology because you may have a yearning to get to the future analysis in a "hurry." I will try to accommodate your interests as best as I can. If you are not interested in sociology, you will instead be mesmerized by the technology analyzed in this book. You will find a huge bounty of military technology beginning in Chapter Four – the chapter on "Super Soldiers." For those in academia, it is important to not overcomplicate warfare analysis. The fight, above all, is comprised of humans and their tools, machines, and data. This book is an effort to expound upon that simple statement. For example, my chapter on transnational crime is a study on how war can be focused on the basic human desires of money and power. Studying transnational criminal organizations and the technology they use, such as their submarines that can haul narcotics from one continent to another, is the portrayal of a tech-savvy social movement.

Analysts such as Peter L. Hickman are skeptical that future warfare will be so dependent on machines and data. He believes warfare will continue to be human and that artificial intelligence will not rule the world. In 2020, Hickman wrote, "First, the glacially paced military change of recent memory suggests battlefields 15 years hence will likely look more familiar than some may think. Second, military analysts have been erroneously forecasting revolutionary change just around the corner for at least four decades. And third, research demonstrates that technological overmatch does not significantly increase the likelihood of military victory."[2]

I hope that my writing will not be regulated to the dustbin of erroneous predictions of revolutionary technology as Hickman warns. The study of war and sociology may save me from this predicament. Sociologist Max Weber leaps to mind when pondering any sociological analysis. Weber is history's most accomplished sociologist, and he will be quoted throughout the book. It is imperative that I explain his views on war and that you understand Weber because he wrote about numerous themes in warfare. His views on victory, righteousness, psychology, morality, and ethics of conflict are profound. Weber was also concerned about the future of warfare and added that it is the "*future* which above all burdens the victor."[3]

Do humans, machines, and data make victory in warfare more or less likely? Do humans have a closer relationship to war and violence than they do to peace and tranquility? Who actually benefits from warfare and who wins the peace?

Weber answered, "For the victors, at least for part of them, the war would have been politically profitable. And the responsibility of this rests on behavior that made all resistance impossible for us. Now, as a result of the *ethics* (emphasis added) of absolutism, when the period of exhaustion will have passed, the peace will be discredited, not the war."[4]

---

2 Hickman, Peter. 2020. "The Future of Warfare Will Continue to Be Human." *War on the Rocks*. May 12, 2020.

3 Gerth, H.H. and C. Wright Mills. 1946. *From Max Weber: Essays in Sociology*. New York: Oxford University Press. Pg. 118.

4 *Ibid*, pg. 120.

War is organized violence fought by social organizations – be they nation-state armies or non-state actors. Military force has become more bureaucratic, as Malesevic wrote, "What characterizes modern armies, is not the personal and emotional displays of bravery but an efficient bureaucratic machinery of war."[5]

The bureaucratization of violence keeps soldiers fighting in-person combat even though there have been revolutions of military affairs over the decades that would seem to place more emphasis on machines than on humans. War is often political, and the violence gets messy for humans, as the great Prussian strategist Carl von Clausewitz reminded us. Weber agreed. "The most important means of politics is violence. There is no politics which in the last instance is not rooted in the use of force, or the threat of its use, and violence is seen by Weber as the raison d'etre of the state's existence."[6]

The sociology of war also lends itself to the study of social megatrends. Various topics in demographics and the sociological operating environment give us clues about how war will be fought in the future. We live in groups and we are socially stratified, so an analysis of demographic pressures such as urbanization, corruption, and migration is necessary.

Sociologist Morris Janowitz wrote, "The institutional analysis of war and peace has to reassess the fundamental similarities and differences between the management of violence in a variety of industrialized nations and developing nations. Global and undifferentiated concepts, like modernization, have failed to help clarify the issue at stake. The routes to 'modernity' are diverse, and students of sociopolitical change must keep in mind the divergent dimensions of urbanization and industrialization and modernization."[7]

---

5 Malesevic, Sinisa, pg. 28.

6 *Ibid*, pg. 26

7 Janowitz, Morris. 1975. *Military Conflict: Essays in the Institutional Analysis of War and Peace*. Beverly Hills, CA: Sage Publications, pg. 12.

In 2010, 51.6 percent of the world's total population lived in cities, by 2020, that percentage had gone up to 55.7 percent, according to the World Bank.[8] That is an eight percent increase in one decade. Conflict-prone states have high rates of urban dwellers. States in which conflict has a higher likelihood, such as Libya, Iran, Israel, Venezuela, Oman, Saudi Arabia, and South Korea – all have urban populations over 80 percent of the total population, according to the United Nations.[9]

The WorldinData.org reported that in 2020, "More than 4 billion people – more than half of the world – live in urban areas."[10] This affects international security as more conflict will also reach cities. Training and doctrine of the world's militaries will emphasize warfare in urban areas. Also, cities have populations of unemployed and idle young people that can be recruited into the military or radicalized to join extremist terror groups.

Each year Transparency International conducts its Corruption Perception Index which scores countries based on their perceived levels of government corruption, according to experts and businesspeople.[11] The least corrupt countries are Denmark, New Zealand, Finland, Singapore, Sweden, and Switzerland. The most corrupt countries are Venezuela, Yemen, Syria, South Sudan, and Somalia. One can correlate these states' corruption rating to levels of peace and war. Top scoring states are more likely to be peaceful, while the most corrupt states are likely to have conflict. This falls into the "Democratic Peace Theory," in which less corrupt democracies rarely fight each other. Corruption

---

8 "Urban Population (% of Total Population)." United Nations Population Division. World Urbanization Prospects. 2018 Revision.

9 "Urban Population (% of Total Population." Country Ranking. United Nations Population Division. World Urbanization Prospects. 2018 Revision.

10 Ritchie, Hannah and Max Rosen. "Urbanization." Our World In Data. Revised November 2019.

11 "Corruption Perceptions Index." 2020. Transparency International.

also plays a role in how well governments can staff their militaries. The more corrupt a state is, the less likely it is able to sustain an ethical, professional, and well-trained group of officers and non-commissioned officers.

Migration is another sociological megatrend that affects the level of security around the world. Migration can often become a death sentence, or at the very least, can rob one of a peaceful life. The United Nations described "the displacements of millions of people due to conflict such as within and from Syria, Yemen, the Central African Republic, the Democratic Republic of the Congo and South Sudan."[12]

Sometimes sociological trends involve healthcare and biodefense. The coronavirus and Covid-19 pandemic has infected over 100 million people and killed over two million. The U.S. military has responded. The U.S. Army and the army and Air National Guard has been deployed throughout the country offering medical screening, testing, and logistics support. The National Guard Covid-19 response has administered nearly three million tests and over 7,000 missions that support testing and screening.[13] Guard personnel have packaged and delivered nearly 200 million meals, over 88,000 tons of bulk food, 29,000 pallets of essential medical supplies, and have driven nearly two million miles in support of Covid-19 re-supply missions in the United States.[14] The active-duty U.S. Army cut down on the troops it supplied to NATO wargames in 2020 because of the pandemic.

The United States is not alone. Covid-19 has affected militaries around the globe. Saudi Arabia called a temporary cease-fire in its conflict with Houthi rebels in Yemen in 2020 because of the pandemic. Israel has been forced to adjust. Its frontline troops have been shifted

---

12 "World Immigration Report." 2020. Center of China and Globalization. International Organization of Migration: United Nations.

13 Olsen, Ken. 2020. "Rapid Response." *The American Legion Magazine*. July 21, 2020.

14 *Ibid.*

to hand out food, to make sure quarantines are followed, to help senior citizens, and to staff healthcare centers. The Israelis also canceled some military exercises. South Korea sent 2,700 troops to conduct similar medical operations to fight Covid-19. India also canceled training maneuvers.

Many global security threats are still geopolitical in nature. President Joe Biden's main worries are China, Russia, North Korea, and Iran. China has a pre-ponderance of power and an advanced nuclear missile program. Russia has leapt forward with military technology. North Korea, after each passing moment, gets closer to the capability of mating a nuclear warhead on a ballistic missile. Iran has "nuclear fever" as well. Iran is still livid about one of its nuclear scientists being assassinated in 2020, likely by Israel. Iran is also facing even more economic sanctions that were tacked on at the end of Donald Trump's presidency. This book will also cover China, Russia, North Korea, and Iran's future weapons, information warfare, drones, and artificial intelligence.

Meanwhile, sociological threats still crop up in the developing world. Societal food insecurity is becoming a global problem and mega-trend. The United Nations stated that 2021 and 2022 will be some of the worst years of famine in at least 50 years. Covid-19 and rising food prices have led to this crisis. The Atlantic Council wrote about a long list of affected countries. "The World Food Program believes that Yemen, South Sudan, Nigeria, and Burkina Faso may already be suffering famine conditions. Afghanistan, Cameroon, the Central African Republic, Congo, Ethiopia, Haiti, Lebanon, Mali, Mozambique, Niger, Sierra Leone, Somalia, Sudan, Syria, Venezuela, and Zimbabwe are not far away from it."[15]

These mega-trends are not often mentioned when examining warfare. This book takes sociological mega-trends into account, but it also

---

[15] Burrows, Mathew. And Robert A. Manning. "The Top Ten Risks and Opportunities for 2021." *New Atlanticist*. Atlantic Council. Dec. 16, 2020.

drills down to the individual soldier and the future of human combat. A chapter on soldier survivability, biotechnology, and the rise of so-called super soldiers will further explicate the future of the individual soldier. We will see gene editing for soldiers in our lifetime and it will be a race to determine which government can breed the super soldiers fast enough.

Chapter One deals with the context of the current global operating environment of warfare with a greater explication of sociology and war. It uses Afghanistan as the main case study to explain the condition of "Endless War," and how the political elites stumble into Endless Wars. It also introduces the notion of the warrior culture in Afghanistan. Chapter One reviews the future of counter-insurgency in South Asia, the Middle East, and Africa. It examines the rise of the Russian brand of hybrid warfare. I also unveil a new concept called the "gamification of war."

Chapter Two examines the future of transnational criminal organizations and their effects on international security. It looks at violence perpetuated by charismatic leaders. It reveals new technology used by narco-cartels with drones, submarines, and tunnels. Chapter Two also highlights the emergence of the deadly Jalisco New Generation Cartel. It explains the nexus between cartels and terror. It describes criminal gangs from Central America, South America, and Russia. The chapter unveils the use of blockchain technology to better combat arms traffickers and it looks at technological answers for responding to wildlife smuggling and poaching.

Chapter Three investigates how a changing climate will require a military response. Climate change is also a sociopolitical struggle that encompasses humans, machines, and data. The chapter will show how climate change and anti-access area denial challenges military forces. U.S. military bases will feel the pain. With climate change, the Arctic becomes a focal point. The British military faces difficult choices due to climate change. Australia, New Zealand, and Canada are priming their forces to deal with a changing climate. Chapter Three also shows how failing and fragile states in Africa are in danger.

Chapter Four looks at biotechnology regarding individual military personnel, and how gene editing can produce Super soldiers. It examines how soldiers are using exoskeletons and illustrates how they could become cyborgs and be connected to computers. It also describes military personnel and how biotechnology and biomechanics will emerge as important aspects of combat.

Chapter Five describes future weapons systems – both nuclear and conventional. It features hypersonic weapons, electromagnetic rail guns, 3D and 4D printing, and 5G and even 6G military networks. It also has the latest on weapons systems from China, Russia, North Korea, Iran, Britain, and Israel.

Chapter Six discusses how quantum computing can revolutionize the battlefield. It asks whether the human mind can control a drone. It has an overview of unmanned programs from the United States, China, Russia, Iran, North Korea, Israel, and the United Kingdom. It examines how robots can lead to advances in logistics and combat capabilities.

Chapter Seven is on warfare in the cyber domain. It asks if U.S. Cyber Command can come to the rescue and whether a government can classify a cyber-attack in the correct manner. It shows how outer space is the new cyber battlefield. It introduces the notion of "perfect storm" cyber-attacks. Chapter Seven describes how blockchain, virtual reality, and artificial intelligence can alter the balance in cyber warfare. It examines how defense contractors can divulge secrets when attacked by ransomware. It also explains how Russian cyber warfare is a one-of-a-kind phenomenon.

Chapter Eight delineates information warfare. Russia, China, Iran, North Korea, and non-state actors are adept at information warfare. Classic information warfare is practiced by Israel and Hamas. Political operatives are using artificial intelligence bots, computational propaganda, human trolls, election meddling, and deep fakes. The chapter also shows how mass media can be part of information warfare and how information warfare can pave the way for a conventional battle.

Finally, Chapter Nine includes the future of artificial intelligence and introduces my novel concept of "Speed War." Speed war means that fighting by months, days, weeks, hours, and minutes could be reduced down to seconds or even nano-seconds. A human blink of the eye can miss a move on the battlefield. Neural networks, deep learning, and extremely big data have led to this state of affairs.

CHAPTER ONE

ENDLESS WARS, COUNTER-INSURGENCY, AND HYBRID CONFLICT

The War in Afghanistan is the Main Endless War

The future of warfare is steeped in sociology. Afghanistan is a prime example. I will focus on Afghanistan since it is the longest war in American history and because other countries in the NATO coalition have been involved to various extents. The war in Afghanistan has been prosecuted so long, that it has become a social organization in and of itself, and it has created its own bureaucracy. Social organization and bureaucracy are both broad tenets of the sociology of violence and conflict. The overarching institutions responsible for the war, such as NATO and the International Security Assistance Force (ISAF), have further bureaucratized the combat and re-building activity in the country. The conflict has become so institutionalized that is has led to charges that it has become an Endless War, another sociological critique. Since 9/11, the United States embarked on an ambitious nation-building project with tens of thousands of Americans serving in the theater. Britain still has around 850 troops deployed in Afghanistan in support roles as of 2021. So, the future of Afghanistan fits the construct of Endless War, even though peace talks with the Taliban have occurred over the last few years. But the Taliban refuse to meet conditions for a complete U.S.

pullout because there is still a risk of further attacks on U.S. and coalition forces.

U.S. President Joe Biden is reviewing the peace agreement that President Donald Trump negotiated with the Taliban in February of 2020. Biden is deciding whether to remove 2,500 American soldiers from Afghanistan to end the conflict. Weber wrote of Endless War in 1915 during World War One. "Every victory brings us further from peace. This is the uniqueness of the situation." He added, "The entire statesmanship of the last 25 years is collapsing, and it is very poor satisfaction always to have said it. The war can now last forever."[16]

Sociology is on display here as Afghanistan is primarily the setting of a cultural war with several different ethnicities that were indigenous to the country even before 9/11. Then ISAF added mainly personnel from the United States, United Kingdom, and Europe. It can be argued that the conflict over the last 20 years has become a boiling pot of different ethnicities. The Soviet experience in Afghanistan is further evidence that sociology matters in this part of the world. The Soviets also struggled with all the different ethnic groups in the country.

Afghanistan Has a Warrior Culture that Dominates the Country

War in Afghanistan can also be attributed to a "warrior caste" system of indigenous fighters trained by Americans, British, and other countries under the ISAF umbrella. The Afghan National Army itself numbers close to 180,000 members. To put this number in perspective, countries such as France, Taiwan, Saudi Arabia, Japan, and Mexico have a total number of personnel between 200,000 and 300,000. So, Afghanistan has a military of respectable size.

To further explicate the sociological theme, a gun culture also

---

[16] Garth and Mills. 1946. *From Max Weber*. New York: Oxford University Press. Pg. 39.

exists in Afghanistan. According to the military data repository MilitaryFactory.com, there are at least 60 different types and nomenclatures of small arms that are on the battlefield in Afghanistan.[17] Many of these are Soviet-era Kalashnikov rifles, but more modern arms have been introduced by the United States, United Kingdom, and ISAF. Judging by the proliferation of small arms over the last several decades, it is safe to say that Afghans have been socialized into warfare. Even without conflict with the Taliban and other extremist groups in Afghanistan and Pakistan, it is difficult to envision a region where complete military demobilization and disarmament could occur.

Small arms contribute to the warrior caste as a social organization in Afghanistan. Many families think owning a gun is as natural as drinking tea. And the family ties to small arms extend beyond the battlefield. Families, clans, tribes, and warlords own guns for protection of homes, crops, personal property, and familial pride. There is also a hint of masculinity associated with owning a gun. Many provincial Afghans would see that their masculinity would be robbed without a firearm.

Weber has addressed the notion of familial caste extensively in his writings about India, specifically caste and tribe, caste and status group, and caste and social rank.[18] This caste demarcation of sociology applies to Afghanistan and parts of Pakistan as well. Therefore, the notion of Endless War, is a cultural phenomenon based on warrior caste and gun culture. "Culture is a prime determinant of the nature of warfare," War historian John Keegan wrote.[19]

One can observe the warrior caste in action, when examining the Afghan fascination with violent sports such as dog fighting, bird sparring, and a combat sport called buzkashi that features horseback riding

---

[17] "Afghanistan Small Arms List (Current and Former Types)." Infantry/ Small Arms. MilitaryFactory.com.

[18] Garth and Mills. 1946. *From Max Weber*. New York: Oxford University Press.

[19] Keegan, John. 1993. *A History of Warfare*. New York: Alfred A. Knopf.

and dead animal carcasses. These so-called "blood sports" have huge gatherings that often attract Taliban suicide bombings.[20]

"These sports provide a mirror of Afghanistan's social and political climate, where money and power trump goodwill and historical alliances and where ethnic divides and tribalism undermine the most well-intentioned governance,"[21] according to Andrew Quilty writing in *Foreign Policy*.

Thus, Afghans become socialized into the very nature of combat at a young age through the fanfare of blood sports. Warfare becomes second nature, and the warrior caste lives on through adolescence and adulthood. This sociology of violence leads to an Endless War mentality.

On the Western side, Lecturer of Political Science and Sociology Sinisa Malesevic calls this development the bureaucratization of coercion. Western governments, through NATO and ISAF, have bureaucratized violence in Afghanistan – leading to an Endless War mindset.

The Bureaucratization of War in Afghanistan

Government agencies in the United States, such as the Special Inspector General of Afghanistan Reconstruction (SIGAR), serves as a watchdog agency over the profligate and often wasteful and fraudulent spending associated with the nation-building in the country. As of 2021, the United States has spent approximately $143 billion on reconstruction, easily eclipsing what was invested during the Marshall Plan.[22] Weber would not be surprised that the U.S. government had to create an extra layer of independent and autonomous bureaucracy to deal with the rampant waste, fraud, and abuse of the American reconstruction experience in Afghanistan. SIGAR is an example of a social organization

---

20 Quilty, Andrew. 2015. "Bloodsport." *Foreign Policy*. June 19, 2015.

21 *Ibid.*

22 https://www.sigar.mil/

that Malesevic calls "ever-expanding bureaucratic rationalism in the Weberian sense."[23]

These social organizations become more powerful over time when it comes to peacekeeping, reconstruction, and disarmament efforts in war zones. Afghanistan will face these challenges in the future. Western governments, particularly the United States and the United Kingdom, feel the pressure to participate in the Endless War concept. No political leader wants to be blamed for "losing" Afghanistan, although some politicians would not mind being the political hero who brings a successful peace agreement between the Afghan government and the Taliban.

Do Not Cut and Run; They Will Come to Your Country and Terrorize You

Western governments also do not want to be blamed for "cutting and running" from a war zone in which there have been countless casualties among civilians and ISAF military personnel. There is also a bureaucracy of coercion among American and British political leaders to not have their young men and women die in vain after fighting for nearly 20 years. In addition, there is a belief that if you do not fight militants abroad, they will come to your country and conduct terror and other forms of violence. The incidence of foreign fighters who have become trained and have experienced combat and are then radicalized into terrorism in Afghanistan have risen to a level that is notable. It is these fears that become socially ingrained in politics, policy, and public opinion when it comes to the war in Afghanistan.

Blood sports, small arms, private property, and the culture of warfare that citizens are socialized into in Afghanistan create a Forever War ethos. The Forever War mentality, among indigenous forces in Afghanistan, and in the White House, Congress, Downing Street, and Parliament must change, but how?

---

[23] Malesevic, Sinisa. 2010, pg. 7.

There is a populist movement in the United States, both on the Left and the Right, that has taken up the mantra of stopping Endless War in South Asia and the Middle East. President Donald Trump used it in speeches. Former British Labour leader Jeremy Corbyn has vocalized his disdain for Endless Wars. Some of this war resistance is driven by self-interest, political zeitgeist, popular sentiment, fear of losing, reticence in giving power to generals and admirals, and the yearning to be re-elected or staying in power. As Weber wrote, "In case of a lost war, the monarch has to fear for his throne, republican power holders and groups having vested interest in a republican constitution and have to fear the victorious general."[24]

The Power Elite Stumble Into Endless Wars

Sociologist C. Wright Mills feared this power elite in warfare, especially the power and dominance of corporations during World War Two. Mills believed that the military elite, generals, and admirals, plus the military bureaucracy, were beholden to corporations. Accordingly, the U.S. government spent enormous sums on the military. Thus, he wrote, "generals advised corporation presidents and corporation presidents advised generals."[25]

Prussian military sage Carl von Clausewitz nearly predicted this corporatist relationship. One of Clausewitz's main contributions, the Trinity, is comprised of the People, the Commander and his army, and the Government.[26] Corporations were obviously not an issue during Clausewitz's time when he theorized about early 19th century warfare. But one could surmise that the concept of People (domestic political opinion and support for warfare) or the civil-military relationship

---

24 *Ibid*, pg. 171.

25 Mills, C. Wright. 1956. *The Power Elite*. New York: Oxford University Press, pg. 212.

26 Clausewitz, Carl von. 1968. *On War*. Translated by Anatol Rapaport. New York: Viking Penguin.

itself, would blend with the notion of government contracts and funding for war.

Clausewitz believed that humans must support a government's prosecution of warfare for it to be successful. In the American experience, the Vietnam War would be an example of how the people did not generally support the war, and Operation Desert Storm, the first Gulf War, would be an example of when the public did indeed generally support military action.

Clausewitz was not known as a sociologist, but his Trinity shows that he had a belief in humans forming social organizations during warfare – one of the main points of this book. Corporations are a natural outgrowth of the Clausewitzian Trinity, and Mills would be vindicated in his view that elitist social organizations are a naturally-occurring "fuel" for warfare, even in the 21st Century.

Opinions About the War in Afghanistan

In polling released in 2020 by the University of Maryland on American views of the war in Afghanistan, the results were surprising. A decent percentage of Americans still support the war, even after 19 years and over 2,000 U.S. military personnel killed in action and over 20,000 Americans wounded in action. 34 percent, a plurality of respondents, supported keeping the current level of U.S. troops in Afghanistan. 23 percent of those surveyed wanted to remove all troops and 22 percent wanted to decrease troops.[27] So a total of 45 percent of respondents believed that the U.S. military footprint should be reduced.

However, only 16 percent said that U.S. objectives have been successful in Afghanistan, while 23 percent thought that U.S. objectives

---

[27] Telhami, Shibley and Stella Rouse. 2019. "Study of American Attitudes Toward Iran, Syria, and Afghanistan," University of Maryland Critical Issues Poll. Study No. 5.

have been unsuccessful. A plurality of respondents, 38 percent, replied that objectives were neither successful nor unsuccessful.

Other polling has been even more negative about the war. A Pew Research survey from 2019 asked Americans if they believed the war in Afghanistan was worth fighting. 59 percent said it was not worth fighting, while 36 percent said it was.[28]

It seems that there is still a stubborn portion of the American population that supports the war. This could be attributed to the belief that the United States has suffered so many casualties that pulling out completely would mean that the losses would be in vain. Others would point to the notion that hostilities by terrorists in Afghanistan would pose a threat inside the United States. In the University of Maryland survey, 42 percent of respondents agreed with the sentiment that Afghanistan is a breeding ground for terrorists that could threaten the homeland. And 42 percent either agreed or somewhat agreed that the United States should negotiate with the Taliban.

There are fewer opinion surveys about the war in the United Kingdom, so published findings are somewhat out of date. Results that are often cited point toward the 2011 British Social Attitudes Survey, in which 48 percent disagreed with the war in Afghanistan.[29]

Perhaps one reason that the American and British public are reticent to support the war is that Afghanistan has little strategic value. It is land-locked and has limited natural resources aside from rare earth minerals. There are very few exports aside from poppy, heroin, saffron spice, white marble for construction, and rugs and other antiquities. Many

---

[28] Igielnik, Ruth and Kim Parker. 2019. "Majorities of U.S. Veterans, Public Say the Wars in Iraq and Afghanistan Were Not Worth Fighting." Pew Research Center Fact Tank. July 10, 2019.

[29] Gribble, Rachel et al. 2015. "Attitudes Toward Iraq and Afghanistan: British Public Opinion After a Decade of War Has Implications for the Viability of Future Missions." London School of Economics and Political Science. Jan. 9, 2015.

Afghan households have no electricity and running water. There is also a mostly uneducated public with numerous illiterate Afghans. Syria, and to a greater extent, Iraq, does have oil. Before both were ravaged by warfare, these countries had a more educated populace with arguably better human capital that could contribute to a more modern and thriving economy.

The Difficulties of Prosecuting a War in Afghanistan

Warfare in Afghanistan is particularly brutal. The terrain, weather, and altitude are often inhospitable. Travel is difficult with few navigable roads and highways. The country is about the size of Texas and 50 percent larger than Iraq.[30] There are numerous languages such as Pashtu, Dari, and Balochi, and many tribal and clannish identities. Neighboring Pakistan is a refuge for terror groups and a place to escape from coalition forces.

The manner in which the war is being fought is even more troubling. Aside from the standard suicide bombings and improvised explosive devices that coalition forces endure in Iraq, there is the use of so-called "Green-on Blue" killings. This happens when extremist militants dress in the uniforms of the Afghan National Army or police and then open fire on unsuspecting U.S. personnel.

Future Warfare in Afghanistan Will Remain Status Quo with Some High-Tech Enhancements

The future of the War in Afghanistan is to continue to help the Afghan National Army clear and hold territory and attrit the Taliban to reduce their effectiveness. This will require better technology. Victor M. Rosello, Dave Shunk, and Michael D. Winstead, writing in the *Small Wars Journal*, called for improved technology in four areas: lethality,

---

[30] Rossello, Victor M. et al. 2010. "The Relevance of Technology in Afghanistan." *Small Wars Journal*. June 16, 2010.

survivability, situational awareness, and mission command.[31] The authors are interested in technological improvements that will be covered later in this book such as more robust use of drones, better personal armor technologies, and links to sensors, to name a few.

They wrote, "Improved thermal and optical imagery, layering of sensors for better target coverage, and more accurate sensing, breaching, clearing of building and tunnels needs to be better. Remote and rapid alerts with images for small units to assist in clearing buildings, remote reconnaissance, detection, and neutralization of booby-traps, landmines, WMD, and other explosive threats are needed, along with the ability to monitor greater areas with fewer soldiers."[32]

Is Peace Possible?

It begs the question that after all these years of war, is peace even attainable in Afghanistan? The future of peace would likely include the Taliban having their own political party in a power sharing agreement. This accord would be anathema to many members of the current political elite and probably unpopular with many policy makers in the United States and the United Kingdom who have favored intervention in Afghanistan. Also, families who lost loved ones to violence from the Taliban would be reticent to allow the extremist group to win the peace.

Nevertheless, the future of peace in Afghanistan is still a power sharing agreement with the government and the Taliban as a political party, similar to the arrangement in Northern Ireland in which Sinn Fein is the political party that was historically associated with the Provisional Irish Republican Army. The future lies in democracy, and Pakistan must also make a commitment to be the catalyst that gets the Taliban to disarm. Pakistan must also agree to take away safe havens in the former Federally Administered Tribal Areas that are now part of the Khyber

---

[31] *Ibid.*

[32] *Ibid*, pg. 8.

Pakhtunkhwa administrative province. Continuing the counterinsurgency fight against the Taliban is unsustainable. The Afghan government cannot stand on its own without U.S. assistance. A permanent cease-fire is needed because two decades of counter-insurgency efforts have mostly failed.

The Future of Counter-Insurgency in South Asia, the Middle East, and Africa

Allow me to take a deeper dive into counter-insurgency to further explain what future warfare in South Asia, the Middle East, and Africa will look like in the coming years. First, one should examine counter-insurgency through the lens of Clausewitz. The Prussian military sage believed that war is an act of violence in which both sides attempt to make their foe submit to their will. Clausewitz's idea that war is about political objectives definitely fits into what is known about insurgency and counterinsurgency. Clausewitz called on us to examine and analyze each conflict on its own terms and encouraged humans to always understand that each conflict has much unique aspects, specifics, and details. Every insurgency is different since the political objectives are different in each insurgency.

Clausewitz warned us to analyze each war as it is and not what it should be. To paraphrase him from his magnum opus *On War*, "Do not make war into something or wish to make it into something, which by the nature of its relations, it is impossible for it to be."[33]

So, he said, analyze each war differently and do not hope to make it into convenient stereotypes. For example, each insurgency is a nail, and we have a hammer or a simple "bumper sticker slogan" for fighting insurgencies such as "clear, hold, and rebuild." This means defeat and clear the enemy out of an area of operations; deploy enough personnel

---

[33] Clausewitz, *On War*.

to hold the terrain; make it safe for the inhabitants; then rebuild it physically and encourage political sustainability. Clausewitz would warn about making this stratagem fit all insurgencies. He called in *On War* for the "military fighting to set the conditions for a political solution."[34]

As Clausewitz cautioned, "Everything is very simple in war, but the simplest thing is difficult."[35] But Clausewitz would say be careful, it will not be such a simple, binary clear-form fight. There could be civilian spill-over deaths. There could be more proxy countries enter into battle with new combatants. There could be a host government failure, or the host government could be seen as corrupt and illegitimate. There could be corruption and poor governance leading to a fragile state with violence across borders as the insurgents find sanctuary. There could be violence and terrorism that goes on for years with no conclusion.

Can a host government or another government partner actually win hearts and minds in counterinsurgency? It becomes difficult when you examine the type of vehicles that American and British soldiers and marines fight in. You have seen ominous photos of body armor, helmets, and sunglasses. These uniforms can be intimidating to the locals.

Military vehicles matter as well. There are up-armored HUMVEES, Bradley fighting vehicles, various U.S. Marine personnel carriers, mine-resistant vehicles, and tanks. What would the local populace think when those vehicles roll around neighborhoods in an aggressive manner?

Even if soldiers go on foot patrols with "soft posture" rather than mounted-vehicle "hard posture" and you incorporate cultural, anthropological, and sociological understanding, winning hearts and minds is not guaranteed. What if soldiers execute other tactics that the experts say will work? Examples of this would be focusing on the indigenous

---

34 *Ibid.*

35 *Ibid.*

population and trying to guarantee the indigenous people's security and safety. The tasks are numerous: work on political reconciliation, implement government reform, and encourage political capacity building. Other tasks include improving government institutions and legitimacy, while only targeting the insurgents and not the population to reduce collateral damage. Friendly forces should constantly provide a communications narrative to host country's voters and the people in the country undergoing the insurgency. This allows the counter-insurgency force to communicate the reasons for fighting. Establishing the end state is required. All these tasks are critical.

Some British soldiers made a point of only wearing berets when they patrolled the streets of Belfast during The Troubles against the IRA. This was done not to intimidate the local populace, but also to show the IRA that British forces were not afraid of the violent environment.

But here are the problems in Afghanistan. It is difficult to defeat the insurgents militarily because of the need to keep casualties low. Counterinsurgency (COIN) campaigns can take ten years or more. Militaries are not that proficient at performing non-military tasks. There still needs to be a concentration of hard power and violence of action. There should be plenty of conventional infantry troops and marines to hold terrain. There is a need for air strikes that happen dangerously close to civilians. There is a need to stratify and isolate layers of insurgents, which is what happened during the U.S. "surge" in Iraq in 2007. Insurgents hide and melt into civilian populace or they use humans as shields. Insurgents seek cover in mosques or disappear in other countries. There is also a need for a lengthy time commitment that goes beyond government-imposed timelines. There are requirements for an open-ended commitment from special operations forces that necessitate a high operational tempo.

Also, the civilian populace in Afghanistan does not have a linear understanding of time and deadlines in the same manner as Westerners do. Stabilization and rebuilding operations cost huge amounts of money and time. Knowing these difficulties, has COIN, particularly the COIN practiced by the United States and British armed forces and NATO allies, failed? One could certainly make that argument.

In Iraq, one of the most difficult unintended consequences of government reform and democratic capacity building was that several former prime ministers of the country are Shias. So, it still comes down to sociology, ethnicity, and religion. Iraqi Sunnis feel that they have been violently retaliated against and discriminated against. Sunnis do not believe the Iraqi government is legitimate or pluralistic. This resulted in many Iraqi Sunnis becoming recruits for ISIS. One could argue that the ordinary citizens in Iraq and Afghanistan believe their government is too corrupt to be a republican democracy. Personal security is not at a level that mitigates all the violence in both Iraq and Afghanistan. All the time and money spent on training indigenous forces has shown only mediocre results at best. After all these years and all this money spent and all the U.S. casualties, the insurgents and terrorists were never totally defeated. These nations are still breeding extremists and there are still terror attacks in the West.

Iraq is part of the endless war construct as well. As of 2021, there were around 2,500 U.S. military personnel in Iraq. They are there to support the fight against the Islamic State, although the country's parliament has voted that all foreign troops be removed, and the prime minister has expressed support for a complete removal as well.

What about the notion of fighting insurgents in Iraq, Afghanistan, Syria, Libya, and Yemen before they come to the West and conduct terrorist acts? There are many who have argued this effectively over the years, particularly the late U.S. Senator John McCain and U.S. Senator Lindsey Graham.

Spokes and Hubs for Counter-Insurgency

The most important current and future counter-insurgency trend in the U.S. military are forward-deployed bases in North Africa and the Middle East. The first and most important base is Camp Lemonnier in Djibouti at the tip of the Horn of Africa bordering Ethiopia. Camp Lemonnier was an old French Foreign Legion Post that now has about 4,000 American and allied personnel. Its focus is on counter-insurgency and counter-terror in Yemen, Gulf of Aden, and East African states such as Somalia, Kenya, Sudan, and South Sudan. U.S. Special Operations Forces and the Joint Special Operations Command serve there.

A smaller marine force is responsible for security. Several conventional aircraft, fighter planes, and drones fly from there. C-130s are available for cargo, troop transport, and airborne operations. Intelligence analysts and clandestine operators, plus CIA paramilitary personnel, are also present. The concept of operations is to coordinate counter-insurgency and counter-terror operations with all the relevant players – so intel analysis and planning can be located with the war fighters.

They all command and coordinate the drone strikes and bomb damage assessment plus targeted assassinations. They also conduct rebuilding, reconstruction, and stability operations. There is one hub in Erbil, Northern Iraq, and one in Al-Asad in Western Iraq. These serve as air bases and both were attacked with ballistic missiles by Iran in 2020. Another hub is up and running in Spain.

The Iraqi bases house the special operations forces who are training and advising Kurdish peshmerga and other moderate Sunni and Shia militias in the fight against ISIS. Marines are there in fire bases too. U.S. personnel coordinate conventional air and drone strikes with bomb damage assessment. The one in Spain is a U.S. Marine operation at the Móron Air Base in the southern region south of Sevilla. The United States signed an agreement with the Spanish government for a permanent base in 2015, which authorized 2,200 personnel.[36] This group focuses on counter-insurgency and counter-terror in North Africa and West Africa. It is comprised of a marine quick reaction force that can be

---

[36] Kitfield, James A. "U.S. Air Power in Africa." *Air Force Magazine*. Jun 1, 2013.

deployed on V-22 Ospreys, an extremely fast tilt-rotor aircraft. V-22s are faster than helicopters and better armored. To maximize mobility, they can land like a helicopter. Along with C-130s, V-22s can get anywhere in North Africa and parts of West Africa quickly. These high-speed aircraft could likely have changed the outcome in the tragic attack in Benghazi in which four Americans were killed in 2012. They can take the fight to al-Shabaab, Boko Haram, and al-Qaeda in the Islamic Maghreb of Sahara, plus operate against Islamic State in the Egyptian Sinai. The marines in Spain also coordinate intelligence and drone operations from bases in Niger and Cameroon.[37]

So, what is the operational strategy behind this? These permanent bases form "hubs" that will spearhead smaller forwarding operating bases called "spokes."[38] The spokes then have better support and are not isolated from the hubs – isolation that could lead to ambushes and other attacks. The hub and spoke concept is an interesting wrinkle in counter-insurgency warfare and it is the future of "small wars" combat. The most important aspect the concept allows is co-location of intelligence personnel with warfighters.[39] This improves logistics, mission planning, command and control, bomb damage assessment, military fires, and combat search and rescue. Both "hubs" and "spokes" do indeed create more bureaucracy and social organization in the military.

However, for those who believe that the U.S. needs to end Forever Wars, there are still military personnel, including contractors, in Iraq. President Joe Biden will need to decide to wrap up U.S. operations in Afghanistan and Iraq, and that means bringing home people who are in harm's way. In Syria, there are usually around 1,000 special operations forces that advise and train approximately 60,000 people – made up of various Kurdish militias, Christians, and Arabs who are against Islamist

---

37 *Ibid.*

38 *Ibid.*

39 *Ibid.*

extremism. U.S. Senator Rand Paul has called this Syria operation another example of Endless War.

Russia Strikes Back: Hybrid Warfare Is Revealed

The future of warfare is ambiguous, and by that, I mean it is grey, or often deemed "hybrid." Russia's Vladimir Putin, during the annexation of Crimea in 2014, created a new social organization. Quickly dubbed "Little Green Men," these menacing figures wore no insignia on their green fatigues. They also wore green or black face masks that gave them an even more mysterious look. Their deployment allowed Putin to have plausible deniability that Russia had sent soldiers to Crimea.

This was an act of low-intensity combat, yet war was not declared. Undeclared war is the future of conflict. It is exhibited by non-traditional use of military force without traditional frontal combat and without large groupings of units that fight face to face. Destruction of people and weapons does not always take place in hybrid warfare.

Hybrid warfare is a mixture of traditional military measures and new, often historically unobserved nonmilitary measures. As Russian General and Chief of the General Staff Valery Gerasimov wrote in his seminal 2013 work on new challenges in combat operations, "The Value of Sciences is in the Foresight."[40] Russian nonmilitary measures include political opposition, economic sanctions, economic blockades, cyberattacks, changing or removing political leadership, and disruption of diplomatic relations.[41]

Military operations are stunted, indirect, and limited. They are asymmetric and often not executed in the physical realm, but operations are instead enacted in the cyber realm and in the information space.

---

[40] Gerasimov, Valery. 2016. "The Value of Sciences is in the Foresight: New Challenges Demand Rethinking the Forms and Methods of Carrying Out Combat Operations. *Military Review*. January/February 2016.

[41] *Ibid.*

Special operations forces play an outsized role in hybrid warfare. They form a vanguard that works in peacetime to advance military objectives. However, these objectives are political, diplomatic, and economic – they are non-military measures. "Winning" is still the overarching goal, but in hybrid warfare, winning does not always mean destruction of the enemy's forces. Instead, the objective is to occupy territory before the West can react, as evidenced by Ukrainian crisis example.

Hybrid warfare is often cited as being part of the current Russian way of war. But hybrid warfare has reared its head in the Middle East too, especially during the Arab-Israel conflict over the last decades with terrorist social organizations such as Hamas and Hezbollah. Both are social organizations that provide not just military muscle, but social welfare benefits to the populace in the form of food, education, jobs, healthcare, and other welfare benefits. ISIS also created a social benefit program for its populace, in addition to its terror and military wing.

But the Russian experience with hybrid warfare is much more acute and transformational. And since there is a Marxist tradition in Russia, one could argue that sociology plays a bigger role in the Russian version of hybrid warfare. Hybrid warfare requires discipline, a particularly important Weberian aspect of conflict. As Weber wrote, "...the separation of the warrior from the means of warfare, and the concentration of the means of warfare in the hands of the war lord have always been one of the typical bases of mass discipline."[42]

Is Putin the war lord in this Weberian aspect of discipline? Putin would certainly be one of Weber's ideal men of power. Or perhaps Gerasimov is the war lord? This seems to be a better fit because numerous military analysts have even dubbed the Russia way of hybrid war as the "Gerasimov Doctrine."

---

[42] *From Max Weber*, pg. 260.

Gerasimov believes that the very "rules of war" have changed. "The role of nonmilitary means of achieving political and strategic goals has grown, and, in many cases, they have exceeded the power of the force of weapons in their effectiveness," Gerasimov wrote.[43]

Franklin D. Kramer and Lauren M. Speranza of the Atlantic Council broke down hybrid warfare into categories. These are "low-level use of force; cyberattacks; economic and political coercion and subversion; and information war."[44] For low-level use of force, the authors described how Russia deploys operatives in other countries to encourage protest and incite civil unrest or violence. Cyber-attacks can disrupt operational networks. Russia uses economic and political means to "exploit weak, open systems to hijack foreign countries' governing and economic institutions and organizations, using corruption to further expand its own spheres of influence."[45]

Information warfare utilizes traditional media and social media to confuse and mislead foreign governments and their citizens by "denying facts, changing quotes, exaggerating, over-generalizing, discrediting, exploiting balance, employing narrative laundering, creating context, drowning facts with emotion, presenting opinions as facts, and using false facts or visuals, misleading titles, loaded metaphors, and conspiracy theories."[46] That is a long list of characteristics and it makes grey warfare a complex state of affairs.

One could argue, and many observers do, that these activities from the Russian hybrid warfare or the Gerasimov Doctrine are nothing new. These skeptics believe that the current form of Russian hybrid warfare is from the Soviet-era, the only difference is that the 2020's have better technology and the Internet.

---

[43] Gerasimov, Valery, pg. 24.

[44] Kramer, Franklin D. and Lauren Speranza. 2017. "Meeting the Russian Hybrid Challenge." Atlantic Council. May 30, 2017. Pg. 4.

[45] *Ibid*, pg. 9.

[46] *Ibid*, pg. 12

However, Gerasimov is more subtle and more intellectually nuanced than his Soviet ancestors. His version of hybrid warfare, judging from the extremely effective Crimean case study, is more effective than Soviet efforts. Crimea was done on the cheap with few personnel and resources wasted. The Soviets, in contrast, often focused on mass mechanized warfare that had little knack for the surprise or quick resolution.

Much of Russian hybrid warfare, according to the Kremlin, was inspired by U.S. regime toppling in Afghanistan, Iraq, and Libya. Russian policy makers and military leaders were especially stung by the U.S and NATO war in Kosovo against the Serbs in 1999. The Russians supported their fellow Slavs in Serbia and they felt that the independence of Kosovo was also a U.S. inspired annexation of territory that belonged to Serbia in the first place. The bombing campaign in 1999 against the Serbs during this conflict was also extremely upsetting to Putin and his allies in the Kremlin.

These past frustrations all tie into the Gerasimov Doctrine and the Russian version of hybrid warfare, according to the Russian linguist Charles K. Bortles. "Gerasimov's view of the future operational environment is in many ways remarkably similar to our own. Like us, he envisions less large-scale warfare; increased use of networked command-and-control systems, robotics, and high-precision weaponry; greater importance placed on interagency cooperation; more operations in urban terrain; a melding of offense and defense; and a general decrease in the differences between military activities at the strategic, operational, and tactical levels."[47]

But hybrid warfare from the Russian point of view is not always kinetic, or even that violent. Cyber operations or information warfare rarely shed blood. So, the Russians could argue that its use of

---

[47] Bartles, Charles K. 2016. "Getting Gerasimov Right." *Military Review*. January/February 106.

hybrid warfare in Crimea, actually saved lives. To be sure, subsequent Russian operations in the Donbass region of eastern Ukraine and southwestern Russia were indeed violent and bloody. Putin would say these skirmishes were unavoidable and simply Russia defending its national interest and borders from Ukrainians who are usually seen by Moscow as rebellious, untrustworthy, quarrelsome, and nettlesome. These beliefs about Ukrainians date back to World War Two.

The West sees the Russia-Ukraine conflict much differently of course. Russia routinely violates international law – that charge is a common refrain. Also, a widespread fear is that the Kremlin could use hybrid warfare again to annex parts of the Baltics, which would trigger Article V with NATO allies and would require a military response against the Russians from NATO members. A glance at a map will tell you that St. Petersburg is dangerously close to Tallinn, Estonia and Riga, Latvia. But according to Gerasimov, the distinctions between offensive aspects of war and defensive aspects of war are blurring. The Kremlin then could engineer a Russian hybrid incursion into the Baltics, and it could be made to be seen as a defensive operation. Since the Baltics have ethnic Russians as part of the population, Moscow could employ special operations forces as peacekeepers to protect compatriots. This could happen with an information warfare campaign that would increase the chances for protest and other domestic unrest with ethnic Russians as victims in the Baltics. Then a hybrid operation would ensue to protect ethnic Russians. A follow-on threat of nuclear weapons becomes one lever that Russia could engage. This condition is known as "escalate to de-escalate."

Public protest, according to Gerasimov, can be considered a part of warfare now. He referenced the Arab Spring as an example of warfare in the 21st Century. "In terms of scale of the casualties and destruction," he wrote, "the catastrophic social, economic, and political consequences, for such new-type conflicts are comparable with the consequences of any real war."[48] The Arab Spring protests did touch off a civil war in Syria, so Gerasimov has a point.

How do countries and their militaries combat hybrid warfare? Understanding the operating environment and being aware of the objectives, tactics, and strategies are imperative. Recognizing that hybrid warfare is often non-violent is difficult for military personnel to understand. It runs contrary to training and world views. Understanding a hybrid warfare adversaries' media strategy is also important. Recognizing misinformation and false news falls under this rubric. Having a counter-social media strategy helps diminish the effects of hybrid warfare. This depends on manipulating the battle space to change hearts and minds. Addressing the needs of ethnic minorities within the targeted country's borders keeps the adversary from stoking ethnic conflict and then using that as an excuse to wage hybrid warfare, an operation that exists between war and peace.

How to Respond to the Cyber Aspect of Hybrid War

The cyber domain is more problematic. Defense against cyber-attacks takes resources from the public and private sector, and often the two do not communicate with each other. Also, the attribution problem rears its head. It is just too difficult to always find the direct and correct culprit that carried out the attack. Next, is the appropriate response. What is the proportionate reaction? Should it be a full-on conventional, traditional, military, and kinetic attack, such as an air strike? Should the victim launch another cyber-attack against the original perpetrator? These are questions that have to be answered at the strategic, operational, and tactical level. And they will be examined in another chapter. These levels of war fighting do not always have aligned interests, objectives, or even budget funding. Attacks on democracy, particularly election meddling

---

[48] *Ibid.*

and the like, do not have a readily understood proportional response. The United States blamed Russia for election meddling in 2016, but little was done except for hand wringing and political rhetoric in the media, and in public discourse, despite numerous financial sanctions enacted by the Americans.

With all the difficulties in defending its multi-pronged techniques, tactics, and procedures, the current form of hybrid warfare that Russia has executed in the past and will in the future, is a new strategy, not old. Skeptics disagree with this assessment, but cyber activities make it new as compared to the pre-Internet Cold War and Soviet-era. Information warfare is also easier to conduct because of the rise of social media – a new state of affairs missing in the Soviet-era. Therefore, the Russian form of hybrid warfare is similar to past strategies and borrows from those, but it is a new phenomenon and likely to be a strategy that is executed again in the future.

The Gamification of War: Leaders Do Not Feel the Pain of Targeted Assassinations

The future of warfare also lies in what I call the gamification of war. Political leaders and the bureaucracies they control are so far removed from violence that they can lose normal sensitivity to warfare. Look no further than the use of drones beginning from when the first Predator unmanned aerial system was outfitted with Hellfire missiles in 2002. Remember, before that re-fit, unmanned aerial vehicles were used primarily for intelligence, surveillance, and reconnaissance. That changed in 2002 when the United States killed an al-Qaeda leader in Yemen by having a Predator drone fire a Hellfire missile at his car.

Targeted assassinations through drones began that day and became a way for the United States to eliminate its enemies remotely. Israel had been conducting political assassinations with unmanned aircraft since at least 2000 during the Second Intifada. Many American drone strikes over the years have been ordered directly from the White House. That was one of the critiques of the Vietnam War and the War in Kosovo – that presidents Lyndon B. Johnson and William J. Clinton approved bombing targets prior to the air strike. This was seen as micro-managing a conflict from the safety of Washington, DC and it had military analysts lamenting that politicians had usurped power from the generals and the admirals in a way that was detrimental to the war effort.

The White House Situation Room allows presidents, military and intelligence leaders, and cabinet members the ability to observe video and audio feeds of real-time combat missions. This technology has created a decision-making environment that provides an anesthetic or numbing effect to the horrors of war. Combat observed in this manner takes on a "video game" alternate reality that gamifies combat. Presidents also have direct control over special operations forces and their own targeted assassinations or "jack pot" raids that capture bad guys.

Is targeted killing by drone or by a special operation illegal? Is it an assassination or an act of war? The 2020 targeted killing of Iranian General Qassem Soleimani, longtime commander of his country's Quds Force, by the United States is an illustrative case study. This killing was ordered by President Donald J. Trump, even though the United States and Iran were not considered to be at war with each other, unless one counts various proxy actions that the Americans have used against Iranian-backed Shia militants in Yemen. The justification for the killing of Soleimani was that the Iranian general had in the past directed actions that have killed U.S. personnel and that he was actively planning further attacks against Americans. So, this was considered a police action to prevent terrorist activity.

Critics have claimed that the Soleimani drone killing violated international law. They posited that the assassination was at odds with the Hague Conventions of 1907, and contrary to a protocol of the Geneva Convention in 1949. Moreover, there is a law on U.S. books via executive order in 1976 that forbids political assassination. Soleimani was a military officer and a legitimate combat target, so the Trump administration defended its action as a situation where self-defense from future attacks against Americans was imminent and a clear and present danger. The administration said it had intelligence to support the killing.

Iran responded by launching ballistic missile and rocket attacks against American personnel at two Iraqi bases in January of 2020. The White House released a photo of a fully-staffed Situation Room that contained principal members (the Secretary of State and the Secretary of Defense, among others) of the National Security Council.

The White House Situation Room was also fully staffed during the original attack against Soleimani. What was going on in people's minds? Did real-time observation technology gamify the drone strike? To an extent, yes. Policy makers are much more likely to approve drone killings when they are removed from the battlefield and safely situated in the basement of the White House. The video feed can almost become a video game. The targeted killing is not risky in terms of American loss of life since the flight was unmanned, but the Trump administration took on much political risk. Taking on this risk is easier when it is conducted by a coercive bureaucracy in the situation room.

Trump, speaking at a fundraiser held after the operation, shared with his audience a minute-by-minute countdown. This shows that Trump was not only proud of the outcome, but that the taking of another life was an awe-inspiring "reality show" type of event with made for television drama. This also echoes his description of the last living actions of ISIS founder and leader Abu Bakr al-Baghdadi, who was killed by a U.S. Army Delta Force raid in October of 2019. According to the president, "Baghdadi died after running into a dead-end tunnel, whimpering, and crying and screaming all the way...a brutal killer, one who has caused so much hardship and death, has violently been eliminated. He will never again harm another innocent man, woman, or child. He died like a dog. He died like a coward. The world is now a much safer place."

"He died like a dog," is an important choice of words. This phrase shows that Trump has made the killing into a reality show-type of dramatization.

This is what I mean when I describe a "gamification" of a targeted killing even though Baghdadi reportedly killed himself. Showmanship and braggadocio is on full display here, according to Trump's words.

Both Trump and his predecessor Barack Obama are presidents who had no military experience and who came into office without a traditional foreign policy background. Both have exhibited skepticism, lack of trust, and frustration at various times at generals and admirals. Obama had a famous photo of him in the situation room with advisers and members of the National Security Council during the raid on Osama bin Laden. This photo showed his cool detachment from the reality of killing. Obama also used drone strikes against militants in South Asia and the Middle East extensively, and even expanded the program to Somalia after increasing use in Pakistan and Yemen. Did ordering drone attacks against groups and individuals make it easier to execute this decision over time? He did broaden the drone targeting program over President George W. Bush's efforts. In 2017, 10 times more drone strikes happened during the Obama administration compared to the Bush team.[49]

The Bureau of Investigative Journalism chronicled the Obama Administration's war with drones. "The Obama administration insisted that drone strikes are so 'exceptionally surgical and precise' that they pluck off terror suspects while not putting 'innocent men, women, and children in danger.'" This claim has been contested by numerous human rights groups, however, and the Bureau's figures on civilian casualties also demonstrate that this is often not the case."[50]

This brings us to a discussion about whether drones create too much collateral damage to civilians and other non-combatants. It assumes that both Obama and Trump have succumbed to the gamification of warfare through their use of drones and special operations forces. Has

---

[49] Fielding-Smith, Abigail and Jessica Purkiss. "Drone Warfare." The Bureau of Investigative Journalism.

[50] *Ibid.*

gamification made civilian deaths more acceptable as the cost of conducting modern warfare? Human rights groups and media investigations have analyzed more collateral damage and a higher number of noncombatant deaths than the Obama administration released to the public. No one wants innocent people to die in drone or special operations forces attacks. But the chances of this happening should figure into the decision-making calculus of whether to order the attacks in the first place. Gamification of warfare makes this calculus difficult still, but one could argue that it is easier to send a drone into action than send people in harm's way.

Whoever is in the White House assumes an awesome responsibility after receiving that first classified intelligence and national security briefing. Obama got his first briefing during the presidential campaign in 2008 and he had another intelligence briefing as president-elect once he got elected in November of that year. It was reportedly a chilling eye-opener for Obama. He later received his briefings via digital tablet computer. Trump, according to the *Washington Post* in 2018, preferred listening to a simple oral briefing rather than a written presidential daily brief, which was a somewhat different delivery method than his predecessors.[51] Trump was notoriously skeptical of the intelligence community in general. President-elect Joe Biden got his official international security intelligence briefing after the election in 2020, even though Trump was contesting the results in court throughout the months after voting ended.

Since the president is powerful enough to control targeted drone strikes and special operations raids, the manner to which intelligence is received can be telling. Obama learns primarily by the printed word and Trump learns via visual stimulation. They both gamified targeted killings. Biden, having been a member of the Obama administration, will likely carry out this concept of gamification.

---

[51] Leomnig, Carol D. et al. 2018. "Breaking with Tradition, Trump Skips President's Written Intelligence Report and Relies on Oral Briefings." *Washington Post*. Feb. 9, 2018.

The future of targeted killings, whomever is in the White House, is not expected to change. Targeted killings have been highly effective over the years during the war on terror and technology will continue to improve as drones advance into "swarming" mode with autonomous features. The situation room, with President Joe Biden, will remain a popular meeting place for targeted killings and their aftermath. Decisions on war and peace can be extremely lonely for the president and a full situation room makes these decisions less lonely and more gamified, especially as the presidency depends more on mass communication through television and social media.

The future of warfare is also prosecuted in the realm of ethics, morality, and humanism, which are major aspects of the operating environment. A human being will always be present in some form or fashion in combat, whether it is designing the weapons system or pulling the trigger. Even though autonomous robots and drones will be covered in this book, the human is still paramount in the operating environment as the 2020s progress.

Ethics and Morality of Future War: Losing Control of the Machine

Most scholarship on the ethics and morality of warfare are covered in Just War Theory. But one of the purposes of this book is to investigate the ethics and morality of emerging technology, particularly artificial intelligence and machine learning, plus the most optimum relationship in terms of ethics and morality with humans and machines. I am most concerned with making sure that the machine can ultimately be controlled by human beings and the importance of having ethical, moral, and virtuous humans train the machine. It is paramount to train the machine in a virtuous manner where the "trainer" is the hero and the ultimate arbiter concerning the behavior of the machine. Keeping it simple helps control the machine. The first aspect of building a machine-learning or AI application is to adhere to basic and uncomplicated principles in mathematical and statistical modeling known as parsimony, elegance, and maximizing aspects of Occam's Razor.

One wants the machine to only do a simple chore or task, but to have that one task have broader uses. This includes the humanist analogy of a manufacturing assembly line that can be shut off when any employee is concerned about something like safety or quality control. One wants to be able to shut down the assembly line when it comes to training the artificial intelligence too. So, the scientist is always in control. What is the biggest fear? The fear is when the scientist is *not* in control. Those who work in the field of emerging technology and international security have to be responsible and ethically and morally strong – to make sure the trainers can shut off the assembly line and make "human" corrections.

To train a program or platform for machine learning or artificial intelligence, humans construct a mathematical model or models that include various algorithms and then they "feed" the model sample data, in which the model is thus trained. So, humans are overseeing this learning process for intelligence programs and machines. It sounds overly simple, but the models must be trained by ethical and moral humans.

Weber wrote of ethics and conduct as they confront humans that, "...we can force the individual, or at least we can help him, to give himself an account of the ultimate meaning of his own conduct. This appears to me as not trifling a thing to do, even for one's own personal life. Again, I am tempted to say of a teacher who succeeds in this: he stands in service of 'moral forces;' he fulfills the duty of bringing about self-clarification and a sense of responsibility."[52]

This is where Elon Musk and others enter the picture. They are worried about losing control of the machine leading to conflict and war from nefarious acts by machines. But can machines think? Not without help from ethical and morally upright humans. Musk founded a nonprofit

---

[52] *From Max Weber*, pg. 152.

called OpenAI in 2015, which later became a for-profit company and research lab when Musk left the project. Musk originally wanted intelligent machine products that yielded to ethics; embraced humanitarian technology; and counter-acted the potential of misuse by other AI companies. According to its corporate web site, "OpenAI's mission is to ensure that artificial general intelligence (AGI)—by which we mean highly autonomous systems that outperform humans at most economically valuable work—benefits all of humanity."[53]

The U.S. Department of Defense also has a center of excellence, established in 2018, called the Joint Artificial Intelligence Center. The center's "holistic approach" is aimed to accelerate the use of artificial intelligence's large and complex problems across the service branches. One aspect of the center's five-stage strategy and holistic approach is to "lead the military in ethics and safety."[54]

Weber would acknowledge the new social organization as a layer of bureaucracy. This is a step in the right direction, even though it is not clear how the Joint Artificial Intelligence Center will deal with ethical and moral dilemmas with AI. The center's web site claims lofty goals, "AI technology will change much about the battlefield of the future, but nothing will change America's steadfast record of honorable military service, individual accountability, and our military's commitment to lawful and ethical behavior. Our focus on AI follows from our long history of making investments to preserve our most precious asset, our people, and to limit danger to innocent civilians. All of the AI systems that we field will have compliance with the law as a key priority from the first moment of requirements setting through the last step of rigorous testing."[55]

This social organization must have oversight over all AI efforts in the

---

[53] Open AI corporate web site.

[54] Chief Information Officer of the U.S. Department of Defense. "Vision: Transform the DOD Through Artificial Intelligence." Lt. Gen. Michael J. Green.

[55] *Ibid.*

U.S. military. It is not clear how this will come about, but it seems there would be rules, regulations, and procedures regarding military AI oversight. AI is like a "12-year-old" that needs constant supervision. For example, the Department of Defense has an outside advisory committee of technology experts called the Defense Innovation Board. Eric Schmidt, formerly the Executive Chairman of Alphabet Inc., once chaired the board. In 2019, The board released a report called the "AI Principles: Recommendations on the Ethical Use of Artificial Intelligence by the Department of Defense."[56] This report recommended that AI be "responsible, equitable, traceable, reliable, and governable."[57] The report also called for an academic body be constituted to study the ethics of AI and to hold an annual conference on ethical oversight issues.

"Human beings should exercise appropriate levels of judgment and remain responsible for the development, deployment, use, and outcomes of DoD AI systems," according to the report.[58] In 2020, the Department of Defense announced that it would follow the report recommendations closely in the future for proper oversight of AI. We will see if this ethics oversight effort can be effective over the next decade.

While the ethical dimensions of AI will also be further examined in Chapter Nine, the global operating environment for warfare remains broad and diverse. The environment for 21st century international security also includes phenomena such as climate change and transnational criminal organizations. These threats endanger humanity and will further dominate the battlespace in the future.

---

[56] Defense Innovation Board. 2018. "AI Principles: Recommendations on the Ethical Use of Artificial Intelligence by the Department of Defense."

[57] *Ibid.*

[58] *Ibid.*

CHAPTER TWO

THE FUTURE OF TRANSNATIONAL CRIME

The future of warfare is comprised of the heightened amount of criminal activity that creeps across borders around the world. Transnational crime sucks the life out of law enforcement because it involves more than one country. It is a murky area between war and peace in which humans are not uniformed soldiers, but they fight like soldiers anyway. Transnational crime includes nefarious activity by narco-cartels, international gangs, arms smugglers, narcotics traffickers, human traffickers, human slavery practitioners, antiquities smugglers, natural resource smugglers and poachers, and transnational wire fraud. This is quite a list of bad behavior to police.

These groups have become social organizations that often recruit new members and leadership when other transnational actors are arrested, captured, or killed. It is natural that humans commit local crimes of want and need, but the transnational character is historically unnatural. Globalization with 24/7 flows of information, finance, technology, culture and global interaction of people, companies, and governments have led to a natural progression of crime, even warfare. This comes from local actors and their ambition to become international actors with global ambition.

Transnational Criminal Organizations as Bureaucracies

Thus, crime is added to the mix wrought by globalization and becomes a sociological phenomenon that flows across borders. Transnational crime is then a major part of the sociological operating environment that will metastasize into the future. Transnational criminals have reaped the benefits of globalization over the years. Criminal social organizations are sometimes bureaucratic and hierarchical, which would fit into Weber's world view. But they also have transformed Weberian ideals of discipline into micro-level solidarity. This solidarity keeps the social organization together and allows it to commit even more crime.

Transnational criminal social organizations are difficult to combat because militaries are geared to state-on-state and government-on-government warfare. Transnational actors do not have sovereignty over entire countries, although one could argue that they are sovereign over certain localities. But militaries are not often set up to eliminate non-state transnational social organizations. In the future, militaries will continue to be ill-equipped to fight these criminal organizations.

Weber was caught up in power states with powerful neighbors during World War One. Weber's view of international relations was one of great power relationships with allies balancing against each other. And, as far as internal politics was concerned, he agitated for a constitutional democracy. But he saw the ups and downs of a country's power, which led him to believe in the primacy and discipline of army organizations. Like Clausewitz, Weber did not recognize non-state actors, so it cannot be said that Weber predicted globalization and transnationalism. He did write of state-level violence, "The state is an association that claims the monopoly of the legitimate use of violence and cannot be defined in any other manner."[59]

---

[59] *From Max Weber*, pg. 334

As Phil Williams wrote, "globalization is not a policy choice; it is a set of dynamic and, in some respects, autonomous processes, which are highly resistant to large-scale interference or inhibition. Globalization might stutter but it is more likely to be consolidated than rolled back."[60] Sometimes, Williams noted, not only are they non-state actors, but transnational criminal organizations are also backed by states in order for them to achieve geopolitical advantage.[61]

But the transnational social organization is a natural outgrowth of Weber's views on bureaucracy and micro-level discipline and solidarity. This makes non-state transnational social organizations immensely powerful in many instances. "Charismatic leaders," are also powerful, which Weber warned about. Transnational charismatic leaders such as Joseph Kony of the Lord's Resistance Army and Joaquin "El Chapo" Guzman of the Sinaloa Cartel come to mind. With charismatic leaders, the future of a transnational organization can be secured because most of the large bureaucracies, like a narco-cartel, have succession plans when their leader is removed, arrested, or killed. In the future, there will be more charismatic leaders because the size of bureaucracies will grow in the most active and successful transnational social organizations.

Charismatic Leaders and Narco-Cultura Lead to More Violence

Most of these bureaucracies are narco-cartels. Charismatic leaders are often so important that when one is eliminated, there is often a power struggle over drug territory that leads to even more assassinations and other types of killings. This is what I refer to as an "active bureaucracy." These types of cartels supply propaganda and information services that

---

60 Williams, Phil. 2017. "The Future of Transnational Criminal Organizations." *Stratfor*. Dec. 14, 2017.

61 *Ibid.*

could be compared to local governments. The result is narco-cultura or criminal culture. Most of this information war is conducted through media organizations, particularly radio stations, television shows, and newspapers. Cartels are glorified through musical ballads known as narco-corridos. Religion is also involved in the culture through the worship of the drug dealers' patron saint Jesus Malverde. Cartels have been known to bribe or intimidate journalists into covering events in a certain manner favorable to the narco-cartels. The reporters advance narco-cultura or refrain from covering certain actions that the cartel does not want covered in the media.

Mexican narco-cartels will continue to dig tunnels to traffic humans, marijuana, methamphetamine, heroin, and fentanyl. They will also get richer. According to the Department of Homeland Security, narco-cartels clear between $19 billion and $29 billion each year.[62] They will continue to be murderous. At least 150,000 homicides were attributed to narco-cartels since 2006 in statistics compiled by the Congressional Research Service in 2018.[63]

Most assume the violence is perpetrated by cartels against cartels or killings done by the government or police in various shootouts and the like. But self-defense militias known as auto-defensas have cropped up in some of the more violent cartel-dominated states such as Guerrero, Michoacán, Tamaulipas, and Veracruz. These Mexican citizens are taking the fight to the cartels and increasing the death toll. This development gives new meaning to non-state actors and warfare in the 21st century. The federal government in Mexico City clearly has no control of domestic violence in its own country.

---

62 "USA-Mexico Bi-National Criminal Proceeds Study." U.S. Department of Homeland Security.

63 "Mexico Drug War Fast Facts." *CNN*. April 3, 2020.

Narco-Cartels and Burgeoning Technology is Difficult to Curtail

The narco-cartels are also growing in their technological prowess. They have long used traditional methods of getting illegal drugs into the United States. Mexican cartels have utilized submarines, catapults, and manned ultra-light aircraft to send narcotics over the border. Now the cartels are entering into the use of modern unmanned vehicles. Cartel drones are flying over the U.S. southern border. To be sure, these drones are small and can only carry ounces or a few pounds of product. But even a tiny amount of fentanyl brought by a hobby drone could be deadly. U.S. Customs and Border Protection fears that fentanyl could be purposefully or accidentally released over crowds to create a terrorism incident. Also, Customs and Border Protection has few ways to counter these small drones, even though counter-drone technologies do exist. Eventually the U.S. government will provide counter-drone methods to its Department of Homeland Security personnel, but by then the cartels will resort to better technology to evade counter-drone efforts. Cartel drones are likely to become autonomous or near-autonomous. In other words, instead of having a human remotely-piloting a drone to cross the border with illicit cargo, drones can be pre-programmed to have a flight plan that does not need a human pilot. This cat and mouse game will grow exponentially in the coming years. Look for manned submarines that have large payloads to become unmanned in the future. It is only a matter of time for cartels to use unmanned submarines.

Popular Mechanics estimated that narcosubs have "exploded nearly tenfold in the last decade."[64] The subs can reach as far as Spain, and definitely reach as far as the United States according to the magazine. Most of them are successful at reaching their destination.

---

64 Mizokami, Kyle. 2020. "Why Our Seas Are Suddenly Swimming With Drug-Running Narcosubs." *Popular Mechanics*. March 4, 2020.

Smuggling narcotics under water is not the only subterranean effort being conducted by narco-cartels. Tunneling to illegally cross borders will become more advanced. The first smuggling tunnel along the Southern Border was discovered in Nogales, Arizona in 1995. Hundreds of tunnels have been found since then. The tunnels are being built by highly-paid and talented engineers from South America who have experience in legitimate mining operations. These tunnels often have high-voltage electrical cables and intricate ventilation systems to allow for even more humans and narcotics to be smuggled. They are equipped with rail and rail cars in order for smugglers to pack underground carriages with even more illegal drugs. Entrances and exits are often hidden inside buildings making them difficult to discover. And they are getting longer. In 2020, authorities found a tunnel that was over 4,300 feet long (almost a mile) from Tijuana, Mexico to San Diego, California. This tunnel was 70-feet deep.

Social Organizations Are Conducive to More Drug Smuggling

Cartels as social organizations have a vertical and hierarchical structure that makes them more conducive to producing organic drugs such as cocaine and marijuana. But synthetic drugs, like fentanyl that is mainly made in China, can be delivered through direct mail, and ordered over the dark web, essentially bypassing Mexican cartels.[65] But the cartels are definitely not out of the fentanyl trade. In 2019, the Mexican military seized 24 tons of fentanyl at the Pacific port of Lázaro Cárdenas in southwest Michoacán state.[66] There are also numerous precursor chemicals of fentanyl that are shipped through

---

65 Dudley, Steven. 2019. "The End of the Big Cartels – Why There Won't Be Another Chapo." *InSight Crime*. March 18, 2019.

66 Asmann, Parker. 2019. "China Fentanyl Ban Yet to Hamper Mexico's Crime Groups." *InSight Crime*. March 18, 2019.

Mexico with cartel blessing, even though China has banned all elements of fentanyl in 2019.

Cartels excel at adapting their illegal drug supply to Americans' tastes, demands, and desires. Cartels have reacted quickly to the change in narcotic preferences as fentanyl started becoming more of a killer of Americans in 2016. "According to statistics from the Center for Disease Control (CDC), there were 19,413 deaths from synthetic opioids in 2016, a 103 percent increase from the 9,580 deaths reported the year before. At the same time, the Drug Enforcement Administration (DEA) found that heroin-related overdose deaths nearly doubled between 2013 and 2016 to more than 15,000."[67]

Not only are cartels flexible in meeting demand, but they are also adept at the Weberian discipline needed to stay together and survive. As Weber wrote, "This discipline is enforced within their own group, for the blind obedience of subjects can be secured only by training them exclusively for submission under the disciplinary code."[68]

Thus, cartels are designed to survive and adapt, to not only their customers' drug habits, but also to interference by government, military, or law enforcement. A question concerning labels has cropped up over the years that asks whether narco-cartels are terrorists or insurgents. Terrorism analyst Scott Englund believes that they are not terrorists or insurgents.[69] Englund wrote that the cartels are not inclined to overthrow governments and that their number on priority is to maximize profits.[70]

Designating the cartels as terror groups would enable the United States to commit more money and resources at combating them. But

---

[67] Asmann, Parker. 2018. "LatAm Crime Groups Adapting to Meet Growing US Drug Demand." *InSight Crime*. Nov. 6, 2018.

[68] *From Weber*, pg. 253

[69] Englund, Scott. 2020. "Mexican Drug Cartels are Violent-But They're Not Terrorists." *War on the Rocks*. Feb. 24, 2020.

[70] *Ibid.*

doing so could also harm relations and economic development, including trade between the United States and Mexico. Since terrorism and insurgencies are politically motivated movements that endanger Americans, the cartels would not completely fit definitions of terrorism and insurgencies.

Los Zetas and the Latest Narco-cartel Jalisco New Generation Perpetuate More Violence

Shipping illegal narcotics into the United States has killed inestimable numbers of Americans. And at least one cartel, Los Zetas, has been found to shower politicians with money to meddle in elections and encourage policy makers to "look the other way" in the border state of Coahuila.[71] The political activity by the Los Zetas cartel was documented by numerous witnesses, even though Mexican politicians denied the accusations. President Donald Trump called for labeling Mexican cartels as terrorist organizations in 2019 when 21 civilians died in a cartel-police shootout near the U.S. border that year. Six children and three mothers were also ambushed and killed in their car by cartel violence in 2019 as well.

The next most violent gang emerge is the Jalisco New Generation group. These bandits once shot down a Mexican Army helicopter with a rocket-propelled grenade.[72] Jalisco has learned to change its supplier of fentanyl from China to India, after the Chinese have attempted to crack down on the drug. The leader of Jalisco is Nemesio Oseguera, known as "El Mencho." He is now the DEA's most wanted criminal with a $10 million reward for information leading to his capture. The money laundered by El Mencho has allowed the gang to diversify into legitimate

---

[71] Agren, David. 2017. "Mexico Drug Cartel's Grip on Politicians and Police Revealed in Court Files." *The Guardian*. Nov. 10, 2017.

[72] Stevenson, Mark. 2020. "In Mexico, a cartel is taking over: Jalisco New Generation." *Associated Press*. March 18, 2020.

hotels and restaurants and real estate firms. These efforts have even resulted in music recording and promotion.[73]

Jalisco is particularly violent. Their victims are dumped in numerous places with acid or lye used to dissolve the dead. "So many bodies have been found in Guadalajara that authorities ran out of space at the morgue and took to moving rotting bodies around in refrigerated trucks until neighbors complained about the smell."[74]

The Nexus Between Cartels and Terror

It appears highly likely that the cartels in the future will be designated as terror groups by the U.S. Secretary of State. The Obama White House National Security Council already stated that terrorists and insurgents turn to transnational gangs as a funding source and get support to perpetuate violence. This could mean, although it is not required, that U.S. active-duty military personnel could be used in Mexico to combat the cartels. This would likely consist of military advisers assisting the Mexican authorities with counterinsurgency and counterterrorism activities similar to what the U.S. conducted against the narco-terror insurgent group FARC in Colombia in 2002 under U.S. President George W. Bush.[75]

Can Mexico Win Against the Cartels?

The current Mexican president, Andres Manuel López Obrador, objects to the terrorism designation. Lopez Obrador, like other Mexican presidents before him, believes his military and law enforcement personnel are sufficient when it comes to fighting cartels. But the facts on the ground run counter to that argument.

---

[73] *Ibid.*

[74] *Ibid.*

[75] Naren, Nichole. 2019. "Trump Wants to Call Mexican Drug Cartels 'Terrorist Organizations.'" *Vox*. Dec. 12, 2019.

Lopez Obrador has stuck with his policy of pacifying the cartels by getting at the root of the problem and fighting poverty with enhanced government social programs in the geographic areas where cartels dominate. This policy has been called "hugs not bullets." Lopez Obrador's strategy has seemed to concede that complete victory over the cartels is not possible and it admits that punitive measures against the cartels have not worked in the past.

Lopez Obrador does make an important sociological point – that cartels are strengthened in communities where there is no economic hope. If one takes a look at a hypothetical Mexican family in one of the states where cartels dominate, the children face a dire situation and have extraordinarily little upward mobility. Parents have to take the good with the bad when it is almost certain their offspring will be affiliated with the cartels in some way. One child in a large family could hope for a college degree that would lead to a teaching position, for example. Other children may have no choice but to farm poppy, process coca, or assist the cartels in other ways. Parents can only hope for one child to emerge successfully from this poverty trap that cartels take advantage of for recruitment.

Cartel members can easily threaten those that join the military or police by putting pressure on family members. For example, say a cartel ambushes a carful of victims and the military responds with reciprocal force. The cartels simply find the barracks where soldiers live with their families and then they threaten and scare those family members to submission.

There is also the corruption that goes along with organized crime. The cartels spread so much money around to businesses and the judicial system that people bow to their wishes. Extortion runs rampant as well. Lopez Obrador wants to fight this type of public and private-sector corruption, but it seems hopeless to approach a pacification strategy without combating the violence that goes along with all the graft inherent in locations where the cartels are all-powerful.

The future of the conflict with cartels is the United States government taking a more active role and this means designating the groups as terrorist organizations and providing in-person assistance from U.S. special operations forces and the CIA. Lopez Obrador's strategy is about two decades too late. There was a point, perhaps when cartels were just focusing on exporting marijuana and cocaine, that a "helping hand" pacification approach would have worked. But now cartels are so ingrained in the sociopolitical and cultural fabric of the nation that there is no way any Mexican government strategy can be successful without the United States security apparatus.

Another way in which the U.S. government could help quell the violence is to crack down on the supply of small arms that flow into Mexico from the United States. So-called "straw buyers" are able to circumvent American federal background checks on arms purchases. These illegal straw buys usually happen at gun shows in border states. So, narcotics flow northward, and small arms flow southward. Until gun show loopholes are tightened in America, the cartels will be continuously armed to the teeth.

Criminal Gangs from Central America, South America, and Russia Enter the Picture

Mexican cartels are not the only transnational gangs that dominate their areas of operations. MS-13 in Central America and The Vory in Russia are gangs that rival the Mexican cartels in the depth of their strength and the violence of their actions. Mara Salvatrucha was spawned in the 1970s in Los Angeles, California. The group was originally dedicated to protecting immigrants from El Salvador, who were struggling to find a toehold in the United States. Now the transnational gang has at least 30,000 members worldwide with around 9,000 in America. MS-13 is involved with narcotics and human trafficking, arms deals, money laundering, murder-for-hire, kidnapping for ransom and other dirty deeds. Members are known for full-body tattoos and tattoos drawn on their faces. The gang is active in Central America, especially in El Salvador. Their rivals, the 18th Street Gang, also known as Barrio 18, has between 30,000 and 50,000 members in the United States alone. They engage in transnational criminal activity in areas similar to MS-13. Both of these gangs dominate the Western Hemisphere.

Other transnational gangs are less well-known. Some have more political nature such as the National Liberation Army (ELN) in Colombia. The ELN espouse a Marxist ideology and have waged an insurgency in Colombia since 1964. There are still around 2,500 of these militants fighting in Colombia. They are considered a terrorist organization by the United States. ELN makes most of its money through kidnapping for ransom and extorting civilians – the revenue from these actions are what the group calls "war taxes."

In Brazil, the First Capital Command dominates criminal activity and is the largest gang in the country. It is active in most of the 27 states in Brazil and is concentrated historically in the State of Sao Paulo. First Capital Command criminal activities run the gamut of transnational crime. They thrive in anything from prison breaks to highway robbery. Their precursor affiliated group, Red Command, once had a left-wing political dimension since some of its founding members were jailed during Brazil's military dictatorship from 1964 to 1985. Red Command uses well-diversified tactics, including arms trafficking and bank robberies, and anything in between.

In the Eastern Hemisphere, The Vory, from Russia, are extremely ruthless. Known as a "super mafia" by Russia analyst Mark Galeotti,[76] this organized crime group, stops at nothing, and also have distinct tattoos. These marking are eight-pointed starts on members' shoulders. They were organized mostly in gulags during the Cold War and

[76] Galeotti, Mark. 2018. *The Vory: Russia's Super Mafia*. New Haven, CT: Yale University Press.

can even trace their origins to the early 20th century. An important concept to understand the Vory is "Krysha," which is translated as the "roof" that protects these criminal gangs. "Thief-in-law," another important Russian concept, is the class of professional criminals that have carte blanche to commit crimes in Russia. They are elite members of the organization. These members are often protected from prosecution.

Transnational criminal gangs as advanced as those described above are almost impossible for governments to combat. The future holds that these groups will dominate their areas of operations. They are simply too ingrained in the cultures of their various host countries.

Weber would have seen in today's transnational gangs an element of discipline and bureaucracy that keeps them together with tight bonds. Weber wrote, "The content of discipline is nothing but the consistently rationalized, methodically trained and exact execution of the received order, in which all personal criticism is unconditionally suspended, and the actor is unswervingly and exclusively set for carrying out the command."[77]

Transnational Gangs are Socialized into Violence

Members of transnational gangs follow orders emanating from a rigid hierarchy. This is the strength of their operations. They also have the discipline to remain silent under police questioning, to not "snitch" on each other, similar to the Italian mafia concept of omerta. Why conduct violent organized crime? It comes as a result of yearning for collective violence. Violence still takes place even though most abhor it. Some of the precursors to crime get incubated in prison. A need for survival and belongingness in a dangerous environment encourages people to join an

---

77 *From Max Weber*, pg. 253

organization that is bigger than themselves. Outside the penal system are economic, employment, and pocket-book concerns. Crime does pay in the developing world. Violence is learned as part of the socialization and indoctrination into the group. Gangsters often want to "be somebody" and a life of playing it straight offers no appeal. Hatred of authority and law enforcement is also a factor.

Thus, transnational crime is a form of warfare since individuals are socialized into collective violence. Malesevic wrote, "To understand war, one has to decouple it from 'intraspecific killing' and other violent action, as what is distinct about warfare is its sociological character – its organizational structure and ideological justification."[78] One could argue that transnationalism is warfare between criminal bureaucrats and street-level bureaucrats – police, judges, constables, gendarmes, and the like.

Then there is organizational ideology for organized violence for people who do not wear a uniform but are martial in character. Transnational gangs, like their military counterparts during battle, strive to control territory or already control territory. Violence becomes an ideology. Older members have socialized other members into the discipline of violence. Battlefield solidarity is heightened. Violence moves across borders as globalization rears its head. Money from illicit enterprises flows. Transnational criminals are non-state actors, but they fight without politics, geopolitical borders, ideology, and other causes of warfare between state actors.

Then what is the overall objective behind transnational gangs? Money and power would seem to be the most obvious drivers of this organized violence. Holding territory and creating a "homeland" would be part of the objective. Survival against other gangs is paramount. Survival against the state law enforcement authority is also

---

78 *The Sociology of War and Violence*, pg. 57

important. Many transnational gangs have no desire to replace government, however some, like Colombian drug lord Pablo Escobar, became Robin Hood-type folk heroes instead. There was a socioeconomic aspect to Escobar, and he had many political and judicial figures murdered in what could be described as "political hits." Escobar was a charismatic leader who was eliminated from the narco-battlefield. But eliminating charismatic leaders does not always decrease the level of violence, as was discussed earlier in this chapter. Escobar built on a culture of violence in Colombia, and he was creative in his methods. It took an effort between the U.S. Joint Special Operations Command working out of the American Embassy in partnership with Colombian national police operators, the so-called "search bloc," that led to Escobar's demise.

Transnational criminals often act in micro-solidarity without charismatic leaders. This is particularly dangerous because they just know what to do and how to do it without direction. Criminals often operate in cells, offshoots, and other types of subdivisions making their detection difficult. But a hierarchy does still exist, and it allows for a bureaucracy even when subdivisions are flat, not hierarchical, and operate without an obvious pecking order.

The Global Gun Trade is Difficult to Stop

Moreover, arms smugglers are a pernicious lot. Guns provide muscle and give confidence and power to organized criminal gangs and cartels. They add to organized crime by making gangsters in many cases outgun competition and law enforcement. Smugglers take advantage of weapons that are legally produced and that are difficult to trace. Many violent crimes that transnational organizations commit are conducted with illicit firearms. Arms trafficking also includes parts and ammunition, which is even more difficult to track. Law enforcement investigatory bodies such as Interpol, have a database of serial numbers of arms along with their make, model, and caliber. Interpol's "iArms" database also "can help identify trafficking patterns and smuggling routes of firearms."[79]

In late 2019, the United Nations Office on Drugs and Crime released statistics based on 2017 data that gave a count on all types of firearms seized by country. The United States, by far, had the most guns taken off the street with a whopping 320,000 seized in 2017.[80] Mexico had nearly 41,000 firearms seized in 2011,[81] but that number had dwindled down to 7,241 by 2017. Costa Rica confiscated 13,301 guns in 2017, which made it the top country of seized arms in Central America. Many of these arms originated from the United States. "The government of Mexico recovered and submitted more than 99,000 firearms to the U.S. Bureau of Alcohol, Tobacco, Firearms and Explosives (ATF) for tracing in the years 2007 to 2011. Of those, the vast majority — more than 68,000 — were sourced to the United States."[82]

Colombia had the most firearms seized in South America with 22,000 taken off the street in 2018. Kenya had the most firearms in Africa at a rate of 9,728 seized in 2017, which was almost 100 percent more than in 2016. Russia had 13,855 guns taken in 2017.[83] Italy took 4,545 firearms off the street in 2017. Spain removed 10,602 guns that year. Most European countries had a low number of firearm seizures. Australia led the way around the rest of the globe with 27,819 guns removed in 2017 that includes nearly 15,000 rifles.[84]

There are efforts underway to counteract the state of arms smuggling

---

79 "Illicit Arms Records and Tracing Management System (iArms)." Interpol.int.

80 "Comprehensive Statistics of Illicit Firearms Trafficking Now Available on UNODC Data Portal." DataUNODC.org.

81 *Ibid.*

82 "Gun Trafficking." Violence Policy Center. VPC.org.

83 UNODC.org

84 *Ibid.*

and proliferation. The Arms Trade Treaty has been in effect since 2014. This treaty was spawned by the United Nations General Assembly. The Arms Trade Treaty is designed to "stop the international transfer between states of weapons, munitions and related items when it is known they would be used to commit or facilitate genocide, crimes against humanity, or war crimes."[85]

In North Africa, where terror groups proliferate, Libya stands out. Libya is a large supplier of small arms to the Sahel states in Western Africa and it ships guns by boat to the Mediterranean sea lanes. Specific target countries and regions include Niger, Algeria, Mali, Gaza, Syria, and the Sinai.[86]

A United Nations envoy estimated that Libya in 2016 had 20 million pieces of small arms.[87] The United Nations imposed an arms embargo on Libya in 2011 when its leader, Muammar Gaddafi, was assassinated. Gaddafi had plans while he was alive to arm its citizens via huge small-arms depots. Crime emerges in countries where the rule of law is in question and where instability reigns. The civil war in Libya has killed thousands and displaced hundreds of thousands of people. It is so dangerous in Libya, that in 2020 the United Nations had to close a refugee agency in Tripoli. This makes for an environment that is advantageous for smuggling small arms. The European Union decided in 2020 to re-engage efforts to enforce an arms embargo against Libya by beginning sea patrols to thwart arms smuggling in the Mediterranean. The Libyan civil war has also seen numerous proxy countries involved in hostilities including Turkey, Russia, Egypt, and the United Arab

---

85 "Killer Facts 2019: The Scale of the Global Arms Trade. Amnesty International. Aug. 23, 2019.

86 Marsh, Nicholas. 2017. "Brothers Came Back with Weapons: The Effects of Arms Proliferation from Libya." *Prism*. National Defense University. Vol. 6, No. 4.

87 Nicholas, Michelle. 2016. "U.N. Approves High Seas Crackdown on Libya Arms Smuggling." *Reuters*. June 14, 2016.

Emirates. This instability is ripe for small arms smugglers to ply their wares in an advantageous manner.

Illicit gun sales can also come from thieves who steal from arms caches and stockpiles.[88] Soldiers or former soldiers sell their weapons to feed their families. The small arms numbers become staggering. "Some 500,000 people are killed each year by the 639 million small arms in circulation, and in some conflicts up to 80 percent of casualties are caused by these weapons."[89]

Is Blockchain Technology the Answer to the Circumvent Flow of Arms?

The future of curtailing the illicit flow of small arms around the world is the use of blockchain technology. There clearly needs to be a better international system in tracking firearms and blockchain could offer answers to the problem. Originally, blockchain was used for cryptocurrency, but now it has grown in use. A blockchain, according to analyst Ameer Rosic, is "a time-stamped series of immutable records of data that is managed by a cluster of computers not owned by any single entity. Each of these blocks of data (i.e., block) is secured and bound to each other using cryptographic principles (i.e., chain)."[90]

Blockchain can be used for a ledger that can help organize the data from criminal background checks on firearms. This allows multiple entities such as hospitals or mental healthcare providers to upload information on individuals who would not be legally able to access guns. Blockchain could also be used to track the sale of a firearm beginning from the manufacturer to the buyer. The technology could aid law

---

[88] Stohl, Rachel. 2004. "The Tangled Web of Illicit Arms Trafficking." *American Progress*. Oct. 12, 2004.

[89] *Ibid.*

[90] Rosic, Ameer. "What is Blockchain Technology? A Step-by-Step Guide For Beginners." *Blockgeeks*.

enforcement in creating databases for small arms purchases around the globe. Ammunition could even be tracked this way.[91]

Blockchain and machine learning algorithms could also be used to track human traffickers and smugglers and those that engage in perpetrating human slavery. Many of these crimes are hidden and unreported. But blockchain would help law enforcement around the globe to discover perpetrators and victims.

Human Trafficking Will Not Go Away

Estimates reveal that there are between 20 million and 40 million people who have been trafficked and are confined in some form of human slavery.[92] According to Human Rights First, "Human trafficking earns global profits of roughly $150 billion a year for traffickers, $99 billion of which comes from commercial sexual exploitation."[93] Most of these victims are women. They are coerced into sex work or forced labor or both. But others are made to enter into marriage, serve in the military or terror/ insurgent groups, forced into criminal activities, or even trafficked for their organs or other body parts. According to the Migration Data Portal, the average age of each victim was 26-years-old in 2016.[94]

In the United States there are 18,000 to 20,000 victims trafficked each year, according to the Women's Center for Youth and Family Services.[95] 16 percent of those abducted were children. The National Human Trafficking Hotline said that "Since 2007, more than 49,000

---

91 Mire, Sam. 2018. "Blockchain In The Firearms Industry: 6 Possible Use Cases." *Disruptor Daily*. Nov. 15, 2018.

92 "Forced Labor, Modern Slavery, and Human Trafficking." International Labor Organization.

93 "Human Trafficking by the Numbers." Human Rights First. Jan 7, 2017.

94 Migrationportal.com.

95 "U.S. Victim Statistics." Women's Center for Youth and Family Services."

cases of human trafficking in the U.S. have been reported to the National Human Trafficking Hotline, which receives an average of 150 calls per day."[96]

Technological Answers to Diminish Wildlife Smuggling and Poaching

Another transnational criminal category that can be tackled with emerging technology is wildlife smuggling and poaching. Drones are already being used to reduce the levels of African poaching by moving herds of animals with ivory tusks, such as driving elephants and rhinos away from poachers. Poaching and wildlife smuggling is a big business. According to PoachingFacts.com, the illegal trade is worth billions of dollars. Prices for ivory tusks are noteworthy. Rhino horns go for over $60,000 a kilo. Raw elephant ivory sells for at least $2,100 a kilo, and elephant ivory in Chinese illicit markets is priced at $730 a kilo.[97]

The World Wildlife Fund is using a software system based on mobile thermal and infrared cameras.[98] The cameras can find poachers and then alert park rangers to their location. The cameras consist of stationary sensors paired with a mobile camera mounted on utility vehicles. The software looks for heat signatures that are comparable to humans. When a "hit" is identified, the information is sent to a game warden and that individual starts a quick reaction team in motion.[99]

Transnational criminal organizations and the activities they perpetrate greatly affects international security. Governments must expend precious time and money to catch and prosecute offenders. These are resources that could be dedicated to developing militaries, defense budgets, and new weapons systems. Transnational criminal gangs are

---

96 "Myths, Facts, and Statistics: Human Trafficking Facts. Polaris Project.

97 Poaching Facts.com

98 WorldWildlife.org

99 *Ibid.*

difficult to combat despite advances in technology. They stick together by maximizing Weberian discipline. They form bureaucracies and hierarchies. Motivated by money over everything else, they violate the rule of law and exacerbate the efficacy of host governments. Human trafficking and slavery is obviously evil and appears that no end is in sight for the crimes.

CHAPTER THREE

A CHANGING CLIMATE AND INTERNATIONAL SECURITY

It was a different type of order. I briefly served in South Korea while in the U.S. Army. During the monsoon season of summer weeks, it rains nearly every day throughout the Republic of Korea. We were used to getting wet and just wearing our soaking uniforms until they dried when the sun came out later in the afternoon. This time we were ordered to wear a wet-weather top, otherwise known as a jacket. This seemed like an odd request since we were so used to being wet. That was in 2001. Flash forward to 2020 and the monsoon season had changed, and jackets were not enough to stop the damage of climate change.

South Korea had to endure the longest wet season in a number of years with 44 consecutive days of rain in 2020. These storms resulted in mudslides, landslides, flash floods, and other catastrophes that killed 18 people. In the future, a jacket is not going to keep you dry and certainly not safe. But that is an example of how countries and their militaries are becoming over-matched. The Republic of Korea (ROK) Army does not have a National Guard to respond to natural disasters like the United States military has. This organization may shift in the future as climate change and new weather patterns emerge. The ROK Army and Marines may have to respond to internal natural disasters which cost time, money, and resources – efforts that take away from the main mission – which is to protect the homeland from North Korea.

International security continues to be affected by climate change, water scarcity, and food availability. "By 2030, the world could face demands for 50 percent more food and energy and 30 percent more water, while their availability becomes threatened by climate change."[100] Climate change is difficult to define. At any given time and use case, it can be global warming and a rise in global temperatures, sea level rising, deforestation, soil erosion, desertification, changing levels of atmospheric carbon dioxide, greenhouse gas effects, icecap melting, lack of precipitation, change in wind patterns, greater number of natural disasters, and glacier melting. That is quite a list of maladies, which shows the difficulty of counteracting its effects. For the purposes of this book, I shall use an "all of the above" definition.

Climate change can affect international security and warfare by endangering military infrastructure and bases, threatening control of sea lanes, increasing the incidence of resource wars, and negatively affecting logistics by making feeding and supplying troops with food, weapons, ammunition, and fuel more difficult. Climate change could create a migration crisis in which developed nations would fall victim to virus and influenza pandemics such as the coronavirus. Climate change also affects training of military personnel, defense research, development, and testing. Climate change hinders movement and helps enemy's anti-access area denial approaches to warfare. Take the critical U.S. military base on Guam. It would be an obvious victim of sea-level rise. The resulting damage to the base would keep U.S. and allied forces from counter-attacking an offensive move from North Korea or China.

---

[100] Werrell, Caitlin and Francesco Femia. 2015. "Climate Change in the UK National Security Strategy and Strategic Defence Security Review 2015." The Center of Climate and Security. Nov. 24, 2015.

Climate Change and Anti-Access Area Denial Challenges Military Forces

Anti-access area denial is an important concept in modern warfare. Friendly forces and opposing forces often jockey to move into a contested location that is favorable to one or the other. Opposing forces then attempt to deny access to the location or area. In the case of Guam, China or North Korea could take advantage of climate change, when rising sea levels in Guam would damage the base. China or North Korea would then be able to deny forces from Guam their access to favorable locations on the map. Guam is a combined naval and air base that houses a number of robust assets. It is a good example of how climate change is affecting combat readiness. Guam has at least four U.S. attack submarines. It also has a rotating squadron of nuclear-capable bombers. There are around 7,000 U.S. Naval and Air Force personnel on the island. It forms the last line of defense for the Pacific Ocean. Guam is already undergoing signs of climate change with drought, rising sea levels, and lower levels of drinking water. The coral that protects Guam from soil degradation and storms is falling to dangerous levels.[101]

U.S. Military Installations Will Feel the Pain

In North America, numerous U.S. naval bases are threatened by climate change. The number is rising each year. Norfolk, Virginia, headquarters of the Atlantic fleet, and headquarters of NATO allied command, is the largest naval installation in the world. It is home to at least 75 ships, 134 aircraft, and 80,000 sailors. Norfolk is already getting damaging floods and sea level rise is a definite risk. "A 2014 Department of Defense study found one and a half feet of sea level rise to be a 'tipping point' for Norfolk; at that point it will suffer significant infrastructure damage and losses in mission performance.[102] Experts predict sea levels will rise

---

[101] *Ibid.*

[102] "2014 Climate Change Adaptation Roadmap." Department of Defense, Deputy Under Secretary of Defense Installations and Environment.

a minimum of three feet-three inches within the next 100 years. Along with sea levels rising, hurricanes are a definite risk to the naval base.

That is not all. "Increased maintenance and repair of installations has been required: wildfires in the Western U.S. impacting Vandenberg Air Force Base and the Point Mugu Sea Range, hurricanes causing damage and delays at Tyndall Air Force Base in Florida, permafrost thawing impacting operations at Fort Greely in Alaska, and rising seas contaminating freshwater supplies at atoll installations in the Pacific."[103]

Michael Klare is the author of *All Hell Breaking Loose: The Pentagon's Perspective on Climate Change.*[104] Klare, referring to the U.S. Department of Defense, said, "Climate change is a threat in their eyes because it's going to degrade their ability to deal with conventional military problems. It's going to create chaos, violence, mass migrations, pandemics, and state collapse around the world, particularly in vulnerable areas like Africa and the Middle East."[105] The U.S. Department of Defense is also one of the largest carbon producers in the world.[106]

Military Forces Around the Globe Turn to Climate Change in the Arctic

Climate change has focused attention on the Arctic as polar icecaps have shrunk. This has resulted in nations' naval access becoming unnavigable. The U.S. Navy is focusing its attention off the coast of Alaska. For the last several decades, the navy had its eyes set on the Persian Gulf, the Indian Ocean, and the Pacific. Now near peer-competitors such as

---

103 Liebermann, Bruce. 2019. "A Brief Introduction to Climate Change and National Security." *Yale Climate Connections*. July 23, 2019.

104 Klare, Michael. *All Hell Breaking Loose: The Pentagon's Perspective on Climate Change.* New York: Metropolitan Books.

105 *Ibid.*

106 Hussein, Murtaza. 2019. "War on the World: Industrialized Militaries Are a Bigger Part of the Climate Emergency Than You Know." *The Intercept*. Sept. 15, 2019.

Russia and China have designs on the Arctic. U.S. aircraft carriers and their strike groups have not navigated the seas above the Arctic Circle during that time. An Arctic security strategy is emerging, and its focus is on training in the region. In 2018, the USS Harry S. Truman participated in exercises in the Norwegian Sea. No other American ship had steamed that far north since 1991.[107] In 2019, the navy took part in a large war game off Alaska called Northern Edge. U.S. Marines and the U.S. Coast Guard took part in these maneuvers. Most of the navy's ships are not configured to operate in icy waters, so operating in the Arctic is limited due to untested capabilities.

The navy and marines are working to keep the newly opened sea lanes in the Arctic open for free navigation as more trade and transit moves through the region. As global temperatures rise and more polar ice melts, a new Arctic defense strategy is being implemented by the United States. Part of this strategy will include tactics from the Cold War. U.S. fighter jets often have to intercept Russian aircraft flying near the coast of Alaska. Russian airplanes also patrol the skies at the opposite end of the Arctic – near Norway. These types of aerial games were prevalent during the Cold War. In these scenarios, there is a heightened risk of accidents or miscalculations that could spark a greater conflict.

Russia is seeking to dominate the Arctic. Its land mass makes up 53 percent of Arctic coastline.[108] Russia has around two million people living in the region.[109] The Russians are aiming for the extraction of oil and natural gas in the Arctic. The Kremlin has focused on an ambitious

---

107 Hughes, Zachariah. "As Polar Ice Cap Recedes, The U.S. Navy Looks North." *National Public Radio*. June 12, 2019.

108 Ellyatt, Holly. 2019. "Russia Is Dominating the Arctic, But It's Not Looking to Fight Over It." *CNBC*. Dec. 27, 2019.

109 *Ibid.*

Liquid Natural Gas project on the Yamal Peninsula and has also given tax breaks for hydrocarbon exploration in the Arctic.[110]

It is understandable that Russia is self-interested in the Arctic. What they are doing can be considered a power grab and an example of self-help – a principle of the realism theory of international relations. Russia has a very obstinate view of sovereignty and nationalism. They are fighting for relevance in their own neighborhood. The oil crash of 2020 encouraged the Russians and the Saudi Arabians to fight for market share. Both decided to increase production and then later to cut it. This makes them "swing producers" that can change the price of oil. But overall oil demand around the world was waning because of the coronavirus pandemic. The resulting price war hurt Russia, which depends on hydrocarbons for much of its economic growth and government revenue. But that is not enough to change their Arctic strategy. This is a case of offensive realism in which Russia tries to change the status quo and dominate more land mass in its own neighborhood.

The Arctic is a playground yearning for an international hierarchy. Canada, Norway, Denmark, Iceland, Sweden, and Finland make Arctic claims for their own national interest. All are fighting for natural resources, although this does not mean conflict is imminent. But it is a version of a 21st Century "great game" of intrigue and power projection in the Arctic with realist principles of self-help, dominion, and sovereignty.

The United Kingdom Fears the Threat of Climate Change

In the United Kingdom the threat is acute, especially for rising sea levels that threaten the island nation. The UK Ministry of Defense also is sounding the alarm on climate change because British military infrastructure is at risk. The Ministry of Defense holds large amounts of

---

110 *Ibid.*

land in the United Kingdom. 431,000 hectares or 1.8 percent of the country's land is controlled by the Ministry of Defense.[111] This is land that houses submarines and other major military arms systems. Training sites, such as those in Kent and Pembrokeshire, are becoming endangered because of flooding.[112] The Royal Air Force installation at Brize Norton and the Royal Navy bases at Plymouth and Portsmouth also face flooding threats.[113]

The UK has to rely on sea lanes to import food and fuel from foreign locations. Its imports come from the Middle East and Asia, so it is paramount that the Suez Canal, the Strait of Hormuz, and the Strait of Malacca, remain open.[114] Natural disasters or the rising of sea levels around these geographical areas would be bad news for Britain. The United Kingdom has already cut defense budgets over the years. Britain spends about $49 billion, a little over two percent of its GDP, on its military. This compares to around four percent of GDP that was regularly spent during the Cold War.

Therefore, the UK faces a choice: increase defense spending to better answer global security threats or cut defense spending to better position the military to survive during a long period of climate change. This may mean new defense cuts for Britain, and it may mean military retrenching. Rising sea levels clearly threaten British military bases on its coastlines. Defense budgets will need to spend money on re-locating and re-purposing existing military bases. These changes cost money – funds that could be spent on new arms systems upgrades and for increasing the

---

[111] Sears, Ben. 2018. "Battling the Elements – Adapting to Climate Change on the U.K.'s Defense Estate." *PreventionWeb*. Dec. 20, 2018.

[112] *Ibid.*

[113] *Ibid.*

[114] King, Ed. 2014. "UK: Climate Change Is a 'National Security' Issue Say Military Experts." *PreventionWeb*. Feb. 20, 2014.

number of military personnel. The British Army is already contemplating cutting main battle tanks from its arsenal.

The British Military Faces Difficult Choices

This begs the question of what is the future of the British military? It seems that now is the time for difficult decisions. The British Army has been undergoing a reduction in force. It was scheduled to presently have 117,000 soldiers in which 30,000 would be reserve troops – or just 87,000 on active duty. By 2020, the number had dwindled down to less than 73,000 actively serving.[115] In 2003, to put this number in perspective, the British Army numbered 102,000.[116] A large contingent of reserve forces would enable the army to respond to natural disasters such as seasonal flooding in the critical southern part of the country. This would also allow the army to respond to rising sea levels that are expected to happen in the future. The Royal Navy will also be needed to deliver the correct number of engineers and logistics experts to respond to any flooding. If there is another threat to the homeland, the British military would be stretched by having to fight on both fronts – a climate change disaster and a terrorist attack – for example.

The British military still has an identity problem and must figure out its priorities in the 2020s. Fighting climate change will have to be one high priority. It must also decide how to balance against competitors like Russia. The British Army is clearly outgunned and outmanned versus the Russian Army. The British have an outdated artillery force, for example. They have few artillery pieces and their most modern artillery systems, like its multiple launch rockets, depend on GPS-guidance that can be jammed by Russian electronic countermeasures systems. Many British units are more inclined to do light infantry tasks and

---

115 McGlennon, Brian. 2019. "Fury as Defense Chiefs Plan to Shrink British Army to Smallest Size in Centuries." *Sunday Express*. Nov. 24, 2019.

116 *Ibid.*

these brigades may have just two batteries of howitzers, while a Russian motor-rifle brigade may have upward of 81 artillery pieces. As is the case with all modern militaries, the British face cyber threats that could disrupt communications and logistics that would keep units from beginning and maintaining a war footing. The British military may have to use weapons systems that are "stand-off," such as rockets and missiles that can be launched from many miles away. The Royal Navy will have two aircraft carriers by 2022 that will enable greater expeditionary capabilities along with stealth fighters like the F-35 that can compete with Russia since the Russian Navy has only one aircraft carrier.

Keeping all this in mind, how will the British military deal with climate change? Training areas are threatened by floods and rising sea levels as discussed previously. Much of its defense efforts are dependent on vehicles, ships, and aircraft that are powered by fossil fuels. It is not clear how the Ministry of Defense will make a transition to renewables that will replace weapons systems running on hydrocarbons. Electric vehicles would be one area in which a transition could be targeted. Drones, depending on their size, have a relatively low level of fuel burn. Forward operating bases can be powered by solar energy. During the war in Iraq, coalition forces used forward operating bases that were powered by gasoline generators. This forced convoys to bring in fuel to power electricity and air conditioning. Insurgent forces then attacked the convoys, so making outposts sustainable can also help with force protection. But these changes alone will not get the British military to zero-percent emissions by 2050. Making changes early will costs less than waiting to act in future years. Using fuel and conserving energy also has cost-cutting efficiencies. Recruiting and retaining personnel is another area in which the Ministry of Defense is challenged since young people often wish to work for an organization that is committed to helping and not hurting the environment.

Climate change also affects the British military's ability to conduct normal operations. Anti-access area denial is usually based on adversary's actions, but climate change can limit force mobility and make certain geographical areas of operations into "no-go terrain." Fossil fuels also cost more than renewables, even though conversion to alternative energy sources requires an upfront investment. To reach these aspirations, the British Ministry of Defense will have to work closely with civilian subject matter experts in order to reach carbon footprint and greenhouse emissions goals.

The Whole of Systems Approach: The Future of the Fight Against Climate Change

Fighting climate change requires dramatic social transformation. The military must be part of that social change. The concept of "Enmity," from the Clausewitzian trinity, is also part of warfare, but that is usually focused on hatred of a human enemy. To win against climate change requires a shift in thinking about what defines an enemy. Climate change can be quantified, but not easily personified. Fighting climate change requires a "whole of systems approach." This is a top to bottom construct and calls for a distinction between friend and enemy and what it means for civil society and the state. As Malesevic noted, "Through warfare the state advanced its fiscal administration, courts and other legal institutions, regional administration, and financial infrastructure while more widespread mobilization of the people, including universal conscription led toward the steady extension of various political and social rights to a wider population, thus enhancing civil society."[117]

This discussion of civil society and state is the crux of the war against climate change since it requires action from the military and the civilian governing structures. This may mean that the civilian populace has to give up some of their individual rights if a whole of systems approach is prosecuted against climate change. This is an echo of Thomas Hobbes

---

[117] *The Sociology of War and Violence*, pg. 73

who believed that the social contract, or the mutual transferring of right, entailed giving up individual rights in exchange for common security. The British people have a history of shared sacrifice dating back to the First and Second World Wars and beyond.

Thus, geopolitics is in Britain's DNA. Not so for Weber. Weber often did not take geopolitics into account when analyzing warfare.[118] But geopolitics does matter in the war against climate change. For example, if Britain is focused on using its military to fight climate change, what if its adversary is ignoring climate change and mobilizing all its resources in warfare against the United Kingdom? This is a frightening scenario since it assumes that all countries will mobilize against climate change when some states take the realist perspective and seek to maximize power, accept interstate warfare, and contend with anarchy as the normal outcome of the global political order. Britain sees climate change and environmental improvement as a post-industrial condition, meaning that it has already gone through an industrial revolution and answered basic human needs of feeding, clothing, and housing citizens to include offering them jobs and healthcare. Other states' views on geopolitics does matter, despite what Weber claims.

Much has been made about globalism versus nationalism in political analysis. With Brexit, Britain has taken on some nationalistic tendencies and de-emphasized globalist inclinations. The fight against climate change is a global phenomenon. Countries such as China, India, and the United States lead the world in carbon emissions. The United Kingdom is a member of the United Nations Framework Convention on Climate Change which was the impetus on the Paris Climate Change Agreement of 2015. It is interesting that Britain voted to leave the European Union yet remains part of the UN framework. So, there is a tenuous balancing act between nationalism and globalism in the country, which makes for

---

[118] *Ibid*, pg. 71.

a curious state of affairs. Most climate change activists believe in a global approach to counter climate change.

The United States, of course, under President Donald Trump, pulled out of the Paris Accord for nationalistic and realist self-interest reasons. President Joe Biden decided America would rejoin the accord. Britain is straddling both world views and it stands to reason that some of its citizenry that would need to be mobilized fully against climate change are skeptical of international agreements that could reduce sovereignty. The military is caught in the middle of this state of affairs, but it seems the country is on board with climate change activism. Former Prime Minster Theresa May, a Conservative, committed the country to a pledge to reach net zero carbon emissions by 2050. In a pre-election poll conducted in 2019, two-thirds of British voters agreed that climate change was the biggest issue "facing mankind."[119] Only 7 percent disagreed, according to the survey. This would appear to show that the many Eurosceptics are not climate sceptics after all.

Polling like this indicates that there is an understandable yearning for the British military to prepare for climate change and become "greener." Civilians will have to buy in fully to the transition away from fossil fuels. There are only five coal-fired power plants in the UK, but they are carbon emitters that will need to change over to carbon-free if climate goals will be met by 2050.

Australia Is Scorched by Climate Change

While the United Kingdom's biggest risk is rise of sea levels during a climate emergency, in Australia it is global warming and lack of rainfall. Each year, high temperatures, strong winds, and low humidity lead to bushfire season. This occurs in summer months and the fires have been going on for centuries, even before Australia was colonized

---

[119] Carrington, Damian. 2019. "Climate Crisis Affects How Majority Will Vote in UK Election – Poll." *The Guardian*. Oct. 30, 2019.

by European explorers in 1606. The first most serious bushfire in the post-colonial country's history occurred in 1851 – one that consumed 5 million hectares in the state of Victoria. A bad drought precipitated the natural disaster. Twelve people were killed along with a million sheep and thousands of cattle. This fire and subsequent deadly bushfires throughout Australia's history are known by the day it burned the worst, so the 1851 blaze was known as the Black Thursday fires. Four other bushfires killed Australian citizens. 173 people perished during the Black Saturday fires in 2009. Mass bushfires in 1926, 1939, and 1967 killed between 60 and 70 people during each occurrence. The Ash Wednesday bushfires in Victoria and South Australia left 75 people dead in 1983.

Beginning in June of 2019, a time known as the Black Summer, bushfires spread rapidly. By November, the flames in New South Wales had exploded. The government quickly called a state of emergency. The fires also hit Victoria, sent smoke to the Australian Capital Territory, and burned in Queensland, South Australia, Western Australia, and Tasmania. At least 33 died and many others went missing. Around 3,000 homes were destroyed or damaged and 46 million acres were consumed by flames.[120] An area the size of Iceland had been scorched.[121] By February 2020, huge torrential rainstorms allowed first responders to control the fires. But smoke created a health emergency as some of the world's dirtiest air descended upon Australians. Smoke entered hospitals and disrupted care, surgeries, and new births. Smoke even reached New Zealand, Chile, and Argentina, while the large plumes could be seen from space. Along the coastline, six hours south of Sydney, residents

---

[120] Calma, Justine. 2020. "What You Need to Know About the Australian Bushfires." *The Verge*. Feb. 13, 2020.

[121] Westrate, Rachel. 2020. "How Bushfires Will Affect Australia's Security." *Lawfare*. Feb. 5, 2020.

were forced to evacuate along the beaches with some people literally jumping in the water to avoid the flames and intense heat.[122]

Three American volunteer firefighters died in January 2020 when their water tanker airplane went down in New South Wales. More than one billion animals also were killed in Australia.[123] Australians endured the hottest day on record during the fires in December of 2019 with temperatures near 106 degrees Fahrenheit or 40.9 Celsius. "2019 was the hottest and the driest year in Australia's history. So, we actually saw temperature records be broken all over the country," Joelle Gergis, a climate scientist at the Australian National University, said.[124] 2019 was 1.52 Celsius hotter than the 1961-1990 average.[125] Continued global warming has scientists concerned that the Great Barrier Reef would be in danger.[126]

Climate change in Australia, especially global warming, was considered the culprit by many. The World Weather Attribution Consortium investigated this round of bushfires and published their findings in March of 2020. The authors of the study wrote that global warming enhanced the chances of fire by 30 percent.[127] They wrote, "If global temperatures rise by 2 degrees Celsius, as seems likely, such conditions will occur at least four times more often."[128]

The crisis began to take on a national security dimension when the Australian military was called out to assist disaster efforts. The

---

122 "Australia's Bushfires Show Dramatic Effects of Climate Change." University of Notre Dame Sustainability Studies.

123 *Ibid.*

124 *Ibid.*

125 Thomas, Michael. 2020. "Bushfire Crisis Shows Australia Needs a Strategic Response to Climate Change." *The Strategis*t. Jan. 14, 2020.

126 Kormann, Carolyn. 2020. "When Will Australia's Prime Minister Accept the Reality of the Climate Crisis?" *New Yorker*. Jan. 15, 2020.

127 Ghosh, Pallab. 2020. "Climate Change Boosted Australia Bushfire Risk By At Least 30%." *BBC*. March 4, 2020.

128 *Ibid.*

Australian Defense Force mobilized 6,500 soldiers and 3,000 reserve troops. "These troops assisted in evacuations, clearing roads, operating emergency medical facilities, disposing of animal carcasses, felling and removing unsafe trees, delivering clean water and food, and maintaining containment lines."[129] The Australian Navy helped rescue people in Victoria and the air force transported fire fighters and equipment.[130]

What if global warming continues in Australia and each bushfire season becomes worse? The military would have to be used again. This requirement would make it difficult for the Australian Defense Force to fight in two different fronts at the same time. Australia lives in a neighborhood with a revanchist China and a threatening North Korea. The United States depends on Australia as a partner to house U.S. Marines in Darwin and as an intelligence partner as part of the "Five-Eye's" shared intelligence network. The Five Eyes stands for an intelligence sharing consortium made up of the United States, United Kingdom, Canada, Australia, and New Zealand.

Australia Must Endure a Shifting Military Strategy

This means, that like the United Kingdom, Australia must examine its military strategy for the 2020s. Devising strategic plans is sometimes easier when there are known competitors or enemies. Late last decade, the United States had its "4 + 1" construct of challenges (sometimes called "2 + 3"), in which the main priorities were mostly based on near-peer competitors such as Russia, China, Iran, North Korea, and terrorism. This was a way to immediately grasp and understand the national military strategy in shorthand. Having a deliberate strategy can drive personnel decisions, budgetary priorities, and weapons acquisition plans. Notice that climate change is not one of the 4 + 1 or 2 + 3 construct of challenges for the U.S. military.

---

[129] "How Bushfires Will Affect Australia's Security."

[130] *Ibid.*

For Australia, its national military strategy is based on the strong alliance with the United States and recognizing that China is a revisionist power, which means that China is striving for more power or a revision to the status quo. This is called offensive realism. Countries engaging in power revisions can sometimes be more prone to engage in conflict. China is definitely projecting power over the Eastern Sea Lanes. But China faces problems of climate change too. The country is resource challenged, whether it is energy security or water security. China is also severely affected by desertification and expansion of the Gobi Desert that threatens waterways. More than 25 percent of its land mass is covered by desert. This affects fresh water supply and the amount of arable farmland to feed its citizens. Plus, desertification creates sandstorms that blast cities in its northern region. Perhaps Australia and China can focus on its similarities to include global warming and resources challenges rather than its differences in power distribution or power competition.

Australia also has to worry about foreign fighters coming back from war zones in the Middle East and North Africa. This means extremist militants who are Australian citizens get radicalized and then leave for Syria, Iraq, Afghanistan, or Libya and then return with intentions of creating attacks in their home country. And like all countries, Australia must prepare for cyber-attacks that threaten critical infrastructure.

The current Australian Prime Minister as of 2020, Scott Morrison, has shown a history of being a climate skeptic and is an avowed supporter of the country's fossil fuel industry, especially coal mining. He succeeded Malcolm Turnbull who had a climate change program that would have attempted to cut Australia's greenhouse emissions. Morrison has conducted interviews in which he has acknowledged that climate change has played a role in the 2019-2020 bushfires, but his government's climate policy lacked details. And Morrison has yet to elaborate on how the Australian Department of Defense would have a role in fighting climate change. Morrison has kept his priority on supporting the country's coal industry. In February of 2020, "Morrison announced

$4 million in federal funding for a feasibility study into a new coal-fired power plant—making Australia 'one of the last developed countries actively considering new coal-fired power stations.'"[131]

New Zealand Has Climate Change in its Crosshairs

Meanwhile, New Zealand's military is making plans for climate change. The Ministry of Defense and the New Zealand Defence force has identified several threats in the climate crisis operating environment: "human security challenges; health-related crises; resource competition; violence from mismanaged adaptation or migration; and land disputes."[132]

New Zealand's military is focusing on joint operations and working with partners to mitigate climate change and improve capacity building. They will increase operational tempo. Defense forces will focus on better collection and sharing of real-time information during a future climate crisis. The MoD will foresee environmental impact on military training. It will also prepare for climate change induced natural disaster responses.[133]

Although some of these actions sound vague and aspirational, they are evidence that the New Zealand military is planning for the worst and training for the coming crisis. It seems that the main thrust of the New Zealand defense response would be for a natural disaster or water shortage and the repercussions and potential mitigation from those types of crises. Concrete steps from the Ministry of Defense would be plans for "Enhanced sealift and airlift capabilities, improved aerial surveillance and maritime domain awareness, as well as increasing the size of the New Zealand Army."[134]

---

[131] Withers, Rachel. 2020. "The Great Australian Cop-Out." *Slate*. Feb. 27, 2020.

[132] "Responding to the Climate Crisis: An Implementation Plan." 2019. New Zealand Ministry of Defense. May 12, 2019.

[133] *Ibid.*

[134] Mark, Ron and James Shaw. 2019. "Defence Climate Change Implementation Plan Released." New Zealand Official Government. Dec. 9, 2019.

Canada Has also Mobilized

Another member of the Five Eyes allied intelligence consortium, Canada, has used its military in natural disasters and extreme weather events that could be argued are the result of climate change. The Canadian military had to respond to only one natural disaster in 2016 – a fire in Fort McMurray. But in the succeeding years more extreme events cropped up that needed a military response. During the next two years, the military in Canada was called out six times for responses to disasters. By the Spring of 2019, "more soldiers were deployed to assist states of emergencies — during floods in Ontario, Quebec, and New Brunswick as well as wildfires in Alberta — than were deployed overseas."[135] Canada is seeing the need to increase its troop level in order to better respond to climate threats and natural disasters such as fires and flooding. The country also must respond to military needs outside the country.

In 2019, Canada conducted an assistance deployment to fight extremist terror and insurgent groups in Mali. An after-action-review determined that in future deployments to Africa, climate change will be even worse on the continent. Canada has also advised countries on peace and stability operations in the Democratic Republic of Congo and South Sudan. This will affect the United States as well, since the Department of Defense has Africa Command with a large presence in Djibouti and it deploys troops in advisory capacities to help countries address violent extremism. Africa has numerous climate emergency problems. Drought, sea level rise, soil erosion and threats to farmland, desertification, water insecurity, disease, and epidemics, and many aspects of climate change will afflict Africa.

---

[135] Major, Darren and Salimah, Shivji. 2019. "Canada's Military Feeling the Strain Responding to Climate Change." *CBC*. June 24, 2019.

Africa Is in Great Danger

Africa is the continent that is arguably most at risk from climate change. Africa has 17 percent of the world's population, but it creates only four percent of total carbon emissions.[136] Not only is draught a threat, but the continent also suffers from too much rain during monsoon seasons that creates dangerous flooding. In 2019, deadly floods that killed hundreds and displaced hundreds of thousands occurred in Sudan, South Sudan, Djibouti, Somalia, Kenya, Tanzania, Burundi, Democratic Republic of Congo, Uganda, and Central African Republic.[137]

Many national and local governments are not sophisticated enough or do not have the tax revenue and operating budgets to address these challenges. Weather patterns in Africa are notoriously difficult to predict. Armies and national police are often undermanned and can sometimes be corrupt, which makes it more challenging to respond to a natural disaster. Much of the economies are often agrarian and farmers are the most hard-hit populations during droughts and floods that destroy crops. Populations are affected by malaria and HIV-AIDS, Covid-19, and other communicable diseases that place a greater strain on governments. Public health systems lack sufficient government budgets and do not have the ideal number of hospitals, doctors, and nurses. These challenges leave inadequate money and resources to governments to address the rapidly changing effects of climate change.

This makes fighting extremist groups more difficult. Al-Qaeda in the Islamic Maghreb operates in Mali, Algeria, Niger, and Mauritania. Al-Shabaab has its area of operations primarily in Somalia, Kenya, Tanzania, and Mozambique. Boko Haram controls territory in northeast Nigeria. Terrorist organizations become stronger when African communities are hit by climate change. When farmland is spoiled because of drought or erosion, young males normally engaged in farming

---

136 "How Africa Will Be Affected by Climate Change." *BBC*. Dec. 15, 2019.

137 *Ibid.*

are more likely to become radicalized and join terror groups. Natural disasters that create migration force people into refugee camps where refugees can more easily become radicalized or influence them to look at more extreme forms of religion. Rising sea levels also make it more likely that afflicted cities on the coasts will have larger pockets of unemployment and poverty, which again makes for a disaffected group of young males that are susceptible to radicalization. Militaries in Africa that are tasked with fighting terrorists must also worry about public health emergencies with outbreaks of Ebola, malaria, and Covid-19.

In the 21st century, Africa will need continued military assistance from countries outside the continent to fight extremist terror groups. It will also need aid and support to address climate change. This is a matter of human security. Human security is an important aspect of international security. Human security is freedom from fear and want.[138] Most Western ideals on international security focus on territorial sovereignty and territorial integrity. But Africans suffer from a lack of human security. They often lack security in "personal surroundings, community, and the environment."[139] Human Security, according to the United Nations, is freedom from violence and harm; freedom from disease; freedom from a plunging level of human rights; freedom from corruption; freedom from corruption; freedom from forced migration; and freedom from an unclean environment.[140]

Thus, climate change leads to a decreased level of human security and this affects Africa to a great extent. Africa will suffer disproportionately compared to the Global North because the continent is less responsible for emissions compared to the developed world. The continent is also water insecure, which increases the chances for conflict

[138] King, Gary and Christopher J. L. Murray. 2002. "Rethinking Human Security." *Political Science Quarterly*. Vol. 116, pp. 585-610.

[139] *Ibid.*

[140] *Ibid.*

over water scarcity "The UN has identified nine river basins in Africa that are at risk for the onset of tensions or conflict, among them the Kunene, Okvanago, Zambezi, Limpopo, Orange, and Nile."[141] Adding to the problem, rising air temperatures tend to evaporate water sources quicker. Plus, a lack of consistent water supply affects the amount of food that is grown, and Africa is plagued by a lack of food security.

In the Central African Republic, the situation with conflict and climate change is particularly acute. The Central African Republic has been in a civil war since 2012. The war is sectarian between Islamic and Christian groups and the government. The main militias fighting each other are called Seleka and Anti-Balaka, but there are several other militias engaged in combat. There have been high levels of atrocities, including religious and ethnic cleansing. According to the "Global Conflict Tracker," from the Council on Foreign Relations, "Reports by human rights groups and UN agencies suggest that crimes committed by both ex-Seleka forces and Anti-Balaka groups amount to war crimes and other crimes against humanity."[142] Conflict is also between groups who work the land as farmers and those who herd cattle, which is an interesting sociological battle between agriculturalists and pastoralists. Both groups struggle amid droughts and floods.

The warring factions and the government have partitioned the country into various areas of control and 2.9 million people need humanitarian assistance.[143] Over 580,000 are internally displaced.[144] And nearly 15,000 United Nations personnel are in the country conducting various operations to quell the violence and help the afflicted.[145] "A peace agree-

---

141 Brown, Oli and Alec Crawford. 2009. "Climate Change and Security in Africa." International Institute for Sustainable Development. March, 2009.

142 "Global Conflict Tracker." Council of Foreign Relations.

143 *Ibid.*

144 *Ibid.*

145 *Ibid.*

ment signed in June 2017 between the government and thirteen of the fourteen main armed factions had little effect, and ex-Seleka and Anti-Balaka militias along with hundreds of other localized groups operate openly and control as much as two-thirds of CAR's territory."[146]

Amidst the violence, the Central African Republic is suffering from climate change. Temperatures are changing. Rainfall levels have shrunk causing droughts in some areas. Increased levels of rainfall in other areas have caused floods to hazardous effect as the country devolves into a failed state. There is not a government infrastructure to react to climate change since central authorities do not control the entire country. "Water availability and agriculture are two key areas of vulnerability in the Central African Republic. There are two extremes when it comes to water — longer dry spells and an increased prevalence of floods," said Denis Sonwa, a scientist and agro-ecologist.[147] In October 2019, flooding ravaged the country, which destroyed 10,000 homes, killed dozens, and affected 100,000 people.[148] A tributary of the River Congo rose to flood levels along 372 miles of shore and crushed houses built of mud-brick.[149]

Citizens in the Central African Republic dealing with conflict and climate change lack government welfare programs to ease the burden for people being displaced without adequate food and water. This is another reason why climate change hits people in Africa unequally. Conflict and climate can be hugely destructive. The Central African Republic is an excellent case study for this phenomenon. So is Syria

---

[146] *Ibid.*

[147] Johnson, Katherine. 2013. "Tackling Climate Change May Lessen Central African Republic Conflict Risks-Scientists." *Forests News*. Aug. 22, 2013.

[148] Haynes, Suyin. 2019. "'No Safety Net.' How Climate Change and Unprecedented Flooding Is Destroying Communities in the Central African Republic." *TIME*. Dec. 24, 2019.

[149] *Ibid.*

after the Arab Spring in 2010. Syria had faced a drought in which many rural citizens migrated to small towns and cities.[150] This put pressure on the Syrian government to respond to the bad economy and to provide jobs and basic services for the migrants. There was also a large population of Iraqi immigrants fleeing conflict in that country. This led to more civil unrest that helped spark the civil war that ravaged the country for a decade. Sudan is another example of when climate change led to a resource-based internal conflict as citizens fight for access to food and water because of drought.

Russia Sees Opportunity in Risk of Climate Change

While it is clear that Africa will have trouble because of climate threats in the coming years, Russia, due to its huge landmass, is also at risk for global warming. Russia endured a warming trend in July 2010 that resulted in a heat wave, wildfires, and crop destruction. 56,000 Russians died. In the future, Russia will have to contend with the permafrost melting in the Arctic and in Siberia. This is a mixed blessing. Permafrost melt can release greenhouse gases in the air that had been trapped by sand, rocks, and dirt over the centuries. However, this could also unlock precious metals and minerals, including more oil and natural gas, and allow Russian extraction firms to benefit from melting in the tundra. Ultimately, Russia could also grow more food as more permafrost melts. Tundra melting will also create new supplies of fresh water that is desperately needed by China. In terms of international security, this could bring Russia and China closer because of new trade relationships.

Fragile and Failing States Will Suffer the Most

More years of climate change in countries that are fragile or failing states could lead to more war, particularly civil wars. Certain academic studies

---

[150] Banerjee, Neela. 2019. "Climate Change Will Increase Risk of Violent Conflict, Researchers Warn." *Inside Climate News*. June 13, 2019.

have found a connection. A group of climate change experts, social scientists, and historians convened by Stanford University in 2019 investigated whether there was a link between civil war, internal conflicts, and climate change. "There was 'strong agreement that the risks go up with more climate change,' said Katharine Mach, director of the Stanford Environment Assessment Facility."[151]

Other studies have made similar findings, although "it is important to note that climate change alone has not been proven to increase the likelihood of discord; however, climate change compounded with challenging economic, political, or social conditions can heighten the risk of conflict."[152]

This is why the U.S. military calls climate change a "threat multiplier." An example would be higher temperatures and civil unrest without a social welfare safety net makes an environment ripe to produce civil war because of more floods, droughts, and wildfires. Researchers from Princeton University and University of California at Berkeley found that more internal conflict was associated with rising temperatures.[153] They concluded that "a rise in average annual temperature by even 1° Celsius (1.8° Fahrenheit) leads to a 4.5% increase in civil war that year."[154]

Future climate change will only get worse. It opens a new front in international security. Governments in the emerging world and the developed world, from strongly-governed states to badly-governed states are at risk. Climate change is a huge factor in the operating environment of humans, and it contributes to a new sociopolitical rivalry that militaries of numerous nation-states must deal with.

---

[151] *Ibid.*

[152] Bhatt, Vishva. "Is Climate Change Causing More Wars?" *The Years Project.*

[153] *Ibid.*

[154] *Ibid.*

CHAPTER FOUR

LIFE ENHANCEMENT, LIFE SUSTAINABILITY, SUPER SOLDIERS, AND BIOTECHNOLOGY

How do soldiers stay alive in battle? The U.S. Army, in Basic Combat Training, teaches trainees to shoot, move, and communicate. In 1999, I went through Basic Training at Fort Knox, Kentucky and learned to do this drill. The idea, like most infantry tactics, is simple in concept, but not easy to do. Soldiers proceed in four-person fire teams as part of a squad. The squad is part of a larger platoon. Two soldiers work together in a kind of a leap-frog movement over any type of terrain.

Start first with cover and concealment. Cover can stop a bullet. Think about a tree to lurk behind or an edge of a building to peek around. Concealment hides you. You want both if possible. Two soldiers yell, "Cover me while I move!" The second two soldiers who are covered and concealed, yell, "I got you covered!" The movers take off to the next covered and concealed position as they scream "moving!" The coverers pop out of their positions and begin firing. This cover fire makes the enemy take notice and hopefully ignore and choose not to engage the movers. By the time the enemy reacts, the movers have already found a new position. The process repeats itself and the fire team leapfrogs to its objective. After rehearsing this basic movement technique, the teams get so good that they can easily anticipate when they move or need to move. The battle drill is highly orchestrated and done so often, it becomes second nature.

This human interaction is an example of the sociology of war at the micro level. I am making a departure here from the orthodox definition of the sociology of war, which is an analysis of the macro level of conflict that affects societies. In combat, the four-person fire team is the society. It is all that matters. It is the meaning of war. You may see only four soldiers interacting, but these personnel do not look at it that way in combat. Why don't they run away, break contact, and retreat? They are glued together like any society – bonded by their training and love for one another. They are even what Weber may have called a tiny bureaucracy. These soldiers believe they are the best in the squad and the best in the platoon. They have unit pride like any polity within a bureaucracy. They are also human in that they are jealous and resentful of one another, while also being jealous and resentful of members in other squads and platoons.

In this book I argue that the sociology of war drives technology and technology drives the sociology of war. This means that even the four-person fire team has wants and needs when it comes to tech. Often the wants and needs include a yearning for more firepower, better bullets, improved night vision goggles, a personal mini-drone and so forth. This four-person society wants and needs better technology. The Weberian discipline leads to micro-level solidarity on the battlefield. Social organizations make soldiers fight by inhibiting them from leaving the battlefield.

Re-visit the interaction among the teammates. Soldiers are continuously shooting, moving, and communicating in battle. These drills are done in training, simulations, and rehearsal. The problem when conducting these techniques in combat is often soldiers produce too much adrenaline that saps strength, quickness, and endurance. The soldiers get tired easily, even when they are extremely fit. Especially if the outdoor temperature is as hot as Baghdad gets in the summer. There is then always a need for soldiers who are fitter, bigger, faster, and stronger.

So-called "super soldiers" fit these criteria. What kind of technology spawns a super soldier? Gene-editing is one option to create a super soldier. Moreover, "QuikClot" bandages increase survivability. Exoskeletons give soldiers extra strength and protection. A computer chip can be installed into a soldier to better monitor vital signs and to generate a more intelligent fighter. This is the idea behind cyborg enhancements. Take your best soldier and scan his brain and create a brain emulation that controls an autonomous weapon. Train the weapon to have greater accuracy from this brain emulation taken from a soldier who is an expert at marksmanship.

This chapter will examine super soldiers, survivability, life enhancement, life sustainability, and the biotechnology of future warfare.

Performance enhancers have been prevalent throughout military history. Wine, beer, and rum were given to conscripts to calm nerves and provide confidence as far back as the Roman empire. The Germans in World War II used methamphetamines to give their soldiers the ability to stay awake and be more alert during long periods of blitzkrieg action. German munitions factory workers during the war imbibed in uppers as well.[155]

Substances to Enhance Soldier Performance are Widespread

The U.S. military currently tests its personnel for illegal drugs such as methamphetamine and cocaine. However, legal performance enhancing supplements, even those forbidden by athletics in amateur and professional sports, are not screened and flagged for violations by the

---

155 O'Donnell, Wes. 2018. "Super Soldiers: Performance-Enhancing Drugs and the Military." InMilitary.com. Aug. 1, 2018.

Department of Defense, although illegal drugs are taboo under the uniform code of military justice. On the other hand, the need to be bigger, faster, and stronger with greater endurance and quicker recovery periods using legal supplements is considered normal in the military. Whey protein, creatine, glutamine, and ginseng products are available at stores at many military bases and posts around the world.

Over-the-counter cold medication has pseudoephedrine, which is a precursor chemical for methamphetamine. These cold meds can give a boost to physical training. More serious supplements such as anabolic steroids are sometimes consumed by U.S. special operations forces and other personnel looking for an edge.[156] It is estimated that up to 25 percent of U.S. Army Rangers used steroids in 2007.[157] To crack down on their use, a commander can order a special drug test to look for steroids.

It stands to reason that other strength-enhancing substances are consumed by U.S. soldiers as well, including a variety of testosterone boosters and human growth hormone. For example, androstenedione, commonly known as "andro" was popular with professional athletes in the 1990s until it found its way on the banned substances list. Andro has been used by military members to increase levels of serum testosterone. This builds strength in the gym, enabling users to lift more weight or do more pullups and sit-ups in military physical training tests. Another of these steroid precursors is called dehydroepiandrosterone.

One line of thinking is that if steroid use is prevalent among certain personnel, perhaps it can be administered in a safer way. Currently military doctors are contemplating more studies to determine the future of anabolic steroid use in the service branches. This research will explore "encouraging further exploration of steroid use, understanding the true prevalence of steroids, understanding the costs and benefits of steroids,

---

156 Pelltier, Chad and Kyle Pettijohn. 2018. *Military Medicine*, Volume 183, Issue 7-8, July-August 2018. Pp. 151–153.

157 *Ibid*

connecting users to trusted sources of information, and collaborating with other organizations to address these concerns."[158]

Then could it be possible that the U.S. military, having mostly ignored anabolic steroid use for years, would someday allow or even encourage its use? One of the rationales for steroid intake is that soldiers lose an excessive amount of weight during combat deployments. This makes it more difficult to carry large amounts of equipment necessary in land warfare. Also, there are minor injuries. Steroids help users recover faster from these types of muscle pulls and tears or ligament damage.

The long-term side effects of steroid use are well-known in the medical community and in popular culture. "Roid rage" and violent mood swings are probably the most serious side effects. Keeping calm on the battlefield is paramount and losing mental control in anger can lead to collateral damage to civilians or other war crimes.

The use of steroids and other related supplements should be studied, but not used or condoned by the U.S. military, even in the special operations community. There are just too many dangerous side effects. Steroids, despite being monitored by any doctor or hospital, ravage the body. Long-term use can make bones brittle, raise cholesterol levels and blood pressure, and create liver problems. Steroid use can also give the wrong impression to young soldiers, that if you cheat, you can win. Over-the-counter supplements such as whey protein, that does not contain banned substances by global athletic bodies, should be encouraged. Good diet and nutrition habits should also be emphasized.

What is the future of soldiers using natural supplements as opposed to synthetic performance enhancers? There is a public stigma associated with those who cheat. The sporting world is littered with athletes who have been caught "doping." Cyclist Lance Armstrong, baseball player Barry Bonds, and others come to mind. The profession of arms often

---

158 *Ibid.*

tops the list of most admired professions. Why sully it with doping or other forms of banned substances? People should have confidence in their militaries. Steroids or other forms of cheating erode this confidence. To be sure, more medical studies should be done. There may be more performance enhancers that do not have the stigma or side effects that steroids have.

But could steroid use keep an individual soldier alive in combat? After all, the idea is to shoot, move, and communicate in the best manner as possible. Surely, being bigger, faster, and stronger is a way to excel on the battlefield. Maybe the answer is focus. So-called focus-medications such as Ritalin and Adderall are used by children, teenagers, and adults for long periods of concentration. These are banned substances in the National Football League, but they have their advantages. Perhaps these medications would allow more focused physical training that could lead to advances in speed and endurance through better training methods.

Nevertheless, the future lies in diverse and more realistic types of combat training. For decades, the military, particularly ground force elements, used timed endurance runs, sit-ups, push-ups, and pull-ups to measure strength and endurance. It took years for the U.S. Army to change its physical training tests and incorporate more battlefield tasks into its testing. Now new events include strength deadlifts and overhead medicine ball throws to replicate motions used on the battlefield.

So far, I have discussed performance improvements in soldiers. What about survivability? After all, soldiers are human and made up of soft tissue that cannot stop a bullet or shrapnel from a suicide bomb. Body armor has come a long way since Vietnam-era flak vests that were used up until the early 2000s. Soldiers now go into combat with vests supplied with Kevlar plates. Their helmets are lighter and have better protection. What is the next evolution in soldier-survivability?

Perhaps supplements and performance enhancers address only part of the problem. The next step is survivability and more strength, speed, and agility. There are drawbacks to the current form of soldier protection. Humans are similar to vehicles. Add more armor and protection, and you get a combatant that weighs too much. Endurance and speed suffer. More armor can also scare indigenous populations in counterinsurgencies. Historically, during counterinsurgencies, British troops often made great pains to patrol dangerous areas without helmets to show they were not a threat to the local populace – so people could see their identity and recognize faces – much in the same way a police officer patrols her community outside her vehicle. She has a bullet proof vest, but she is not dressed in riot gear. However, refraining from using heavy body armor has its drawbacks in terms of survivability. There is no armor to stop a bullet or shrapnel during her outdoor patrol.

Exoskeletons: The Next Logical Step in Survivability and Performance

Enter exoskeletons. Take a trip to Hollywood to understand them. The Star Wars stormtrooper is the most obvious example with an outer shell of a uniform covering nearly all exposed parts of the body. Many die in combat in the various Star Wars movies with a well-placed laser blast, but one could see the benefits on a future battlefield. However, the same rule applies: more protection equals less speed and maneuverability. From my personal experience using body armor and helmets, the less weight the better. And the stormtrooper exoskeleton would add more weight. Currently, it appears that the Star Wars exoskeleton is more for recruiting and for the "gee-whiz" factor that could enthrall potential enlistees. It is likely not a practical solution.

Another film, Elysium, starring Matt Damon, had an interesting take on the exoskeleton. Damon's character was exposed to a high-level of radiation that threatened his life. To overcome an evil band of future ruffians, he succumbed to an exoskeleton suit installation to level the playing field with his enemies. The radiation was going to kill him anyway and the bad guys had similar suits. The film showed that a space-age metal outer skeleton not only provided protection, but gave humans a boost of power, strength, and jumping ability.

Hollywood science fiction aside, this contraption in reality would be semi-robotic and give soldiers more survivability and mobility. The Elysium-style exoskeleton has metal slats that could be made of titanium. These slats fit on the anterior side of arms and legs – the same way a pin-stripe runs down the side of pants or a shirt. The slats are connected by a joint at the elbows, shoulders, hips, knees, and ankles. The idea is that this artificial enhancement will get better leverage with power. It can achieve more torque on vital kinesiological movements such as jumps, springs, kicks, punches, and chops. A mixed-martial artist, using an Elysium-style exoskeleton, would likely be twice as effective. The system would help soldiers in close-quarter combat, traveling over difficult terrain, and in shoot, move, and communicate situations on the battlefield.

Defense contractors have been waiting for the right moment for exoskeletons and it appears the U.S. Army is finally interested. The 10th Mountain Division has been testing the Lockheed Martin ONYX exoskeleton.[159] It looks similar to the Hollywood version from the film Elysium discussed earlier. Lockheed released a video of a soldier springing over a pile of rocks, and it appears the exoskeleton is giving this person a performance boost. Further research and development will be done by the U.S. Army Natick Soldier Research, Development and Engineering Center.[160] Sarcos Robotics introduced its exoskeleton in 2019. The U.S. Navy and Air Force are using the Guardian XO for shipyard activities and logistics operations. The Guardian XO exoskeleton can help its wearer lift 200 pounds.[161]

---

[159] South, Todd. 2018. "This Army Unit will be first to test an exoskeleton that lightens combat load." *Army Times*. June 5, 2018.

[160] *Ibid.*

[161] Tangermann, Victor. 2019. "The U.S. Military is Buying a Brutal-Looking Powered Exoskeleton." *Futurism*. March 19, 2019.

The exoskeleton has many downsides. The first is mass-production of the prototype. How would it fit different body types? Soldiers come in all shapes and sizes. How long does it take to put on the suit? Fighters often need to be combat-ready in moments. One cannot easily sleep in the suit, so it would have to be removed before and after every mission. This means that combat units would each require a load-out area like a sports locker room to prepare for battle with the suits – not always practical in remote locations. Infiltrating exoskeleton-outfitted soldiers into combat zones from airplanes and helicopters is another problem. Airborne operations would be difficult with the added weight. The suits take up more space in already-cramped helicopters during air assault operations.

Exoskeletons also have an inertia problem in movement. In other words, it will probably take longer to go from full-stop to full-speed, even though exoskeletons allow users to run faster when inertia is overcome. If a soldier is standing still, would the suits give him enough of a burst of speed to accelerate or does the acceleration take longer to develop from a stationary position? A live hand grenade at a soldier's feet illustrates this principle of physics. A soldier freezes and then decides whether to move or jump on the grenade. Would the exoskeleton impede sudden movement, or would it allow the combatant to move faster? These questions will be addressed in the battle labs, but inertia and gravity may get in the way of these grand designs.

Cost is another question. As with many acquisition and procurement programs in the U.S. military, producing just a few of the suits is often more expensive than mass production. This is the marginal cost conundrum. A suit is only cost-effective if each extra unit produced is cheaper than the prototype. Many procurement programs are cancelled due to this marginal cost conundrum. They are too expensive during testing and then mass production is never achieved to get the cost advantages of economies of scale. Say goodbye to the exoskeleton if it is not adapted in mass quantities.

Many of these problems will be addressed in testing and training. Despite the downsides, exoskeletons will be part of some U.S. ground force units in the near future. They can prevent injuries such as knee and ankle sprains. They can give soldiers more confidence with the added strength and power. They are an advantage in close-quarters combat. They can make relatively smaller body types and soldiers with less strength more effective. They will be less expensive over time. Soldiers will eventually adapt to taking them off and on.

Can You Breed Super Soldiers?

Exoskeletons are on the outside, but what about inside the soldier? A gene-editing technology that has already shown tremendous medical breakthroughs has some wondering if cancer and HIV in civilians can be defeated by genetic engineering. But despite the optimistic headlines, the technique known as CRISPR is also becoming an emerging international security threat. CRISPR, stands for "clusters of regularly interspaced short palindromic repeats." CRISPR could someday enable U.S. adversaries to genetically-engineer bioweapons or even create super soldiers to dominate future battlefields.[162]

Scientists in China are racing ahead. They have already modified human embryos, cloned a dog, and spliced genes in monkeys and mice.[163] Meanwhile, some American biotech firms are exporting CRISPR technology for legitimate scientific discovery around the globe. But their sales efforts sometimes target customers in China who may be conducting beneficial civilian research or developing sinister military applications.

---

[162] The following CRISPR section from page 11-15 is reprinted from a partial excerpt from the Atlantic Council from the author's article: Brent M. Eastwood. "Gene-Editing in China: Beneficial Science or Emerging Military Threat?" Atlantic Council's *Future Source Blog.* July 13, 2017.

[163] China Academy of Sciences. 2017. "China Produces World's First Cloned Dog Using Gene Editing." July 7, 2017

What Are the Details of CRISPR?

CRISPR is a laboratory process that edits DNA. The technique is based on a figurative "pair of molecular scissors" from an enzyme called Cas-9 that can focus on amending specific DNA for a desired effect in the targeted genome. Doctors and researchers can then "remove, add, or alter the genetic sequence," according to YourGenome.org. Moreover, the CRISPR-Cas9 "system currently stands out as the fastest, cheapest and most reliable system for 'editing' genes," according to the Wellcome Genome Campus website, a bioscience research institute in Cambridge, England.[164]

While most CRISPR research is devoted to benevolent advances in medicine and science, former Director of National Intelligence James Clapper was quoted in a threat assessment report that U.S. enemies could use the technique for nefarious purposes.[165]

After that warning, Atlantic Council's Foresight, Strategy, and Risks Initiative Director Mathew Burrows said during a forum that the "speed of these scientific developments...continues to outpace the ability for us to prepare."[166]

In 2018, a Chinese scientist used CRISPR to genetically modify babies. In 2019, the Chinese were working on their third baby that has been gene-edited. Also, that year, researchers at the University of Pennsylvania were conducting a CRISPR study to treat two patients with cancer.[167]

---

164 Eastwood, Brent M. 2017. "Gene-Editing in China: Beneficial Science or Emerging Military Threat?" Atlantic Council's *Future Source Blog.* July 13, 2017.

165 Clapper, James R. Director of National Intelligence. 2016. Statement for the Record: Worldwide Threat Assessment of the US Intelligence Community. Testimony given to the Senate Armed Services Committee. February 9, 2016

166 *Ibid.*

167 Stein, 2019. "First U.S. Patients Treated With CRISPR As Human Gene-Editing Trials Get Underway." *National Public Radio.* April 16, 2019.

Gene Editing as an International Security Threat

In an Atlantic Council panel on gene editing in 2016, Dr. Pierre Noel, a professor at the Mayo Clinic and a non-resident fellow at the Brent Scowcroft Center on International Security, agreed the technique could be a threat. "It's possible that in the future, as the technology becomes more sophisticated, countries may be able to implement gene-editing technology to design...super soldiers...with great muscle force and strength."

The main concern about gene-editing and its potential danger is the ease of obtaining CRISPR toolkits for less than $50. In 2017, the web site Futurism.com chronicled how organizations routinely distribute the kits around the world.[168] Addgene, a nonprofit DNA molecule repository in Cambridge, Massachusetts, has sent "thousands of CRISPR toolkits to researchers in more than 80 countries," according to Futurism.[169]

Is Chinese CRISPR Research for Military or Civilian Use?

One of those countries is China. Chinese researchers use Addgene frequently. They have made over 10,000 requests for CRISPR plasmids (separated DNA molecules) and hundreds of deposits of plasmids in the Addgene repository.[170] The organization also has a distributor in Beijing.

Russian researchers work with Addgene too and the nonprofit helps scientists navigate Russian customs. Addgene, to its credit, has numerous safeguards in place to ensure that its products are used for legitimate science. Researchers must show evidence that they are working in academia or in other valid research laboratories. Addgene also does not ship to "Cuba, Iran, North Korea, Sudan, and Syria."[171]

---

168 "In Just a Few Short Years, CRISPR Has Sparked a Research Revolution." May 28, 2017. *Futurism.*

169 *Ibid.*

170 From addgene.org corporate web site

171 Addgene.org

While Russian scientists from the Skolkovo Institute of Science and Technology (Skoltech) have shown modest success conducting CRISPR experiments testing bacterial immunity,[172] it is China that has become a global leader.

Chinese researchers at a biotech firm in Beijing announced they cloned a dog using gene editing in 2017. Genome experts believe that China is either ahead of the United States in CRISPR breakthroughs or is closely behind.[173] That year, China began using CRISPR techniques on a human with cancer.

There is so much gene-editing research being conducted in China it is difficult to pinpoint the primary sources. It is also not easy to discern whether the research in China has civilian, military, or defense applications. The secretive Academy of Military Medical Sciences and the Third Military Medical University are the most likely defense labs. These DARPA-like institutions handle medical studies for the People's Liberation Army, and both are feverishly pumping out CRISPR research.

Chinese military scientists are using the technique to produce proteins of human blood called albumin in baby pigs. Military researchers are improving CRISPR gene splicing with their own innovative light-induced editing systems. Other studies focus on improving cancer drug resistance. The Chinese military is also investigating removing Hepatitis-B virus DNA with CRISPR.

The main civilian CRISPR laboratories appear to be affiliated with Chinese Academy of Sciences, particularly its Institute of Neuroscience at the Shanghai Institutes for Biological Sciences. These centers alone have dozens of labs with at least 50 scientists each who could be working

---

[172] "Russian Scientists Discover New Features of Bacterial Adaptive Immunity." July 5, 2016. *Russia Beyond.*

[173] "China, US Race to Develop 'Gene Editing' Technology That Could, If Approved, Revolutionize Medicine." *Bloomberg.* February 24, 2016.

on gene editing at any given time. And that estimated number is just in neuroscience. That does not count all the Chinese CRISPR researchers who are toiling in human bioscience or animal biology. These civilian scientists are speeding through experiments with monkeys and mice. But more worrisome are Chinese CRISPR breakthroughs in human embryos. Alternatively, the United States has banned CRISPR techniques conducted on human embryos.

Meanwhile, China is clearly pursuing dual-use genetic engineering technology. Beijing likely plans on becoming the undisputed global leader in gene editing for its military and civilian medical and scientific communities. As Burrows has said, the speed of the technological advances in this field is astonishing, and future growth will continue to be difficult to track and analyze. The CRISPR tool kits are cheap and easy to get. Each day more scientists around the world are obtaining various services and products that help them splice genes.

The development of Chinese "super soldiers" is here, and these concerns should be taken seriously and monitored closely. It is plausible that the People's Liberation Army would be interested in improving soldier survivability and CRISPR has that potential to someday improve human performance on the battlefield. For example, in late 2020, John Ratcliffe, then the U.S. Director of National Intelligence, revealed that China was indeed testing human subjects for super soldier-type modifications to their biologically enhanced capabilities.[174] And do not forget Russia. The Russians may lag behind the Americans and Chinese in gene-editing research, but Vladimir Putin is always looking for a new military edge.

It does not seem that Iran is interested in developing or acquiring CRISPR technology. That would probably be seen as a taboo to believers in Shia Islam. North Korea, on the other hand, has a proclivity for

---

[174] Dilanian, Ken. 2020. "China Has Done Human Testing to Create Biologically-enhanced Super Soldiers, Says Top U.S. Official." *NBC News*. December 3, 2020.

acquiring technology that it cannot develop at home. It is more likely that North Korea would go after CRISPR as it would be interested in super soldiers. Terrorists often lack the laboratories or the expertise to develop their own CRISPR techniques. Their main goal is to acquire weapons of mass destruction, so gene editing is likely lower on the list of wants and needs.

While authoritarian, despotic, and rogue governments have no qualms about gene editing research that requires cooperation and permission for research, the United States is different. American medical ethics are strict and require permission from human subjects before experiments can begin. Authoritarian countries may not be affected by medical ethics and this is the fear in CRISPR research in rogue countries. China and Russia have different norms and medical practices, so it may be easier for them to conduct gene editing on live human beings. They could have the edge then in the race for super soldiers.

CRISPR is not going away anytime soon. The risk-reward ratio is a satisfactory gamble to many governments and militaries around the world. The gene editing kits make it a cheaper enterprise and the reward for such a cheap investment is high. Failure can be ignored or learned from and success can be replicated. Most of the time, research and development in CRISPR simply requires the use of a laboratory. There is no hazardous or biomedical waste. It is also difficult to monitor the advances in research on any given day.

Journalists are having trouble keeping up with the story. It may fall on the U.S. Department of Defense to monitor developments out of research organizations such as DARPA or the Office of Net Assessment – a think tank inside the Pentagon. Various health and medical-related commands inside the Department of Defense, not to mention the U.S. intelligence community, are likely trying to keep up with new developments in the enterprise.

Also, it is difficult to distinguish between commercial, academic, and military uses of CRISPR. Where is the research actually produced?

Is it for the public good? Is it for profit? Or is it for defense purposes? China shows that their CRISPR projects are occurring in a spider's web of defense-related research and development facilities sponsored by the People's Liberation Army. American research is assumed to be for the public good so far. But American private firms, including a bevy of startups, are making money off CRISPR kits. It is only a matter of time before CRISPR enters the defense world full-time. These will be the questions that must be answered going forward.

So how long until gene editing produces super soldiers? The horizon looks to be five to ten years. Gene editing can create bigger, faster, stronger people. It can make their blood clot faster if they are wounded. It can take the best genes from the best soldiers and replicate them into one. Those who run fastest, lift the most weight, have the most stamina, and shoot the best could be replicated. We will see gene editing for soldiers in our lifetime and it will be a race to see which government can make the super soldiers fast enough.

Cyborgs: Soldiers Connected to Computers

Another way to create a super soldier is the conversion of a fighter into a living-connection to a computer. The idea is to implant a chip into a human being so vital information from the human brain or other type of electronics is connected. This is the so-called "Iron Man" concept in which an operator can "talk" to a central processing unit set up in a remote location. DARPA, which has been working on the cyborg concept since around 2016, has put at least $62 million into the project.[175] DARPA rarely releases public information on its projects unless there is some type of public relations gain or if they think the project will come to fruition, so the cyborg concept is likely maturing toward wider adaptation.

The most immediate advantage of a computer chip implant is the

---

[175] Browne, Ryan. 2016. "U.S. Military Spending Millions to Make Cyborgs a Reality." *CNN*. March 7, 2016.

ability to monitor a soldier's vital signs. This leads to the survivability of a human on the battlefield. Combat medicine could thus receive a boost if a medic can talk to doctors in real time about the status of a soldier when he or she is wounded. This would help triage an individual, especially in a mass casualty situation. Medics on the ground would get real-time information on who to save first and who has already expired. Evacuation could then be better coordinated and doctors at hospitals and medics on helicopters would have a more realistic chance at saving the patient if vital signs are relayed. A cyborg connection could also tell where the wound is located. Sometimes, when evaluating a casualty in the heat of battle, it is difficult to know where the bullet or shrapnel has entered the body. A cyborg could answer questions such as whether a bullet has damaged vital organs or where it has entered and exited. This allows medics to determine if the bullet has left an external wound instead of lodging in the body.

Implanted chips could also aid in the healing process. Traumatic brain injuries, vision, and hearing-related injuries could also be monitored and even diagnosed in a more efficient manner if the soldier's brain is connected to a computer. The computer could then send digitized images and auditory signals back to the patient to aid in recovery. Doctors could also get a better reading on traumatic brain injuries. Implantable cyborg chips have the potential to become so-called "labs on a chip," in which actual medicine could be released into the soldier. This could include artificial adrenaline or pain relief medication. Perhaps even a local anesthetic could be administered through a lab on a chip. The chip would allow medics to proceed with a battlefield surgery before wounded personnel have to be transported to a hospital.

"The implantable device aims to convert neurons in the brain into electronic signals and provide unprecedented 'data-transfer bandwidth between the human brain and the digital world,'" according to DARPA.[176]

---

[176] *Ibid.*

The DARPA implant would be the size of "two nickels." The implants have implications for exoskeletons as well. The electronic signals, by communicating with the brain, could potentially control exoskeletons in a more efficient manner. I discussed the inertia problem earlier, in which the exoskeleton would be slow to accelerate and difficult to surmount the physics of movement and gravity. An implant could perhaps overcome this inertia.

Implants could also aid in communication with the central computer. Battle plans could be developed and adjusted on the fly. Mission planners at forward operating bases would get immediate feedback on the success or failure of a mission and adjust tactics, techniques, and procedures.

With implanted chips, the road can be paved for the development of a fully armored Iron Man-type of suit. Stormtrooper-like armor is cumbersome and too heavy to put on. It would have the inertia problem too. A static object in the physical world has trouble accelerating.

And how practical is an Iron Man-type suit? It would take years to develop. What is already in public use is the jet pack suit from the British company Gravity Industries, which has built what it claims is the world's fastest jet pack. Founder Richard Browning is sure it has important military applications.

But the chip implant is the first step in this cyborg arc of adaption. The implanted chip also raises the issue of who or what is in control of the soldier. In the shoot, move, and communicate example, a soldier is relying on years of training to be effective. Her own brain and body are making the decisions on when and how to shoot, move, and communicate. If this is controlled by an implanted chip linked to a computer, does that mean a central authority could end up calling the shots on what a soldier does on the battlefield? Could the soldier over-ride the chip or even remove the chip if she is given an unlawful order?

These types of issues frighten observers such as Elon Musk, as the human element becomes sacrificed to the machine and computer world. The Elon Musk-type assessments of the danger of artificial intelligence will be analyzed in a later chapter. But it is safe to say that an implanted chip in a soldier that is connected to a computer that later leads to an Iron Man-type of armored suit for combat is frightening to some.

Are Soldiers Ready for Implantable Devices?

This calls for an ethical discussion. When one joins the military, this person gives up many individual rights for the well-being of the team or unit. This is often referred to as the needs of the military. Biomedical solutions become an issue early on in a soldier's career. He or she must succumb to a bevy of shots, immunizations, and inoculations. When I first enlisted in the military, the anthrax vaccination caused much controversy. Some soldiers refused to take the shot because of real or imagined harmful side effects. Envision the pushback of implanting a chip into a human being. The current size of the chip that DARPA is working on is the size of two nickels. That is not tiny. Although it stands to reason that the chips will decrease in size over the years of research and development, soldiers, and even their family members, may protest this type of injection.

Most soldiers when they enlist are only 18 or 19-years-old. At this point, brains and bodies are not fully mature. Will cyborg implants cause side effects in an immature brain? Could this affect the growth of the human body or the intelligence of a person with a cyborg implant? These are long-term questions for the military medical research community.

What are the norms, ethics, and morality of cyborgs? What type of training is administered to medical staffs to allow them to determine what is right and wrong when it comes to controlling a human with a cyborg implant? Perhaps a cyborg implant controlled by a computer could be programmed with an over-ride function in which an improper or unethical order could be ignored. This could be helpful in avoiding battlefield atrocities or violations of the Geneva convention and war crimes.

In Iraq and Afghanistan, soldiers have been confronted with numerous difficult moral decisions. This usually happens in counterinsurgencies with murky rules of engagement. Who is friendly and who is a foe? Who is a threat and who is not a threat? Recent war crimes in the U.S. Army have involved a platoon leader who was in charge when troops fired on three alleged insurgents riding a motorcycle. The unit had just been attacked by a suicide bomber using a motorcycle in order for the terrorist to quickly get in close to friendly troops and detonate a bomb. This platoon leader ordered his troops to fire on the motorcycle riders, but the dead riders were found later to have no weapons or bombs on their person. The lieutenant had to make a split-second decision and it resulted in a murder charge, a court-martial, and jail time.

Perhaps a computer-controlled cyborg chip could have prevented this event by providing real-time intelligence on whether the motorcycle riders were a legitimate threat. The surveillance intelligence could come from a drone relaying overhead information to computers to aid the friend or foe decision in rules of engagement that is so difficult on the battlefield.

Of course, the opposite scenario could happen. The computer-controlled cyborg chip could go haywire and give the command to shoot in the same situation – a mistake that would violate the rules of engagement as well. Then thorny legal and moral questions arise. Who then is responsible for the war crime, the soldier or the chip?

Cyborgs are an interesting idea. Chips connecting humans to computers and other electronic devices have many advantages in battlefield medicine. Lab on a chip technology could save lives for soldiers wounded in combat by allowing exfiltration to be more successful in treating a casualty before the individual can get to a hospital. A computer chip could solve the inertia problem in exoskeletons and even lead to an Ironman-type combat suit. But the downsides of a chip implant are prohibitive. Soldiers may refuse the implant and there are ethical and moral risks to a computer over-riding a human's decision-making process or to determine when the correct time it is to cancel an unlawful order from a computer. And most important, who trains and programs the cyborg chip and computer? Hopefully, these are ethical scientists and technicians who do not have wicked plans for the resulting cyborg.

Cyborgs will not become a reality anytime soon. There are just too many obstacles. Developing the science may be a bridge too far. In this day of reduced U.S. military budgets for research and development, it would be difficult to fully fund the necessary work to make them viable. Their future would depend on Congressional funding and there does not appear to be the need for these types of super soldiers at this time. There would be some public and media backlash on the full use of a cyborg Iron Man-type warrior on the battlefield. However, chip implants that monitor a soldier's health and vital signs do have a chance at becoming a viable supplement to battlefield medicine. There would be some pushback by soldiers who would refuse the implant, but the benefits could result in saving lives and better medical treatment of combat-wounded individuals.

The Dawn of "Ems" and International Security

The pluses and minuses of cyborgs are something to ponder. But nothing comes close to the future envisioned by Robin D. Hanson. Hanson is one interesting man. He is currently an economics professor at George Mason University, just do not try to pigeon-hole him. His interests lie everywhere and in everything. He has a doctorate in social science from Caltech, plus master's degrees in physics and philosophy from the University of Chicago. Hanson cut his teeth as a research programmer for Lockheed Martin and NASA. Now he probably has one of the most complete visions of the future in the world.

His book, *The Age of Em: Work, Love and Life, When Robots Rule the Earth*,[177] is a death-defying, no apologies ride to the future. What is an "em," you ask? Hanson has created a brave new world for them. The following quote is from his book's home page:

"Many think the first truly smart robots will be brain emulations or ems. Scan a human brain, then run a model with the same connections on a fast computer, and you have a robot brain, but recognizably human. Train an em to do some job and copy it a million times: an army of workers is at your disposal. When they can be made cheaply, within perhaps a century, ems will displace humans in most jobs. In this new economic era, the world economy may double in size every few weeks."

Hanson does not delve too deeply into the world of what his ems will contribute to the future of international security, but Hanson's ems, if they do come to fruition, could be the advent of a robot intelligence analyst. Scan the brains of the CIA's best analysts and then hook the scans up to a computer and you would have a stellar analyst. Imagine an intelligence analyst who did not have to be trained or paid and who would work 24-7 with no complaints. This em analyst would not replace the humans; it would just be in the office with the human analysts. Think of how much data could be processed by an em. All-source intelligence – signals, electronic, human, open web – would all be accessible by the em analyst. This could help the National Security Agency as well.

Let me take the em idea further and examine how else this could be applied to security. How about taking your best, most elite military personnel: SEAL Team-6, Delta Force – and scanning their brains? Take the best shooters in the U.S. military and make an em to teach marksmanship. Ems would likely not have a future on the battlefield. They would be better behind the scenes in a training and advisory role. Ems do not need to be actual robots – they should be hooked up to a

---

[177] Hanson, Robin. 2018. *The Age of Em: Work, Love and Life, When Robots Rule the Earth*. New York: Oxford University Press.

computer and retain a back-office role in the military. Of course, that is the conundrum. If they become so useful, the next logical step is to make an em into a robot. I do not want to get too far ahead because there will be a chapter on robotics and drones in this book. So, I want to focus on ems as a supplement to military and intelligence personnel – not to replace humans. Hanson would probably say they are going to replace humans anyway, so get ready.

The U.S. Army wants to use augmented reality and virtual reality night vision goggles. Augmented reality is a supplement to a live view while virtual reality is a complete departure that immerses the user into a separate visual world. They would combine a "digital visual augmentation system; tactical assault kit-enabled end user device; tactical radio; weapon sights; and small unmanned aerial vehicles to provide capabilities not possible with analog systems," according to army researchers described by military electronics analyst John Keller.[178]

DARPA has been shooting for so-called "smart contact lenses" for years. They think they have found the answer developed from the French engineering school IMT Atlantique. Military personnel could use them for augmented reality while performing combat surgery or for drivers and pilots who are at machine controls for long periods of time.

Elon Musk's startup Neuralink began in 2016 to develop brain-machine interfaces. In 2021, its goal is to "develop ultra-high bandwidth brain-machine interfaces to connect humans and computers. Practically, this materializes as a chip that is implanted into the brain to achieve a 'sort of symbiosis with artificial intelligence' that can significantly preserve and enhance our brains," according to Arnav Lehiry.[179]

---

[178] Keller, John. 2019. "U.S. Army Investigates Making Night-vision Goggles Double as Virtual Reality and Augmented Reality Devices." *Military Aerospace and Electronics*. Oct. 28, 2019.

[179] Lahiry, Arnav. 2020. "Will Elon Musk's Neuralink Shape The Future Of Humanity?" *The Oxford Student*. May 19, 2020.

This brings us to what Peter Thiel, in his book *Zero to One*, calls the human-computer hybrid.[180] Thiel recounts his experiences at PayPal when he and his engineers had created an internal program that could spot credit card fraud. Fraudulent charges were hurting PayPal's bottom line. In an early deployment of commercial machine learning, the machine found and eliminated the bogus credit card transactions. It was a hybrid system which required human input and analysis working with the software. Thiel prefers this type of human-computer interaction and replicated it later into the publicly-traded enterprise Palantir, which is a secretive company that gained many satisfied customers using its data science system for the federal government. Palantir has ventured out to working with clients in the private sector, but they still claim that humans, not automation, control the software.

This is an illustrative point on the need for human interaction in a world that is fraught with automation. It may also be a cautionary tale to those calling for more advanced robots such as ems that would be autonomous. I support the human-computer hybrid and not the complete evolution to robotic ems that Hanson calls for. This is mainly for ethical and moral reasons, but also to make sure artificial intelligence does not control humans. It assuages Elon Musk's constant calls to beware of an all-powerful artificial intelligence takeover – something I will be discussing in a later chapter.

The human-computer hybrid versus complete autonomy of machines is something to watch out for as international security evolves and goes for the next big thing. It could lead to accidents and miscalculations that can escalate into conflict quickly.

Robotic weapons have been used in South Korea along the demilitarized zone for years and there have been no accidents so far, at least none reported in the mainstream media. If ems evolve, and brain

---

[180] Thiel, Peter and Blake Masters. 2014. *Zero to One: Notes on Startups and How to Build the Future*. New York: Crown Business.

scans are focused on replicating the best marksmen in the military, it stands to reason that more weapons will be roboticized. Ethics plays an important role in this development. What would constitute a war crime if a robot were handling the weapon? Even the most highly trained elite soldiers make mistakes in warfare. President Donald Trump pardoned a handful of military personnel accused of murder on the battlefield. Guilty or not, how does one decide on which brain to scan and emulate? Special operations forces are already vetted psychologically during their security clearance background check, and at other times for their mental well-being. But you never know what can happen to even the most elite operators after constant deployments in conflict zones.

Could an em tell right from wrong in warfare? Probably not. That is why the human-computer hybrid is so important. Keep the em as a back-office enhancement to human workers. My rule of thumb would be one em per office, organization, or what the military calls a forward operating base in a combat zone.

On the whole, I like ems. Hanson has created the most comprehensive plan of action for a futuristic society I have ever seen. Hanson has a huge vision for ems that encompasses daily life, politics, sociology, economics, business, and labor. Some may call that far-fetched, but his big vision is appreciated.

Yuval Noah Harari, author of *Sapiens* and *Homo Deus*, has visions of futuristic superhumans as well. Harari is not sure how superhumans will develop but believes that they are an essential part of human development. "The notion of superhumans is using bioengineering and artificial intelligence to upgrade human abilities. If they use the power to change themselves, to change their own minds, their own desires, then we have no idea what they will want to do."[181]

---

[181] Interview with Yuval Noah Harari. Nate Hopper. 2017. "How Humankind Could Become Totally Useless." *Time*. Feb. 16, 2017.

Biotechnology Inches Into Combat

Beyond super-humanism and into biotechnology, James Jay Carafano and Andrew Gudgel, writing for the Heritage Foundation, define biotechnology as "...any technological application that uses living organisms to make or modify products for explicit use, specifically through DNA recombination and tissue culture."[182]

I have discussed DNA recombination in the previous section on CRISPR gene editing. CRISPR, often referred to as synthetic biology in biotech circles, is such a revolutionary technology, it stands on its own. Biotechnology is a much broader topic in terms of soldier survivability and enhancement. Sometimes biotechnology is, of course, used to maim or kill enemy combatants or civilians. One synthetic biological threat that keeps threat planners at the Pentagon up at night is the possibility of a bad actor getting access to a virus such as smallpox or strain of influenza and turning it loose on a group of people.[183] This was the fear with the coronavirus that ravaged the world in 2020 and 2021 – that it was the result of a Chinese bioweapon experiment in a Wuhan military lab. Although it is not clear how the coronavirus developed in China, the Covid-19 pandemic is an example of the need for defenses against biological weapons.

Most dual-use biotechnology research and products will have to be borrowed from the private sector. But national laboratories under the auspice of the U.S. Department of Energy have provided multitudes of biotechnology research over the years. Unfortunately, many of these government-sponsored advances have not made it over to the U.S. military.

---

182 Carafano, James Jay and Andrew Gudgel. 2007. "National Security and Biotechnology: Small Science with a Big Potential." *Heritage Foundation Policy Backgrounder*. Number 2055. July 23, 2007.

183 Regalado, Antonia. 2018. "U.S. Military Wants to Know What Synthetic-Biology Weapons Look Like." *MIT Technology Review*. June 19, 2018.

Nanotechnology is a case in point. Carbon nanotubes, one of the great advances in nanotech, are carbon hexagonal lattices or strips rolled into a tube. The best example that could relate to soldier survivability would be "carbon nanotubes acting as scaffolding for bone growth."[184] It is not clear if this civilian research will ever make it to the Pentagon, but perhaps it should. The implications for soldier survivability would be obvious. Bullets and shrapnel shatter bones and even simple fractures of legs and arms are an unfortunate side effect of training and combat. Imagine how much carbon nanotubes could improve bone density, strength, and healing. However, nanotechnology has seen better days. It was all the rage in the 2000's and it just could not break through to broad commercial or military use. It entered what the U.S. defense procurement community calls the "valley of death" between research and development and actual products, techniques, and procedures – a common malady in military acquisition.

Carafano and Gudgel make this point about biotech – that "Congress and the Administration should not only be aware of the growing biotechnology field, but also act to ensure that the private sector remains competitive by streamlining the federal government's capability to fund and adapt new technologies."[185] Avoiding valley of death in procurement requires the White House and Congress to make research and development – along with adaptation with the soldier as the end user – a priority. Sadly, biological applications of nanotechnology did not make it to fruition.

One of the best examples of a biotechnology product that did make it across the valley of death from research to reality is the hemostatic

---

184 Haddon, Robert C. Laura P. Zanello, Bin Zhao, and Hui Hu. 2006. "Bone Cell Proliferation on Carbon Nanotubes." *Nano Letters*. Vol. 6, Issue 3: pp. 562–56.

185 Carafano, James Jay and Andrew Gudgel. 2007. "National Security and Biotechnology: Small Science with a Big Potential." *Heritage Foundation Policy Backgrounder*. Number 2055. July 23, 2007.

device QuikClot. QuikClot does just what its name says – it stops bleeding quickly. It is gauze for combat casualties, and it is also used in the civilian world. 6 million units of QuikClot gauze has been sold to the military since its inception.[186] QuikClot works well because of kaolin, an inorganic clay and silicate mineral, which accelerates the clotting process as soon as the gauze hits blood in need of coagulation. QuikClot dates back to 1984 when it advanced beyond powdered form and passed numerous military testing programs after 9/11.

QuikClot is what one of my former colleagues at The George Washington University Elliott School of International Affairs, David Malet, cited as a biotechnology success story.[187] Making the journey from laboratory to battlefield is fraught with risk and missed opportunities and downright failures. Malet has researched some interesting nuggets in his definitive work on biotechnology and security. One project being investigated by U.S. military researchers is brain dexterity that "speeds up reflexes and cognitive processing of soldiers and pilots through electrical or chemical stimulation."[188]

That sounds vague but also promising. Fighter pilots are said to live and die by the so-called OODA Loop. That stands for Observe, Orient, Decide, and Act. All aspects of OODA feed back into each other when flying a combat mission. Anything that speeds up the OODA Loop more adroitly is better for aerial combat. Once again, we have the question of ethics. Just who is serving as the human guinea pig when certain brains are getting electrical and chemical stimulation? Chemical stimulation in pill form would likely be better accepted by human research subjects than electrical stimulation of the brain.

Unfortunately, as discussed before, authoritarian governments such

---

[186] QuikClot corporate web site.

[187] Malet, David. 2016. *Biotechnology and International Security*. Lanham, MD: Rowman and Littlefield.

[188] *Ibid.*

as China, Russia, and Iran have less concern about medical ethics, so experimenting with the brain waves of human beings could accelerate at a faster pace in those countries compared to the United States.

Biomechanics to the Rescue

Speaking of acceleration, someone has to study the speed or quickness of an individual soldier, without all the modern gear holding him or her back. This is where the study of biomechanics comes in. The Center for Military Biomechanics Research, according to the federal government data repository Data.gov, is focused on soldier movement. It is described as, "a fully equipped 5,000 square foot biomechanics research laboratory with a 12-camera Qualysis infrared video motion analysis system. It also contains a unique patented dual-force platform treadmill that measures x, y, and z forces and torques on individual feet during walking. There are also six portable Myomonitor EMG systems to measure muscle nerve activity, as well as metabolic carts to measure oxygen consumption to determine locomotion efficiency."[189]

This lab is secretive. There is not much available about its activities on the open web. But it is safe to say that someone is seriously looking at soldier movement. It would not be surprising if exoskeletons are being discussed there.

The University of Virginia is more transparent about its biomechanics research. Its Center for Applied Biomechanics has been working for the Pentagon in vehicle protection. The lab made a name for itself investigating the U.S. military's Mine-Resistant Ambush-Protected vehicles or MRAP's. When MRAPs were first deployed, occupants were still being wounded by improvised explosive devices. This was a huge disappointment and defeated the purpose of the entire MRAP procurement

[189] Data.gov

program. Then the DOD had University of Virginia check out the problems.

A team of Virginia researchers led by principal scientist Rob Salzar said, "These are not the kinds of intrusion injuries you see in a typical accident. Because of the thickness of the armor, the floor might move just half an inch, but it has been driven by 500 to 1,000 Gs of force. This causes complex injuries at the point of contact, the foot and ankle as well as the pelvis."[190]

The Virginia researchers went to work. They created their own blast simulator and an advanced crash dummy to replicate IED strikes – all to focus on their main mission of increasing soldier survivability and performance through the study of biomechanics. The Pentagon will be integrating this research into improving the protection of MRAPs.

Other biotechnology applications are amazing. The "Quantum Stealth" product jumps to the forefront because it turns things invisible. The technology developed by Hyperstealth Biotechnology Corp. is a "material that renders the target completely invisible by bending light waves around the target. The material removes not only your visual, infrared (night vision) and thermal signatures but also the target's shadow," according to the company's CEO, Guy Cramer, on the company's web site.[191]

China Takes a Crack at Biotechnology for Combat

China synthetic researchers in the military have also gone to work in biotechnology as well. They keep these experiments under wraps, but you can read into what the PLA is doing by examining their overall biotechnology strategy for dominance. For example, according to the Jamestown Foundation think tank, after various mergers of agencies,

---

[190] University of Virginia Center for Applied Biomechanics web site. http://www.centerforappliedbiomechanics.org/research/military/

[191] http://www.hyperstealth.com/Quantum-Stealth/

China's Academy of Military Science has been re-organized into separate research institutes underneath a lieutenant general with a PhD in engineering.[192] This change came straight from President Xi Jinping, the Jamestown Foundation reported in 2019.[193] The key entity is the Military Medicine Institute. Instead of just focusing on pure research in fields such as chemistry and biology, the Academy of Military Science is seeking to blend research and military doctrine.[194] The reorganization also allows for greater coordination between the military and civilian universities – similar to the United States when the Pentagon gives research grants to academia.[195] That means they are getting into applied research that drills down to the common soldier. If they are changing their research focus to real military use, then biotech is one of the areas in which they want to dominate.

China does not do anything without a strategy or a focused goal in mind. In this case, it is survivability of the soldier. The experiments with biotech will be done in conjunction with computer-brain emulations or cyborgs. This is where the super soldiers come in. It is all part of a greater research strategy coming from the PLA's reorganization of the Academy of Military Science. That is the big change that Western militaries should take seriously. Pure research for the sake of knowledge-building has changed in China to developing technology for aspirations such as soldier survivability. They want research to be adapted into military doctrine, hit the battlefield, and get down to the individual soldier instead of their military researchers just publishing academic papers. Although publishing is still encouraged. Much of their prior pure research entered into the death valley. The Chinese do not want biotechnology to fall by

---

192 Wuthnow, Joel. 2019. "China's 'New' Academy of Military Science: A Revolution in Theoretical Affairs?" Jamestown Foundation. *China Brief.* Vol. 19: No. 2. Jan. 18, 2019.

193 *Ibid.*

194 *Ibid.*

195 *Ibid.*

the wayside and just be the subject of academic papers. There is a real Chinese strategy to get these experiments to the point of having tangible applied repercussions for the individual soldiers.

In any military, those serving give up individual rights for the good of the entire organization. Authoritarian governments take this to extremes. Alternatively, in the U.S. military, individuals can refuse to carry out an unlawful order. It is a volunteer military as well. For those who do not want to give up their individual rights, they can choose not to serve. China has features of their military that differ. Soldiers are conscripted and have a much more communal hierarchical structure. Orders are often carried out without question and without regard as to whether they are legal or not. If the PLA orders a human subject to be part of an experiment for biotechnology, that order will be carried out. They are always going to have a large number of human subjects for experimentation. That is less likely to happen in Western militaries which are more democratic and less authoritarian. The Chinese have this huge advantage in biotechnology because they will have so many ready participants in soldier survivability and super-soldier experiments. In the United States, if a family member knew that their loved one was in the military and became the subject of a biotechnology experiment, they would contact their Member of Congress, tell the media, and there would be a Congressional hearing with generals and admirals called up to testify about the dangers and ethics of using military human subjects in experiments. Congress could cancel the program and forbid the practice. The Chinese do not have to deal with that scenario. This allows them to take medical risks and push ethical boundaries without any political repercussions. It is a huge advantage in their research – unlimited attempts at getting it right with human subjects. They will eventually get it right and take biotechnology to new levels for soldier survivability.

The United States and other Western governments should not relax ethical controls for experimentation on human subjects, even if means giving the advantage to the Chinese. Individuals in Western militaries serve for many different reasons, but they do not sign up to be medical guinea pigs. As discussed earlier, let me examine again the controversy over the administration of the anthrax vaccine that some thought contributed to "Gulf War Syndrome" in the U.S. military. That was just an immunization shot. Some refused to take it and were discharged for refusal. A simple immunization shot had large ethical repercussions and some negative medical implications for certain individuals. Imagine the implications for being a human subject in a biotechnology experiment. It would be too controversial. Fortunately, the media and legislators would be investigating it if even one U.S. soldier sounded the alarm. And rightly so.

China has the ambitious biomedical strategy, the leadership, the military objectives, the means, the money, the medical resources and researchers, the time, the political will, numerous human subjects not bound by Western ethics, a compliant media, and limited legislative oversight. That is a recipe for dominance in biotechnology that can lead to greater soldier survivability and a huge advantage on the battlefield.

But the United States also needs a national strategy in biotechnology, according to National Defense University's Diane DiEuliis. DiEuliis is a deep thinker on all things related to biodefense and biotechnology. "The uncertainty about the program's future is consistent with the lack of a holistic overarching Pentagon strategy for incorporating biotechnology products into deployable tools for the warfighter," [196] she wrote. "This stems from a traditional and instinctive linking of biotechnology to medicines and force health protection. But today, biotechnology's benefits extend far beyond that area — it can now also deliver materials, sensors, and fuels. The disparate components of biotechnology can also be seen in the way the Defense Department siloes this field of science

---

[196] DiEuliis, Diane. 2018. "Biotechnology for the Battlefield: A Need for Strategy." *War on the Rocks*. November 27, 2018.

— many different agencies touch different parts of the proverbial elephant that is biotechnology."[197]

Thus, the United States has its work cut out for it when it comes to competing with authoritarian countries and biotechnology on the battlefield. Adversaries like China have already developed their strategy and are acting on it quickly.

Despite these worries, China is indeed acting to tap the brakes on rogue medical engineering. A biophysicist named He Jiankui, who claimed to have made the first babies using CRISPR, was sentenced to three years in prison in 2020 for breaking Chinese law on medical practices. This is a positive development for international security. The sentencing should send a warning to Chinese scientists who conduct research at a network of PLA hospitals that could use CRISPR to create an unfair advantage on the battlefield.

Weber would not have been surprised. Bureaucratic power has reared its head in China. Perhaps the "humanity" in Chinese jurisprudence has promoted a belief in the sociology of war at the macro level. And perhaps the Chinese are putting the brakes on CRISPR and other attempts at super soldier development for ethical reasons, and this is a positive development from Beijing.

---

[197] *Ibid.*

CHAPTER FIVE

FUTURE WEAPONS SYSTEMS

For humans to create a war machine, even if it is enhanced by biotechnology, a Weberian bureaucracy is required to accumulate scarce resources and compete with other elements of the non-military bureaucracy. Two forces are in play at once. Bureaucratic pressure to spend more money on weapon systems and realist self-help in an anarchic global system. Technological change is an obvious outgrowth of this state of affairs. Emerging technologies add to weapons systems in a competition with near-peer rivals around the globe. The United States and the United Kingdom face revisionist powers and extremist terror. Rivals such as China, Russia, Iran, and North Korea are innovating in their militaries as well. The quest for the latest weapons systems is a global contest in which the realist system fans the flames of self-help.

Two major technology movements are emerging. Hypersonic glide vehicles, along with lasers, are new weapons systems that are hot commodities. For militaries to communicate better, 5G networks are also rising to the top of the heap on countries' wish lists. New aerial bombers and improved nuclear submarines will be introduced in the coming years.

American innovation locations such as Silicon Valley, Austin, and Boston are playing a greater role in building emerging technology and boosting defense acquisition. Look for the Pentagon's Defense

Innovation Unit, headquartered in Silicon Valley, to play a greater role in transferring technology from the private sector to the acquisition of new war machines. The Defense Innovation Unit starts the technology transfer process with a military problem that flummoxes the Pentagon, then the unit poses the problem to start-ups in Silicon Valley, Austin, and Boston, where the Defense Innovation Unit has satellite offices. The idea is for the brightest minds, who would not normally be working in defense, to take on an intellectual challenge to bring the latest innovations to the military. These civilians could be better recruited with student loan forgiveness and other incentives. The unit can award its own contracts instead of relying on the antiquated and slow-moving acquisition bureaucracy and present-day defense procurement system.

Why not create entire military bases in these innovation centers? Former Defense Innovation Unit director Raj Shah has called for this.[198] It would help recruit innovative talent to work on solving defense problems full-time. Soldiers and marines could train on the new technology as it comes to fruition. Currently, U.S. defense acquisition experts are embedded overseas with soldiers, marines, sailors, and airmen. They witness military problems first-hand. The personnel on the ground then tell the acquisition workers what is needed, and this information is sent back to the Pentagon.

A better solution would be the acute military requirements be sent back to the Defense Innovation Unit to act in real-time. Universities and their academic eco-systems would play a role in the new bases. Silicon Valley has Stanford and UC-Berkeley. Boston has Harvard University and a host of other colleges and universities. Austin has the University of Texas flagship campus. There would be what Weber called "solidarity" in these innovation centers that would be an improvement on the current defense bureaucracy. These new bases would attract people who

198 Barnett, Jackson. 2020. "Ex-DIU Leader Call for Tenfold Increase in DOD's Budget for Emerging Technology." *Fedscoop*. Feb. 5, 2020.

would not consider a career in the military. There is precedent for a base in Silicon Valley. Outside of San Jose, California, a recreational area known as Mount Umunhum was the location for Almaden Air Force Station during the Cold War before it was shuttered in 1980. Most of the facilities have crumbled since then, but it would be an area that could be used for a military base. NASA's Ames Research Center and Moffett Federal Airfield in Mountain View in Silicon Valley would be a better choice for a full-time military base focused on innovation. The Defense Innovation Unit already has its main office in Mountain View. There would be synergies with NASA, and it would be an obvious location for the U.S. Space Force. But these types of concepts require political will and money. There has not been the type of budgetary outlays that would enable new military bases dedicated to innovation.

Research and Development efforts have seen budgets ebb and flow, although this is beginning to change. The latest Fiscal Year 2021 National Defense Authorization Act contains a generous Research, Development, Test, and Evaluation budget request from the executive branch. The line item is now $106.6 billion, its highest in history. This includes $7 billion in advanced capabilities and emerging technologies.[199] This category is comprised of hypersonic missiles, artificial intelligence, 5G/microelectronics, and autonomous platforms. $3.2 billion of this requested outlay will be dedicated to hypersonics. There is also a line item for a system that can sense when an enemy's hypersonic glide vehicle or hypersonic cruise missile is launched. $841 million is earmarked for artificial intelligence – eight percent more than the previous year. $1.7 billion will be set aside for autonomous platforms and human-machine capabilities will be prioritized. Budgeting for 5G networks will be $1.5 billion for fiscal year 2021.[200] But despite this robust spending request, it is clear the United States military needs to invest more in

---

199 FY 2021 National Defense Authorization Act.

200 *Ibid.*

emerging technology over a number of subsequent years. This requires Congress and the White House to set high priorities dedicated to this goal.

Hypersonic Weapons Are a Priority

The arms race for hypersonic missiles is a major part of the 2021 defense budget. Hypersonic weapons are extremely fast – similar to a ballistic missile but can be maneuvered like a cruise missile.[201] Hypersonics fly along the edge of space at MACH 5 or at 3,800 miles per hour to MACH 10 or 7,500 miles per hour. Some models can hit even higher speeds approaching MACH 20 to MACH 30. This makes the weapons harder to track by adversaries' sensors and radar. The high speed and maneuverability make them different from existing ballistic missiles since regular missiles have a predictable trajectory that is easily tracked by missile defense systems. Ballistic missiles also fly lower since hypersonics are traveling in the atmosphere while ballistic missiles fly in lower earth orbit making hypersonics more difficult to defend against. Hypersonics can carry nuclear or conventional warheads. Hypersonics are sometimes called glide vehicles because they can burst from the last stage of a missile fired from the ground or from submarines. They can also be released from an aerial bomber like a cruise missile. The ultra-high-speed comes from the so-called Scramjet propulsion system. "A Scramjet engine is an engine that uses 'air breathing' technology. This means that the engine collects oxygen from the atmosphere as it is traveling and mixes the oxygen with its hydrogen fuel, creating the combustion needed for hypersonic travel."[202]

But hypersonics do not always need their own propulsion systems. They can be dropped by an airplane or ballistic missile to glide toward the target. These weapons are also known as hypersonic glide vehicles or

---

201 "Hypersonic Weapons Basics." 2018. Missile Defense Advocacy Alliance.

202 *Ibid.*

a concept the Americans call tactical boost glide. "The deadly projectile might ricochet downward, nose tilted up, on layers of atmosphere — the mesosphere, then the stratosphere and troposphere — like an oblate stone on water, in smaller and shallower skips, or it might be directed to pass smoothly through these layers. In either instance, the friction of the lower atmosphere would finally slow it enough to allow a steering system to maneuver it precisely toward its target."[203]

Hypersonics are usually not that large – between five and ten feet long and 500 pounds – but they pack a powerful punch. "The missiles' kinetic energy at the time of impact, at final speeds of at least 1,150 miles per hour, makes them powerful enough to penetrate any building material or armored plating with the force of three to four tons of TNT."[204]

In the future, Americans could use these weapons to take out Russian or Chinese rail or road-based nuclear-weapons launchers. They could be utilized for destroying enemy radar sites that control air defense systems. If accurate enough, and there are questions about their accuracy, hypersonics could be used for targeted assassinations of enemy political leaders.

Hypersonic Weapons from Near-Peer Competitors Are a Threat to the United States

Meanwhile, the United States has to be concerned about its own weapons systems being targeted. Aircraft carriers would be endangered by hypersonic missiles fired by China or Russia. With hypersonic missiles coming to these three countries – the United States, China, and Russia, the leaders controlling the missiles, will need to have some kind of ethical decision-making calculus on first or second use. Hypersonics are so fast that there is not a lot of decision-making time to figure out whether

---

[203] Smith R. Jeffrey. 2019. "Hypersonic Missiles Are Unstoppable. And They're Starting a New Global Arms Race." *New York Times*. June 19, 2019.

[204] *Ibid.*

to launch or not launch a counter strike. For example, a nuclear-armed hypersonic missile first-strike attack from Russia could give decision-makers only 15 minutes to decide whether to retaliate with a nuclear salvo. In the future, hypersonics may have to be part of non-proliferation deliberations on their potential for first-use and other arms control considerations.

It is not just Russia and China that are building hypersonic missile programs. France and India have programs in development and Australia and Japan are conducting research into the new weapons systems. The Japanese have plans for a hypersonic glide vehicle and a hypersonic cruise missile. They are also using scramjet technology for propulsion. The Japanese seek a high-explosive armor piercing warhead that could potentially attack Chinese shipping – particularly a Chinese aircraft carrier. These developments make the Asia-Pacific a flashpoint for hypersonics with rivals China, the United States, Japan, and Australia all having plans for the weapons systems. So, this global arms competition is running unabated and only the size of military budgets stand in the way of development.

The United States is developing two main hypersonic missile programs to be fully operational by 2022. They are both conventional and non-nuclear at this point. Russia and China are pursuing both nuclear and conventional hypersonics. The U.S. Department of Defense is focusing on a glide vehicle called the Advanced Hypersonic Weapon. It was successfully tested in 2011 by hitting a target 2,300 miles away.[205] Lockheed Martin's program is much more ambitious. The Falcon Hypersonic Technology Vehicle 2 is designed to go MACH 20, which is 13,000 miles per hour. Both the Advanced Hypersonic Weapon and the Falcon Hypersonic Technology Vehicle are part of the Pentagon's "Prompt Global Strike" concept, which would enable the United States to launch a hypersonic missile anywhere in the world within an hour.[206]

---

205 Hypersonic Weapons Basics.

206 *Ibid.*

Hypersonic missiles are not without disadvantages. At such high speeds, the body of these crafts heat up considerably. This negatively affects the accuracy of the weapons. Testing is expensive, difficult, and noisy. There are few missile ranges in the United States that can effectively test a hypersonic weapon. Sonic booms from MACH-5 to MACH-15 flight are considerable, so the Pentagon is struggling to find testing grounds that can accommodate the new missile technologies. The tests can cost around $100 million.[207]

Meanwhile, Raytheon is developing technologies that can serve as counter-hypersonic missiles. "Raytheon Missiles and Defense is working with the government and industry to develop layered solutions aimed at detecting, tracking and ultimately defeating modern hypersonic weapons."[208] Friendly missile defense forces must be able to defeat hypersonic glide vehicles and cruise missiles from Russia and China. Look for this cat and mouse game to play out in the coming years as hypersonics become more prevalent. Currently, the United States has little protection against a potential hypersonic missile attack from Russia or China.

The advent of hypersonic weapons is changing warfare. The future of war will be stand-off missiles that will allow rival countries to pick off targets from afar without having to deploy frontline troops. Already, the United States Marine Corps is changing the way they fight. The marines are retiring their Abrams main battle tanks and shedding most of their field artillery. Instead, the Corps will focus on long-range rocket artillery for the stand-off fight. Since World War Two, the marines had long used an island-hopping strategy and technique in which they were accustomed to preparing and training for amphibious warfare. Now they are prepping for what I call the "stand-off missile fight," in a potential

---

[207] *Ibid.*

[208] Hypersonic Weapons Overview – Raytheon. https://www.raytheonmissilesanddefense.com/capabilities/hypersonics

future conflict with China. To be sure, there are still numerous island chains in the South China Seas such as the Spratly and Paracel Islands in which the Chinese have military bases. Subi Reef and Fiery Cross Reef, for example, have high military strategic value for the Chinese. But these reefs are tiny, and the marines feel that the tanks and heavy artillery will not be needed, instead opting for rockets. The main marine system is an armored truck with a six-tube launcher called the HIMARs or High Mobility Artillery Rocket System. The marines will also use naval strike missiles and a new variant of the Tomahawk cruise missile.

These changes will continue to be a factor in future warfare, although not every U.S. service branch is making such drastic changes as the marines are. But if China develops its own hypersonic missile before the Americans, there will be a dangerous lag in time that will favor the Chinese. And it appears that the United States will not be fully ready with a hypersonic weapon until 2022. However, testing is going according to plan for the Americans – for the most part. In March of 2020, the United States had a successful test of the common hypersonic glide body that launched in Hawaii and hit its target. The common hypersonic glide body "will form the basis for hypersonic weapon systems fielded by both the army and navy. According to the Department of Defense, C-HGB will comprise a hypersonic weapon's 'conventional warhead, guidance system, cabling, and thermal protection shield.'"[209]

Hypersonic weapons face two overarching considerations – ethics and arms control. There must be ethical scientists and civilian military leadership, all the way up the chain of command to the national command authority, who build and control these weapons. China and Russia are making them nuclear-capable, and the United States is sure to eventually follow suit. Nuclear proliferation conjures up deep ethical and moral problems. Deciding on whether to engage in first-use or

---

[209] Mizokami, Kyle. 2020. "The Pentagon's Hypersonic Weapon System Passes a Critical Flight Test." *Popular Mechanics*. March 24, 2020.

retaliatory nuclear strikes is one of the deepest dilemmas in war and peace. Hypersonics have created a new arms race that is sure to continue throughout the decade. Once they are developed more broadly, the general public will catch on and will likely have pockets of protest as they are tested. So, there is a budding protest movement probably in store for hypersonics. Negotiations for arms control are another factor. The Russians and the Americans are bound by the New START treaty in which they are limited to 700 deployed intercontinental ballistic missiles and submarine-launched warheads along with limits of 1,550 nuclear warheads. China is not bound by this treaty, although there are calls to make the country a signatory. Nevertheless, both Russia and China are working toward nuclear-capable hypersonic missiles. This will require more difficult and fraught negotiations to limit nuclear proliferation. The best course of action would be to re-negotiate the New START Treaty and add hypersonic nuclear warheads to the limitations of the accord. It is imperative that China be added to the treaty as well.

Modern Lasers Enter the Mix

One potential defense against hypersonic weapons is the use of a laser. Lasers have a long history of military application in the United States, having first gone into research status in the 1960s. The most successful role for lasers has been in using them for range-finders and designating targets. Range-finders measure the length from a firing point to a target. Laser designators inform and help laser bombs find their target by enabling a sensor to retrieve the signals that are reflected into the sky.

Making lasers into weapons has proved to be difficult, but much progress has been made in research and development over the decades. Historically, lasers have been forced to depend on chemical mediums such as oxygen-iodine or fluorine-hydrogen to make the intense energy to form the laser. This compound could explode the laser during use.

Now lasers can be powered electrically by fiber optics.[210] This allows lasers to be built much smaller and lighter than those built with chemical mediums. The U.S. Air Force can then aim for having lasers mounted on the wings of small jet fighters. The "ammunition" would be limitless since new energy is constantly produced.[211] However, hand-held laser weapons are a long way off. The amount of energy needed is too great for such a small weapon. Also, hand-held laser weapons produce too much heat for an individual soldier to handle.

Lasers have assisted multitudes of American soldiers and marines over the years. MILES gear (Multiple Integrated Laser Engagement System) allows trainees to have realistic battle simulations between a "blue" or friendly force versus a notional or "red" hostile force to make mock battles. Personnel wear sensors around their bodies that pick up a laser-activated by blank ammunition in weapons. When there is a "hit" on the MILES sensors, the soldier's sensor buzzes, and that person is considered hit and notionally killed or wounded. MILES gear can even be set up on a tank. This type of laser tag has allowed for very realistic training for U.S. military personnel over the years.

Other military laser systems have not been as successful. The U.S. Air Force had high hopes for its Airborne Laser program. This was based on the Strategic Defense Initiative, the so-called "Star Wars" system for missile defense during the Reagan administration in the 1980s. Later, during the George W. Bush administration, the Airborne Laser Testbed was mounted on a 747 aircraft called the Boeing YAL-1 to destroy incoming enemy missiles with a laser blast. The Airborne Laser Testbed was designed to send a laser beam "15 inches of diameter on the missiles' skin," and the hit would heat up and rupture the enemy missile

---

[210] "Chapter 4, Military Applications of Lasers; Science Clarified." *Science Clarified.*

[211] *Ibid.*

by weakening it and forcing it to break up from the stress of flying at such high speeds.[212]

Although it was tested successfully against a target in 2010, the Airborne Laser program proved to be awfully expensive. The program life span cost over $5 billion. Going forward, each YAL-1 aircraft equipped with the Airborne Laser would set the air force back $1.5 billion a piece with an additional operating cost of $100 million per year, according to Secretary Robert Gates in 2011. Moreover, the airplanes had limited range and would have to constantly fly in orbit over Russian or Chinese airspace to be effective. This limitation proved unrealistic and the program was canceled in December 2011.[213]

Despite these difficulties and setbacks, lasers are still popular with the U.S. military and will be used in the future. Sometimes lasers can be utilized as non-lethal weapons to help with crowd control during mass protests. The U.S. Joint Non-lethal Weapons Directorate Program has a directed-energy induced Plasma Effect concept. These plasma effect lasers can take a protester and target him or her with direct energy that heats up their skin without damaging it until protesters disperse. The program also features very bright lights to "blind" protesters and "talking plasma balls" to communicate to demonstrators that now is the time to get off the streets. The program plans to have sound waves pass through the laser. The lasers used for crowd control have very high-energy with a short pulse rate that removes electrons from gas – creating a plasma effect or plasma ball. These crowd control techniques would be used to protect bases and outposts from protesters and others who need to disperse with non-violent means. There are also plans to mount the directed energy generators on vehicles to have the capacity for mobile crowd control. The directed energy beams can be utilized to create

---

212 *Ibid.*

213 Hodge, Nathan. 2011. "Pentagon Loses War to Zap Airborne Laser From Budget." *The Wall Street Journal.* Feb. 11, 2011.

continuous audio "flash bang" grenades to stun crowds into submission. This is accomplished by creating ultra-loud noises in order to make protesters give up ground and leave the premises.

In terms of defense from enemy unmanned aerial systems, the U.S. Air Force has leapt ahead. In the second quarter of 2020, the air force announced it had a directed energy weapon that could take out enemy drones. Dubbed THOR (Tactical High-Power Operational Responder) by the Air Force Research Laboratory at Wright-Patterson Air Force Base, scientists claim the Raytheon system is able to eliminate swarms of attacking drones. Research on THOR started in 2018, when the Vice Chief of Staff of the air force called for a directed energy response to adversarial remotely piloted-vehicles. Testing continued in the following years at White Sands Missile Range, New Mexico and Fort Sill, Oklahoma. By 2022, the air force and Raytheon will have a sound road map to eliminating enemy drones by laser.[214]

The U.S. Army also wants to deploy lasers to take out enemy drones, rockets, and mortars. The service plans to outfit its Stryker armored personnel carrier with a 50-kilowatt directed energy weapon also by 2022. The army believes the laser can definitely be mounted on a vehicle, the challenge, according to the Army's Rapid Capabilities and Critical Technologies office, is to maximize the energy throughput of the lasers. This will be a critical testing and research path over the coming years.

The entire Pentagon wants to get into the counter-unmanned aircraft systems business. The Department of Defense is investing $404 million in Fiscal Year 2021 on this branch of testing and research.[215] An additional $83 million will be spent to buy the finished systems. The U.S. Navy is the furthest along in its directed energy program. Since 2014, it has deployed a laser weapon on board the USS Ponce. This weapon can

---

[214] Cohen, Rachel S. 2020. "Overseas Directed-Energy Demonstration Underway." *Air Force Magazine*. April 8, 2020.

[215] FY 2021 National Defense Authorization Act.

engage and kill enemy drones. The navy also has what it calls an "optical dazzler" that can interfere with the sensors on an adversary's drone and wreck its flight path. In 2021, a new and more powerful 60-kilowatt laser will be deployed on the USS Preble. This directed energy weapon will have counter-drone capabilities. Not to be outdone, the U.S. Marine Corps is getting into the counter-unmanned vehicle game. Its ground-based air defense program is buying the compact laser weapons system which comes in 2-, 5-, and 10-kilowatt variants. Unfortunately, the marines plan to field a man-portable counter-unmanned aircraft system has not worked out. The system's weight and power requirements were not realistically sound.

One of the problems with the Pentagon's various laser systems is that they duplicate effort among the different service branches. This is a common malady in defense acquisition when the branches compete against each other for attention and funding with Congress. Another problem is to make sure these lasers do not accidentally target a commercial aircraft and cause damage or danger to civilians.

Meanwhile, defense contractors are feeling the itch to get military-use lasers deployed with soldiers, marines, sailors, and airmen. Lockheed Martin won the contract for a High Energy Laser Tactical Vehicle Demonstrator mobile direct energy platform that will come to fruition in 2022 for the U.S. Army. Lockheed Martin claims to have worked on lasers for 40 years. The defense contractor believes directed energy capabilities such as rapid firing and inexpensive cost per shot are an improvement over conventional interceptors for missile defense that are often inaccurate and more expensive per salvo when fired.

Most laser systems have focused on counter-drone or counter-incoming rocket, mortar, or artillery fire. Can lasers be used for more offensive tactical value? For example, could a laser be fitted on a main battle tank to supplement its regular gun? Emerging threat analyst Kyle Mizokami of *Popular Mechanics* thinks that lasers are not quite ready to be deployed on tanks. I would like to make a special acknowledgement and give credit to Mizokami and *Popular Mechanics* because I will make several references to their work in this chapter. There are many aspects that hinder use of lasers on tanks. It is not clear how a laser would burn through an enemy tank's armor. It would likely take at least five seconds, according to Mizokami.[216] While the laser is trying to forge through another tank's outer protection, the main conventional turret could shoot two rounds. Mizokami also pointed out that a laser's strength is affected by the atmosphere. "As a laser beam travels through tiny droplets of water in fog, ice crystals in snow, and ash from fires, the laser strikes them and rapidly loses coherency. An adversary facing laser-armed tanks might lay smokescreens filled with tiny particulates that block vision and reduce the power of any laser that passes through them. Chemical energy guns, on the other hand, would not lose any of their hitting power at all."[217]

Perhaps lasers are a better fit for larger platforms such as ships and airplanes. General Dynamics is racing ahead with the U.S. Navy to make improvements on the laser that was installed on the USS Ponce in 2014. That aging laser was only 30-kilowatts. Another ship – the USS Dewey – has a 60-kilowatt Optimal Dazzling Interdictor that enables the directed energy rays to interfere with enemy sensors on vessels, airplanes, and incoming missiles to obstruct their flight.[218] The new laser that will be installed on the USS Little Rock will be five times more powerful than the USS Ponce and two and a half times more powerful than the one on the USS Dewey. The Little Rock is a smaller ship – a littoral combat ship – but the laser will be a large and robust 150-kilowatt system. It will now be the fourth naval ship to deploy a laser. The 150-kilowatt laser is made for blasting drones and small aircraft. In May of 2020,

---

[216] Mizokami, Kyle. 2020. "So...Should We Put Lasers on Tanks?" *Popular Mechanics*. March 19, 2020.

[217] *Ibid.*

[218] Mizokami, Kyle. 2020. "The Navy's Smallest Warship Gets a Big Laser Gun." *Popular Mechanics*. Jan. 14, 2020.

the amphibious ship USS Portland had a successful test of a solid-state laser against an unmanned aerial vehicle target. The laser was able to disable the target drone.[219]

It could also be used to attack small, swarming craft that the Iranian Islamic Revolutionary Guard Navy utilizes.[220] In the second quarter of 2020, President Trump ordered the U.S. Navy to destroy armed Iranian speed boats that have been harassing U.S. Naval shipping for years in the Persian Gulf. Since the order was announced on Twitter in April 2020, it was not clear what the rules of engagement would specifically be, in other words, what would constitute a clear and present dangerous threat that would give the U.S. Navy the impetus to fire on the patrol boats and destroy them. This would certainly be an act of war if carried out. If the Iranian patrol boats fired first at the American ships, then that would constitute an aggressive act that could be considered warlike and thus fit for a warlike answer. It is interesting that despite the rise of near-peer competitors such as Russia and China, the future of warfare is still in the Persian Gulf, after decades of the United States attempting to shape events there.

Naval lasers are not just confined to the surface fleet. U.S. submarines are looking at adding laser weapons, although lasers do not thrive underwater. Water scatters light and absorbs the directed energy. So, the lasers would have to be used when a submarine is steaming on the surface. This could help with defenses from enemy airplanes and drones.

Lasers are here to stay, and they are the future of warfare. Other countries will be fielding lasers as well, which I will examine later in this chapter.

---

[219] *Ibid.*

[220] *Ibid.*

Electromagnetic Railguns are Fascinating Weapons

The U.S. Navy, in addition to lasers, is looking for alternative styles of weapons, one of which is the use of electromagnetic railguns. Functioning as a large electrical circuit without gun powder, they send a kinetic energy warhead 5,000 miles per hour or MACH 7.5 at 20 to 32 megajoules with a range of 110 miles. At these speeds, railguns can defend against cruise missiles and ballistic missiles, which are valuable capabilities in the South and East China Sea since the Chinese have an enormous amount of shore-based cruise and ballistic missiles that are aimed at U.S. naval shipping near the coast of China.

The weapon produces 1,200 volts in ten milliseconds which makes a pulse-forming network.[221] This results in a network of capacitors that will release the energy to propel the projectile. The projectile weighs 45 pounds and accelerates to 5,000 miles per hour in an astonishing one one-hundredth of a second. This is three-times the speed of conventional weapons. Since the warhead is made up of kinetic energy, it does not use explosives. The ultra-high speed enables the warhead to knock out cruise missiles and ballistic missiles with kinetic energy. The railgun can fire at a rate of 10-rounds per minute at a cost of $25,000 per round.

Another exciting development for the navy is that the guided projectiles used in railguns could also be fired from a conventional powder gun. This program is called "gun-launched guided projectile." These projectiles do not fly as fast as the rounds fired out of the railgun, but they would take advantage of existing military weapons. In other words, the guided projectile could be fired from already existing conventional land-based howitzers and shipborne powder guns.[222]

---

[221] Osborn, Kris. 2019. "Why the Navy Wants a Long-Range Electro-Magnetic Rail Gun." *The National Interest*. Oct. 28, 2019.

[222] "Navy Lasers, Railgun, and Gul-Launched Guided Projectiles: Background and Issues for Congress." Congressional Research Service. Feb. 26, 2021.

The railgun needs at least five years to develop, and the research and development required is always subject to the ebb and flow of Congressional funding. The railgun is not yet ready to be deployed on U.S. Naval ships and it only received $9.5 million of funding for fiscal year 2021. But the navy sees its value especially in air defense to defend its shipping in dangerous potential conflict zones in the Middle East and East Asia.

3D Printing and the Future of the U.S. Military

Since the new weapons like the railgun take years to design, what if parts or aspects of the design could be pre-fabricated with a 3D printer? 3D printing, also known as additive manufacturing, is the future of the U.S. military and it is seeing a large uptake in the service branches, particularly in the army. 3D printing exports material layer by layer to create three-dimensional items. 3D printing has been used in the front lines at maintenance depots to make new parts and tools that were needed by the army in a hurry. Congress earmarked $42.5 million to the Pentagon for advanced manufacturing, additive manufacturing, and 3D printing for fiscal year 2020.[223] The army approved a policy in 2019 to use 3D-printed parts in new and used weapons. This has an obvious advantage when it comes to keeping tanks, armored personnel carriers, and helicopters in service. It is estimated that the Department of Defense has built thousands of parts using 3D printing.[224]

There are a multitude of uses for 3D printing in the military. Concrete 3D printers can build barracks for soldiers to sleep in. Sometimes the parts that are printed are mundane. Toilet seats in cargo planes that can cost $10,000 would cost only $300 with 3D printing.[225] But it is

---

[223] National Defense Authorization Act FY 2020.

[224] Weisgerber. Marcus. 2019. "Pentagon Remains Bullish on 3D Printing, Despite Regulatory 'Slog.'" *Government Executive*. Dec. 23, 2019.

[225] *Ibid.*

small replacement parts that make the most sense for 3D printing to be enormously beneficial to the military. From simple fasteners and plastic caps to more complicated parts for weapons systems, 3D printing has enormous potential. "Parts made with 3D printers tend to be lighter than their traditional counterparts, which can provide greater range for the fuel in a vehicle, or create space for more ammunition; while lighter, newer production designs can create parts that are actually more durable that their traditional counterparts."[226]

However, defense contractors would rather have the military spend more on defense procurement done the old way because 3D printers could rob them of lucrative contracts for spare parts. Also, the Pentagon needs an overarching strategy and policy for 3D printing. That is why the Department of Defense has established an army 3D printing and additive manufacturing center of excellence at the Rock Island Arsenal in Illinois. Remember the hub and spoke concept for COIN in a previous chapter? Well, there are hubs and spokes for logistics and acquisition as well. Rock Island Arsenal will be the "hub" of additive manufacturing for the military. Then the "hub" will branch out to other 25 "spokes" or various depots, plants, and arsenals to better coordinate 3D printing throughout the army. This should eliminate duplication of effort around the army service branches concerning additive manufacturing. The hub will then bleed down to various divisions in the army. The 25th Infantry Division in Hawaii and the 2nd Infantry Division in South Korea are setting up pilot programs with the Rock Island arsenal and actually beginning to print in 3D on demand. The idea is to have a "digital thread" so the various army divisions can pull up already approved drawings and print them for parts.[227]

---

226 Mehta, Aaron. 2019. "Why the US Army Must 'Get Religion' on 3D Printing." *Defense News*. Dec. 7, 2019.

227 Judson, Jen. 2020. "US Army Developing Process for Using 3D Printing at Depots in the Field." *Defense News*. Feb. 4, 2020.

One of the best examples of the value of 3D printing is its potential to create body parts for wounded soldiers. Cadets at the U.S. Army Military Academy at West Point are working on the invention of "bio-printers" which could print parts of the body such as bone cartilage and blood vessels.[228] These body parts would be printed with stem cells that could forge into a human body and prevent rejection of the part. Another group of cadets are working on "bio-bandages" that are printed from the cells of a wounded soldier. The bandages would be combined with stem cells to create a quick-healing bandage for burns and other types of wounds for quick clotting and the elimination of some types of scarring.[229]

Cadets are also working on different bio-printing projects such as blood vessels, a working meniscus, and a human liver. This is purely for research purposes at this point, but someday the goal is to get these parts accepted as a transplant into the human body. The idea would be for a 3D printer to be located at aid stations and mobile military hospitals so a wounded soldier could use his or her own collagen. Collagen is a protein in the human body that produce bandages or cartilage. Research from these experiments could also be used to create 3D printed body armor to stop a bullet or shrapnel.[230]

4D Printing Is Coming to a Defense Contractor Near You

4D Printing is even more exciting than 3D printing. That is no typo. 4D refers to printing that has a fourth dimension – time. This means that fabricated objects can change their shape over time. These printed materials can transform their shape in response to a specific stimulus introduced to the fabrication. The stimuli include changes in temperature or

---

228 Mizokami, Kyle. 2020. "3D Printed Body Parts Could One Day Help Wounded Soldiers." *Popular Mechanics*. Feb. 20, 2020.

229 *Ibid.*

230 *Ibid.*

adding light, water, magnetic fields, chemicals, and other environmental changes. After the stimuli is added, 4D printouts can smartly change their shape over time in a predetermined manner – usually to fold or unfold.

"During the 4D process, a geometric code is added that contains 'instructions' on how a shape will move or change once triggered by a stimulus. This preprogramming step enables the creation of smart, responsive objects that can adapt to specific environmental factors."[231]

An object is first 3D printed and then components are made to react a certain way with the stimuli. If 4D printing calls for the material to fold and unfold, for example, then the military application would be making a barracks or building a forward operating base for soldiers. Building a bridge for combat is another use case. Constructing these structures by hand normally would take longer and would be a heavy lift logistically. The stimulus could be a change in temperature with sunlight, then the 4D structure would assemble itself under the principle of smart materials.

4D printing can also be used for medical applications as well. Hydrogels are one example. Hydrogels are dispersed with water acting as the stimulus. They are three dimensional networks that can serve as carriers of cells for tissue engineering. 4D printing can produce a smart gel from changes in temperature that could aid in battlefield medicine because hydrogel can help create living tissue and human organs. This would be an excellent material to work with in conjunction with the 3D printed organs being investigated by the army officer cadets discussed earlier.

3D and 4D printers will likely be operating near battlefields soon. They simply have too many advantages not to be put to use for military applications. 3D printers are cost effective. They can be purchased off

---

231 "What Is 4D Printing, Anyway?" *AMFG*. Feb. 5, 2019.

the shelf for military use in many different models under $1,000. 4D printers are not "for sale" at this time. They are still in labs in research and development stages. But being able to change the shape of 3D printouts is a valuable technology with many military applications.

5G Military Networks Will Transform Security Across the Board

3D and 4D printing require stable and fast information technology networks to securely send digital blueprints to warfighters working in supply and logistics in order for more effective printing. The U.S. Department of Defense is hard at work bringing 5G mobile communication networks to fruition. 5G networks are around 20 times faster than existing 4G networks. They can handle bigger pipelines of data that have higher volume, veracity, and latency.[232] Latency refers to the speed of return communications. Currently, the U.S. military relies on communication via satellite relays. 5G is terrestrial and thus has a quicker turnaround. The Pentagon asked for $484 million in 5G funding for fiscal year 2021.

According to Avionics International, 5G "is a critical technology to the Department of Defense" and "enables high bandwidth, real-time, densely-connected networks, which represent many of the use cases central to defense command, control, and communications," said Charles Clancy, vice president of intelligence programs at MITRE.[233]

The idea behind 5G and military networks is to increase the level of situational awareness for personnel in the field and in command centers. 5G networks will not only help 3D and 4D printing, but they will also assist in the accuracy of hypersonic missiles. 5G networks will also help the advent of augmented reality and virtual reality for the U.S. military.

---

[232] Harper, Jon. 2019. "Defense Department Forging Path for 5G Adoption." *National Defense*. Dec. 6, 2019.

[233] Wolfe, Frank. 2020. "Pentagon Seeks Ramp Up in 5G Investment, What Does it Mean for Military Avionics?" *Aviation Today*. Feb. 14, 2020.

This will improve training and also boost levels of situational awareness in mission planning. F-35 pilots already have elements of augmented reality in their flight helmets. Maintenance is another area 5G networks can better assist the warfighter. So-called "smart" warehouses combined with augmented reality and sensors would allow seamless re-supply to get parts, food, and ammunition to the front lines.[234]

Joe Evans, the Pentagon's technical lead for 5G, said in a *National Defense* article, "One of the problems with 4G and even Wi-Fi types of technologies is they really weren't designed to be having tens of thousands of individual wireless devices talking to the cell site or the access point," he said. "What 5G is doing is essentially increasing that scale. And so, from a single access point, you can now track greater volume of individual items in the warehouse [and do] the finer grain tracking."[235]

5G enables dynamic spectrum sharing. This means that since 5G has the capability to be so broad-based in use, the military can share it with defense contractors and make collaboration easier. Research areas such as artificial intelligence will grow with the various offices working together and breaking stovepipes of redundant bureaucracies between the military and civilian defense contractors. This is a big step forward for U.S. allies in NATO and other alliances if other countries are able to adapt to 5G networks as expected.

The Pentagon has initiated four 5G pilot programs at military installations across the army, navy, air force, and marines. Testing and development will be in augmented reality and virtual reality, smart warehouse concepts, and dynamic spectrum-sharing experiments.[236]

In the future, 5G technology can help with autonomous and swarming drones because 5G can enable rapid communications

---

[234] "Defense Department Forging Path for 5G Adoption."

[235] *Ibid.*

[236] Tucker, Patrick. 2020. "Pentagon Wants to Start Testing New 5G tech Soon." *Defense One*. Feb. 26, 2020.

between sensors in the air and ground command and communications. Intelligence, surveillance, and reconnaissance can also be improved due to "increasingly high-bandwidths to process, exploit, and disseminate information from a growing number of battlespace sensors. This could provide commanders with timely access to actionable intelligence data, in turn improving operational decision-making," according to the Congressional Research Service.[237]

Charles Clancy of the think tank MITRE believes the air force will benefit with the new communication technology. "With respect to 5G and military aviation, there are many use cases, 5G's millimeter wave technology could enable a new class of high-bandwidth air-to-air and air-to-ground communications. The Internet of Things features in 5G could be used for secure fly-by-wireless avionics, dramatically reducing aircraft weight. Secure, ubiquitous ground connectivity could fundamentally change how ground logistics, operations, and maintenance are performed."[238]

The B-21 Raider: America's New Stealth Bomber

Communication with the latest generation of aircraft and other weapons systems will be essential with the 5G technology. Take, for example, Northrop Grumman's new bomber – the B-21 Raider. This will be put into service in 2022. It took until 2020, but the air force finally released an image of the airplane.[239] This is the first new American bomber since 1988. There are two other bombers in the air force that are the workhorses – the stealth B-2 Spirit and the conventional B-1 Lancer. I have

---

[237] "National Security Implications of Fifth Generation (5G) Mobile Technologies." Congressional Research Service. Jan. 26, 2021.

[238] "Pentagon Seeks Ramp Up in 5G Investment, What Does it Mean for Military Avionics?"

[239] Mizokami, Kyle. 2020. "The B-21 Bomber Is the Coolest Plane We've Never Seen." *Popular Mechanics*. Feb. 3, 2020.

seen the B-2 in action, and it is like a flying wedge that glides effortlessly in a sweep of air beneath its mono-wing. The new B-21 Raider is a flying wedge too, but it is smaller and sleeker – with an outer stealth coating that reminds you of the nice smooth curves of the F-22 stealth fighter. That is the whole idea behind the B-21 Raider. There are no vertical shapes on the airplane, just the smooth flying wing – the best way to make it stealthy and evade enemy radar.

The B-21, if all goes to plan, will defeat surface-to-air missile systems like the Russian S-400 and competing stealth fighters that the Russians and Chinese launch into the air to protect their countries. The B-21 will also fly at a higher altitude than the B-2. The new B-21 will cost $654 million each and the air force plans to buy 100 of them. The bomber will undergo its first flight likely in 2022.[240]

Growler Unmanned Airplanes Fill the Void

While the B-21 will have a live pilot, other U.S. military service branches will have unmanned aircraft, but these are not drones. These are former navy airplanes that are going to be converted into unmanned airplanes. The navy is taking some of their older EA-18G Growler electronic warfare jamming aircraft into unmanned aircraft.[241] They announced that it had successfully tested the unmanned version in 2020. The way it works is that one EA-18G Growler is flown from a live pilot and that aircraft controls the other two unmanned ones. While specifically manufactured drones are ubiquitous, this is the first time the U.S. military has tried to convert manned airplanes into unmanned crafts.

This all makes sense when one understands the capability and mission of the Growler. Growlers fly out ahead of navy fighters to take out enemy missile defense systems. The Growler is based on the F/A-18F

---

240 *Ibid.*

241 Mizokami, Kyle. 2020. "The Navy's Surprise Unmanned Fighter Is a Glimpse of War's Near Future." *Popular Mechanics*. Feb. 5, 2020.

Super Hornet. It has a pilot and an anti-radar crewman on board. The Growler has a large jamming pod to foil enemy radar and it is equipped with anti-radar missiles. Since it has a dangerous mission flying out ahead and often alone, having an unmanned version has obvious advantages – if one is shot down – two crewmen are not lost.[242]

It is somewhat surprising that the navy is going unmanned in this manner. The branch has been way behind the air force when it comes to drone development. The navy's MQ-25 Stingray is a carrier-based drone, but this craft is a tanker instead of a fighter or bomber. So, this foray into unmanned flight by the navy will have an interesting conversion cycle.

Standoff Weapons Will Dominate the Battlespace

Another gun that is causing heads to turn from the U.S. arsenal is called C-RAM. This stands for Counter-Rocket, Artillery, and Mortar. C-RAM is an ultra-high-speed firing system that can protect against enemy counter-fires. It is a radar-controlled rapid-fire 20mm gun that sends an awe-inspiring 4,500 rounds per minute down-range to counteract enemy rockets and artillery and mortar rounds. C-RAM stays on a trailer and can be a mobile system that is fired remotely. "When a threat is spotted, the weapon system automatically detects, evaluates, tracks, engages, and conducts battle-damage assessment," according to SOFREP.com.[243] One can grasp immediately how important it is to have a system that can protect against enemy rocket and artillery fire.

Lockheed Martin has a weapon system in store for the army that aids the ground-to-ground fight. The Precision Strike Missile has a range of at least 300 miles. It is compatible with existing army launch systems such as the M270 multiple launch rocket system. The missile

---

242 *Ibid.*

243 Allamazoglu, Stavros. 2020. "C-RAM: The Weapon System Behind the Video that Went Viral." *SOFREP*. May 20, 2020.

system is part of the army's long-range precision fires aspiration.[244] That means upgrading the current tracked-vehicle Paladin 155mm howitzer system with its Excalibur rocket-assisted projectile. This projectile gets the Paladin's range out to 44 miles, but the army wants to improve on this range because near-peer competitors such as Russia and China can field artillery with longer ranges. The Paladin will eventually have a longer gun tube to improve its range.

Taking the precision fires concept down to the lowest level – the individual soldier – is the "smart fire control tool." This enables a rifle to be fired only if a hit is guaranteed. The weapon works with an artificial intelligence system that lines up the target automatically and then the trigger cannot be fingered to fire until the targeting system is perfectly aligned, then the soldier is able to fire with a guaranteed hit of the target. This way there will be few if any errant shots.[245]

The Threat from China Has the Americans Taking Notice

Individual soldiers in the United States, no matter how accurate their firing, are outnumbered by the Chinese. China's People's Liberation Army (PLA) is the largest in the world – numbering over two million active personnel. China's Navy has the most total assets in the world. But despite the numerical advantage, China is not resting on its laurels. China is not afraid to improve its major end items and weapon systems to dominate the United States. First, China is acquiring electromagnetic railguns – just like the United States Navy. China state-run media brags that railguns are coming soon and at least one has been spotted on a Chinese naval ship. The railgun program is reportedly in prototype mode, but the technology will soon be ripe.

---

[244] Goure, Dan. 2020. "Army's Newest Long-Range Fires System Isn't New, But It Will Be Effective." *Real Clear Defense*. Dec. 2, 2020.

[245] Roblitzski, Dan. 2020. "US Army Considering Rifle That Only Fires When Hit Is Guaranteed." The Byte. *Futurism*. Jan. 31, 2020.

At the individual soldier level, the Chinese have a rifle that can shoot around corners. This allows a soldier to have cover and concealment behind a wall or other structure, and to fire while staying hidden. Taking things to extremes, China has its own Mother of All Bombs, enormous explosive devices that can be delivered by air. There are Chinese "carrier killing" missiles. The stealth drone program is taking off, which will be explained in detail in the next chapter. The next generation J-20 stealth fighter has been mentioned before.

China is America's number one adversary, according to many defense practitioners and experts. Chad Sbragia, then deputy assistant defense secretary for China, speaking to Congress in 2020, said, "In most of the potential flashpoints in the Indo-Pacific region — the Taiwan Strait, the South China Sea, the Senkaku Islands or the Korean Peninsula — the United States may find itself in a military crisis with China."[246]

China has an advantage when it comes to weapons systems development and procurement. It has a culture of shared sacrifice that enables an attitude that "we are all in this together." The idea of Maoist continuous revolution is still in effect. It helps to have an adversary to promote continuous revolution and China has a target in the United States. There is a missile gap between the United States and China with the PLA fielding more missiles in the Far East with greater ranges than the American military. So, in the future, by 2025, the U.S. Marine Corps will be transformed and will use Tomahawk cruise missiles, that are normally fired by ship or airplane, into "ship killer" teams.[247] These teams will shoot converted Tomahawk missiles that can be fired on land at People's Liberation Army Navy (PLAN) ships. The future of fighting in the Far East will be mainly done by standoff missiles.

---

[246] Gertz, Bill. 2020. "China's Military Buildup, Global Ambitions on Collision Course with U.S., Pentagon Official Warns." *Washington Times*. Feb. 20, 2020.

[247] Woody, Christopher and Ryan Pickrell. 2020. "The Marine Corps Wants a New Ship-killer Missile." *Business Insider*. March 11, 2020.

China in the future will try to bring Taiwan fully under its orbit and reunify so there is no chance that Taiwan will become independent. Hong Kong, if Beijing gets its way, will also have no chance at being an independent democracy. China will keep consolidating gains over various rocks and reefs in the East and South China Sea. China will continue to be allies and a "big brother" to North Korea. Beijing will resume building upon its military bases in Pakistan and Djibouti.

China's Navy will continue to develop its role as a "blue water" maritime force able to project military power around the world outside its current neighborhood. By 2025, China could have at least three aircraft carriers in service.

Retired Navy Capt. Jim Fanell, a former Pacific Fleet intelligence director, told Bill Gertz of the *Washington Times* that, "Despite this all-to-common failure to recognize China's strategic intentions, the fact is China has and continues to build a naval force that if left unchallenged will not only be sailing the seven seas, as it is today, but will increasingly be able to achieve sea control in the global maritime commons as early as 2030, and potentially even sea superiority by 2049."[248]

China is also developing "directed energy weapons, advanced space weapons, electromagnetic railguns, high-powered microwave weapons, or even more exotic arms," according to former Deputy Secretary of Defense Robert O. Work.[249]

China has an advantage in its military-industrial complex because of its dedication to investing in research and development to develop dual-use technologies that can be used by both the civilian sector and for defense purposes. This means that it can put its best and brightest minds on projects in artificial intelligence, quantum computing, 5G,

248 "China's Military Buildup, Global Ambitions on Collision Course with U.S., Pentagon Official Warns."

249 Ioanes, Ellen. 2019. "China's Military Power May Surpass the US's Faster Than You Think, Thanks to Six Shrewd Strategies." *Business Insider*. Aug. 26, 2019.

and hypersonic technologies, and have advances in those areas track right into military-use scenarios. China wants to degrade American command, control, and situational awareness. China's nuclear warfare capabilities have increased with advances in intercontinental ballistic missiles and submarine-launched ballistic missiles. It could double the size of its nuclear forces by 2030.

China has made serious improvements to its electronic counter-measures and jamming equipment. These information denial aspects look to interrupt U.S. 5G technology and networks. Most of the electronic warfare assets are ground-based, but some are based on drone platforms. The PLA has a new Strategic Support Force. This group is responsible for space, cyber, and electronic warfare.[250] The idea behind this force is to supplant the United States as the most technological adept force in East Asia by 2030 or sooner. China has noted that the United States cannot prosecute warfare without its information technology-based intelligence, surveillance, and reconnaissance systems. China wants to focus its Strategic Support Force to degrade these capabilities, which the Americans are so dependent on.

China is building on its hypersonic glide vehicle technology that it started in 2014. The DF-17 missile will pave the way for Chinese hypersonics.[251] This will be a vehicle that is launched by a conventional missile. The vehicle then detaches during flight as it is dropped to fly at MACH 5 or 3,800 miles per hour. The glide vehicle is nuclear-capable, and the Chinese hypersonic technology is ahead of the United States. The Americans also do not have plans to make their hypersonic missiles nuclear-capable; they are high-explosive only at this point.

---

[250] Williams, Ian. "More Than Missiles: China Previews its New Way of War." CSIS. Oct. 16, 2019.

[251] Episkopos, Mark. 2020. "Why China's DF-17 Hypersonic Missile Is So Dangerous." *The National Interest*. Nov. 17, 2020.

Like the Americans, the Chinese are focusing on laser weapons, particularly airborne lasers. These laser pods are mounted on a fighter jet and can be used to attack an enemy airplane or strike an incoming missile. The Chinese also have a ground-based laser system for air defense that is called the LW-30. Lasers are deployed on People's Liberation Army Navy (PLAN) ships. In early 2020, the PLAN reportedly shot out a "dazzler" laser at an American reconnaissance aircraft. The laser shot was intended to blind pilots, crew, and sensors aboard the airplane. The laser came from a PLAN vessel. The U.S. Navy then put out a statement, "Weapons-grade lasers could potentially cause serious harm to aircrew and mariners, as well as ship and aircraft systems."[252]

Once again, the Chinese military is matching the American Department of Defense weapons systems for weapons systems. The Chinese also have a new stealth bomber that is similar to the B-21. This is a stealthy flying wedge they have worked on since 2016. The Xian H-20 flies at supersonic speeds and can deliver nuclear weapons with a payload of 45 tons. The next-generation bomber has a range of 5,300 miles. This is twice the range of China's version of the B-52.[253] U.S. military bases in Guam, Japan, and the Philippines fall under this range.

Almost mirroring the United States step by step in weapons procurement, China has a non-lethal weapon for crowd control. The so-called sonic weapon uses "focused waves of low-frequency sound," according to the *South China Morning Post*.[254] The weapon reportedly brings about "extreme discomfort, with vibrations in the eardrums,

---

[252] Pickerell, Ryan. 2020. "A Chinese Destroyer Fired a Weapons-Grade Laser at a US Surveillance Aircraft, US Navy Says." *Business Insider*. Feb. 27, 2020.

[253] Chan, Minnie. 2020. "China's Long-Range Xian H-20 Stealth Bomber Could Make Its Debut This Year." *South China Morning Post*. May 4, 2020.

[254] Chen, Stephen. 2019. "Chinese Scientists Develop Handheld Sonic Weapon for Crowd Control." *South China Morning Post*. Sept. 19, 2019.

eyeballs, stomach, liver, and brain."[255] This development comes as China seeks to thwart democracy protesters in Hong Kong.

Always looking to eclipse the United States military, China is developing not only 5G networks for civilians, but in the future, it will be forging 6G wireless technology. Again, this is no typo. 6G will have zero latency and perform ten times faster than 5G. The Chinese Ministry of Science and Technology published an article in 2020 that outlined Chinese plans for 6G.

"If 6G technology is introduced into the military, it will surely have a major impact on military practices, such as war formation, equipment development, and battlefield communications. Promoting the gradual application of 6G in the military might be one of the major focuses for the Chinese armed forces to adapt to the new military changes in the future," according to Peter Suciu of the *National Interest*.[256]

6G technology has numerous military applications for the Chinese. It would help with targeting and sensors. The People's Liberation Army would have an easier time setting artillery pieces and lining up targets. Chinese spy planes could communicate faster to home bases on the ground. It would have lightning-fast effects on logistics allowing the People's Liberation Army to have just-in-time delivery for food and ammunition.

Could the Chinese conduct a "Pearl Harbor" attack on U.S. critical infrastructure? Peter Pry, an expert on electromagnetic pulse warfare (EMP), thinks this kind of EMP attack is plausible. Pry, part of the EMP Task Force on National and Homeland Security, wrote a report on this type of attack in 2020. The report said, "China has built a network of satellites, high-speed missiles, and 'super-electromagnetic pulse'

---

[255] *Ibid.*

[256] Suciu, Peter, 2020. "5G Is Old News: China Wants 6G For Its Military." *The National Interest*. April 28, 2020.

weapons that could melt down the U.S. electric network, fry critical communications, and stifle aircraft carrier groups."[257]

Russia Flexes Its Muscles

While it is easy to marvel at the Chinese military modernization, do not forget Russia. Vladimir Putin has a vote in this arms race with the United States and NATO. The Russians are just as determined as the Chinese. Russia has been belligerent since the annexation of Crimea in 2014. They have pushed back against Western sanctions by developing even more weapons systems in a sprint to even the score with the West, and particularly the United States. Russia started its military modernization efforts in 2008, way before the Crimean annexation. This was the height of oil prices and Russia invested revenue from this energy windfall, at least partially, on its military. Operationally, they took their military beyond the "Near Abroad" and deployed it to Syria in 2015 to show off its capability and global reach. The United States for decades wanted to keep the Russians out of the Middle East where Moscow always had designs to improve its warm weather port in Syria. The Obama administration was helpless to stop the Russian incursion into Syria and did not appreciate its historical significance.

By 2020, Russia had achieved everything it set out to. It kept the Assad regime in power. It made sure the United States did not intervene. And it increased the regime forces command of formerly rebel-held territory. The resurgence of Russia blinded many in the West who were used to countries in Europe and Eurasia playing within the rules of the Western international political order. Putin had no such illusions when it came to walking in step with the international community.

Russia has always had a thorny sense of sovereignty and a fanatic desire to protect its territorial interest in its Near Abroad. This strategic

---

[257] Bedard, Paul. "China Develops Weapons to Fry US Electric Grid, Eyes High-Tech 'Pearl Harbor' Attack." *Washington Examiner*. June 18, 2020.

culture means that the Russian military strives for modernization and to widen the gap with advances in artificial intelligence, robotics, drones, hypersonic missiles, and stealth technology.

Russia has leapt forward in hypersonic technologies. In 2020, Russia's president oversaw noteworthy missile tests in the Black Sea and hypersonic missiles were featured during these naval drills. Russia's military has already sprinted past the pack to become a leader in hypersonic missile technology. During the Black Sea naval drills of 2020, Putin watched Russian MiG-31's aim their Kinzhal hypersonic missiles at practice targets on land. These missiles fly at 27 times the speed of sound. Putin claimed that other versions of Russia's hypersonic missiles are nuclear-capable.

The Russians also have a hypersonic glide vehicle that is launched off an intercontinental ballistic missile. The Avangard, the world's first that is operational, can fly at 27 times the speed of sound – the fastest on earth.[258] The Russians claim the Avangard can make complicated maneuvers during its attack phase and that it can reach the United States and elude American missile defenses.

Not everyone is sounding alarm bells. The *Bulletin of Atomic Scientists* pointed out that American missile defense systems are primarily designed to stop conventional missile attacks from Iran and North Korea, not necessarily to combat threats from near-peer competitors such as Russia or China.

According to the Bulletin's Andrew W. Reddie, "In reality, the systemic consequences of hypersonic missiles will be minimal to nil, and the narrative that Washington is 'behind' in a hypersonic arms race fails to consider the different strategic challenges facing China, Russia, and the United States..."[259]

---

[258] Marcus, Jonathan. 2019. "Russia Deploys Avangard Hypersonic Missile System." *BBC*. Dec. 27, 2019.

[259] Reddie, Andrew. "Hypersonic Missiles: Why the New 'Arms Race' Is Going Nowhere Fast." *Bulletin of the Atomic Scientists*. Jan. 13, 2020.

I lean toward the more alarmist view – that Russia is leaping forward in hypersonic weapons technology and that this is a troubling development for international security since Putin is personally involved in their development. To be sure, capability does not always mean intent to use. Putin often looks to bolster national prestige with new weapons programs in order to remind the world that Moscow is always relevant. But Russian hypersonic missiles are here to stay, and the United States and NATO should take notice. Moreover, it is clear Russia is ahead of the Americans in hypersonic technology.

Russia has an advantage in land warfare with its main battle tank. The T-14 Armata has an unmanned turret that is automated, which keeps the crew safer. This turret is the first of its kind and the Russians believe the tank itself can be fully autonomous without a crew inside. The new smoothbore 154mm gun can fire 10 to 12 times a minute.[260] It will be operational in 2021 and it has a bigger cannon that what NATO fields on its main battle tanks. It also has an exterior armor system that can withstand an incoming round at the speed of MACH 5.

The next-generation T-50 fighter plane has many advantages. It is made of lightweight, stealthy material that allows it to perform 9G moves for up to 30 seconds. This maneuverability is better than what the United States features in its fighter planes. The U.S. F-22 Raptor can still carry more missiles and is stealthier than the T-50, but NATO has been alerted and the T-50 will be a stout competitor in the future.

The Russians are developing new attack helicopters with anti-tank weapons consisting of advanced missile and rocket launchers. More troubling are the improvements to Russia's nuclear weapons program that has new capabilities in its land-launched mobile carriers and upgraded submarines to deliver nuclear weapons well within range of North America. The RS-24 Yars mobile ICBM launcher has several independent

---

260 "T-14 Armata Main Battle Tank." *Army Technology.*

warheads making it difficult for air defense systems to shoot down. It is also accurate to 820 feet.[261] For submarine-launched ballistic nuclear missiles, Russia will have eight new next-generation Borei-class "boomer" submarines in service throughout the 2020s. But that is not all on the submarine front, Russia also has a new next-generation attack submarine to go along with the nuclear weapon-equipped "boomer." Since Russia has one of the largest fleets of submarines in the world, it is looking to replace its diesel-powered subs with a new nuclear-powered class of boats. That is where the Laika-class comes in. The Laika will be equipped with guided torpedoes, anti-ship missiles, and land attack cruise missiles.[262] The Laika is larger than its U.S. counterpart, the Virginia-class boats. It also has a top speed of 35 knots, which makes it world-class.

Russia has a laser weapons program too to stay in step with the Americans and the Chinese. The Peresvet ground-based laser is designed to take out incoming missiles and airplanes. It can also blind enemy sensors and destroy drones. The system came on-line experimentally in 2018 and will be the basis for future directed energy efforts by the Russians. Vladimir Putin has bragged that lasers "will determine the combat potential of the Russian Army and Navy for decades ahead."[263]

Another system is making waves. The Russians have a "dazzler" light system that is designed to be pointed at the enemy to startle and blind them in order to disrupt hostile fires from weapons pointed at the Russians. Dubbed the Filin 5P-42, it officially uses technology that maximizes visual optical interference. The weapon can also reportedly cause nausea, vomiting, and hallucinations.[264] The system is currently

---

261 Van Allen, Fox. 2017. "Russia's Deadliest New War Machines." *C|Net*. Jan. 29, 2017.

262 Mizokami, Kyle. 2020. "Russia Unveils Laika, Its Next-Gen Nuclear Attack Submarine." *Popular Mechanics*. Feb. 24, 2020.

263 "Putin Hails New Russian Laser Weapons." *Associated Press*. May 17, 2019.

264 "5P-42 Filin: Russian Navy Fits Warships with Hallucinogenic Weapons." *The Week*. Feb. 6, 2019.

aboard the Russian naval vessels Admiral Gorshkov and the Admiral Kasatonov.

While Russia has made great strides in its military modernization efforts and is keeping up and jumping ahead of the United States in many categories, it is woefully behind in aircraft carriers. Russia has only one aircraft carrier. This carrier, the Admiral Kuznetsov, has been a maintenance nightmare and is often in dry dock and not combat effective. In fact, it was dry-docked for the entirety of 2020. Equally embarrassing for the Russians was when one of their dry docks sank in 2018.

Russia is as strong or stronger than the United States in hypersonic weapons, lasers, and tanks. Like China, Russia has a communal culture and attitude of self-sacrifice that makes it very reactive when it comes to keeping up with and surpassing competitors like the United States. This communal nature also helps the weapons procurement process. A strong, charismatic leader, like Putin, encourages a feeling of prestige and power projection with new armaments. Most troubling is the Russian incursion into the Middle East. It shows a mobility of forces that Russia has not shown since the Cold War.

North Korea Refuses to Be Left Out

A Cold War still does exist at the Demilitarized Zone in the Korean peninsula. North Korea continues to be belligerent in its "purple rhetoric" of bombast and braggadocio. Mercurial leader Kim Jong-Un, even though there was a diplomatic rapprochement with President Donald Trump, is still difficult to bottle up. Kim Jong-Un is one of the most dangerous leaders on the planet and President Joe Biden will have to devise a credible new plan for North Korea. In the second quarter of 2020, Kim briefly moved away from the public eye and rumors were rife about his demise. He later appeared, after much speculation on his health, at a fertilizer plant photo opportunity. This seemingly minor event revealed that once again the Western world knows little about the daily goings-on in the country of 25 million. The other question mark is North Korea's line of succession to power that often focuses on Kim's sister Kim Yo-Jong as the heir apparent. It is not clear if Kim Yo-Jong would be ready to pick up the mantle of leadership without a power struggle that would put the world on notice. This country is a nuclear power, after all, with a huge conventional military. The big unknown would be how North Korea would react in a power vacuum. As Kim Jong-Un approaches middle age, his health will be a concern. He is overweight, and reportedly is a heavy drinker, smoker, and all-around glutton. Kim Jong-Un is also ruthless – having ordered death sentences on his uncle and additional grisly death orders to members of his uncle's family.

If Kim Jong-Un happened to die, it could leave an opportunity for hardliners in South Korea to move toward unification with the North. This would create a situation where numerous North Koreans would move as refugees to China. China would be likely to step into the power vacuum to push South Korea aside and refuse efforts to unify. The Chinese are not inclined to serve an exodus of North Koreans into their country. But China would still want to shape facts on the ground, especially when it comes to who controls the North's nuclear weapons, its chemical and biological weapons, and its powerful missile program. Unification is unlikely as long as Kim Jong-Un is healthy and firmly ensconced in power, however, it becomes more likely, if he is out of the picture due to his ill health or death.

Much has been speculated about the future of nuclear arms in the North, but less is said about the conventional rocket forces and huge number of artillery pieces aimed at U.S. forces and South Korean military personnel, along with civilians in the South of the peninsula. The rockets and artillery can also reach Seoul and its suburbs putting South Korean civilians at risk.

North Korea's missile forces are the largest concern and Kim Jong-Un is always quick to announce an advancement or some form of progress on the country's missile program. While North Korea enjoyed better relations with the Trump administration, it took advantage of this impasse to leap forward in missile development. The biggest threat are inter-continental ballistic missiles that can reach the United States. Also, many missiles that would be fired from North Korea can reach American forces deployed in Guam, Japan, and the Philippines.

While tests of some missile systems were suspended since the diplomatic outreach by Trump, it is likely that Kim Jong-Un will order more tests of missile systems in the future, particularly ICBMs and submarine-launched ballistic missiles (SLBMs). The North has tested rocket engines in December of 2019, probably for ICBMs. And the North is close to fielding a fully operational SLBM. Look for tests on missile engines and other types of propulsion tests to continue into the 2020s and for Kim to field full tests on those missiles in the coming years, especially when it comes to mating a nuclear warhead onto an ICBM or SLBM. That is Kim Jong-Un's main goal. When it comes to vehicle re-entry into the atmosphere, a critical aspect of nuclear-equipped ballistic missiles, observers of the North's missile program believe their ICBMs are maturing. The DPRK is also working on the miniaturization of nuclear warheads which is an important step toward mate-ability, or a nuclear device mated on a ballistic missile. North Korea will have a mate-able nuclear-equipped ICBM this decade. Kim Jong-Un already has an estimated 60 nuclear devices.[265] It is only a matter of time before a nuclear-equipped ICBM can threaten the United States and its allies. The current rocket/ missile systems in North Korea are liquid-fueled, but there are plans that these weapons will be solid-fueled, which allows a quicker launch that helps defy missile defense systems and early warning.

In the future, how could the United States intervene to stop the North's march toward a nuclear-equipped ICBM? This would require

---

265 Brewer, Eric. 2020. "North Korean Nuclear Threat Is Here." *The Hill*. Jan. 9, 2020.

that stealthy American fighters and bombers be able to evade the North's missile defense systems. Analysts at the think tank Center for the National Interest investigated this question in 2020. They interviewed various experts on North Korea and got detailed answers.

"They have a mix of old Soviet SAMs, including the S-75, S-125, S-200 and Kvadrat, which are likely in more or less good condition," Vasily Kashin, a senior fellow at the Center for Comprehensive European and International Studies at Moscow's Higher School of Economics told *The National Interest*. "They used to produce the S-75 themselves—and those could have received some significant upgrades. In addition to them, since the 2010s they are fielding an indigenous modern SAM system which is called KN-06 by South Korea and the U.S."[266]

The rest of the air defenses are relatively old and limited. They have conventional air defense cannons and man-portable rockets, which would not be effective against U.S. airplanes. But what the North lacks in quality, they make up for in numbers. The North has "many thousands" of pieces of conventional air defense artillery.[267] The DPRK also has around 40 MiG-29 fighter interceptors, which are really no match for U.S. F-35s and F-22s. So even though the Americans have a decisive advantage in the air, they could plausibly lose aircraft to the North in an air war over the Korean peninsula.

Iran Seeks to Dominate the Middle East

While Kim Jong-Un's has endured questions about his health and his hold on power, the Iran's Supreme Leader, Ayatollah Ali Khamenei, has an even more tenuous hold on power. Iran has internal dissent for a number of reasons. In 2020, when Iran's air defenses were on high alert after the United States killed Iranian military leader Gen. Qassem Suleimani

---

266 "Try This On For Size: Could North Korea Kill an F-35?" TNI Staff. *The National Interest*. Feb. 18, 2020.

267 *Ibid.*

in a drone strike, the Iranians mistakenly shot down a Ukrainian airliner that killed 176 civilians. This shoot-down happened as the Iranians twice fired rockets into Iraqi bases that held American military personnel. 32 Americans were wounded with traumatic brain injuries in the attack.

Iranians took to the streets to protest the destruction of the Ukrainian jet. People demonstrated across the nation. There is no clear leader or opposition movement that stands for a group of ideals or philosophy. The people are expressing their unhappiness and frustration, but they are not necessarily trying to overthrow the Supreme Leader. Many reformists who were barred from running in the parliamentary elections of February 2020 stayed out of the election because they were forced to the sidelines by the Guardian Council. The election turnout was low as reformists refused to vote for the slate of hardliners. The turnout was the lowest in the history of Iran since the revolution. Conservative hardliners won 230 seats in parliament out of total of 290.[268] So it is clear that conservatives and ultraconservatives have a hold on power.

This affects international security in that numerous members of parliament will likely support future military strikes against the United States military in Iraq. It is unlikely that there will be regime change in Iran in the coming years. The domestic opposition, despite the protests, is too weak without a strong leader. Communication among the opposition is limited because the authorities can shut down the Internet any time there is a threat to the power of the Supreme Leader. In terms of the sociology of warfare, Iranian power holders are a good example of what sociologist C. Wright Mills called the power elite. Conservative elites have formed a vanguard of power in the parliament and in the group working directly for the Supreme Leader and the office of the

---

[268] Azizi, Arash. 2020. "Factbox: The Outcome of Iran's 2020 Parliamentary Elections." Atlantic Council. Feb. 26, 2020.

president and countrywide network of clerical commissars who serve the Supreme Leader.

The strongest aspect of the Iranian military is its missile and rocket program. As the Center of Strategic and International Studies wrote in 2020, "Iran possesses the largest and most diverse missile arsenal in the Middle East, with thousands of ballistic and cruise missiles, some capable of striking as far as Israel and southeast Europe. For the past decade, Iran has invested significantly to improve these weapons' precision and lethality. Such developments have made Iran's missile forces a potent tool for their power projection and a credible threat to U.S. and partner military forces in the region. Iran has not yet tested or deployed a missile capable of striking the United States but continues to hone longer-range missile technologies under the auspices of its space-launch program."[269]

Iran is improving the propulsion and aerodynamics of its missiles and rockets with a new guidance system. Fortunately, most of the rockets and missiles the Iranians field are "dumb" without laser or GPS guidance systems, although this will change in the future. Presently, the Iranians do have the Fateh-110 system that is guided by GPS. This missile can reach American, Israeli, and Saudi Arabian military sites in the Gulf region with relative ease. They have strategically placed them in hiding places around the country. Many of them have mobile launchers or they are deployed underground with a network of tunnels.[270] Iran's missiles are far from perfect. In May 2020, Iranian friendly fire from a missile severely damaged one of its own naval vessels in an accidental strike that killed 19 sailors and wounded another 15 in the Gulf of Oman.

Iran has a strong elite group of fighters known as the Islamic Revolutionary Guard Corps and its vanguard, the Quds force. These personnel wage proxy wars in places like Yemen and support the terror group Hezbollah in Lebanon, who are fighting in Syria's civil

---

[269] "Missile Threat: CSIS Missile Defense Project." CSIS.

[270] *Ibid.*

war. Hezbollah has about 150,000 rockets pointed at Israel. The IRGC also supports terror and insurgent movements in Iraq and Afghanistan.

The Iranian Navy has small craft that swarm enemy ships such as the U.S. Navy vessels that patrol the Strait of Hormuz. 3,000 to 5,000 of these mini-boats are able to take on enemy shipping.[271] The Iranians also have an extensive number of naval mines throughout the Strait of Hormuz – 5,000 of them.[272]

Iranian missile defense is extensive. Iran shot down an American drone in 2019 with its Sevom-e-Khordad system. The future of Iranian missile defense comes from Russia such as the advanced SA-20c system and S-300 defense interceptors, although the Russians have refused to sell the Iranians its vaunted S-400 system. Iran also has its own military laser program for air defense in which it is manufacturing its own lasers. The directed energy units are designed to take out American and Israeli drones.

Iran is not at the apogee of its military power. It still makes mistakes when it comes to deploying and employing forces, but it will continue to threaten its neighbors and persist in waging Shia proxy wars against Sunni-led governments. Regime change is not likely in the coming years, even though there is internal unrest. The opposition is loose and unpredictable without a unifying theme or strategy. The regime does experience fear both internally and externally. This makes it a candidate for more self-help in a realist security dilemma. That means it will continue to invest in new weapons systems.

---

[271] Leadon, Brad. 2020. "Iran's Military Power is Boosted by Unconventional Tactics and Proxies in Strategic Locations." WRAL-TV. Jan. 9, 2020.

[272] *Ibid.*

Terrorists Enter the Realm of Technology

Iran is a state-sponsor of terrorism and terrorists also are consumers of technology, although not to the extent of nation states. Terror groups are more dedicated to the future of information warfare, weaponization of social media, drones, cyber-crime, and other exploits, which will be covered in other chapters. But the terrorists have the deadliest advantage when it comes to communication. Terror attacks must be coordinated, synchronized, and calibrated. Even lone wolves often communicate in some manner while pondering and devising an attack. Cell phone apps such as WhatsApp, Signal, and Telegram allow end-to-end encryption. Terrorists have figured out ways to not leave digital "fingerprints," according to Ilan Berman writing for *The National Interest*.[273] They use the dark web through devices such as Tor or imageboard forums like 8chan. They use "burner" disposable phones for one-time usage and then these burner phones are thrown away.

Many terror attacks, however, are decidedly low-tech. Crude bomb-making, hostage-taking, driving trucks into crowds, mass shootings, and other unsophisticated means will always be popular. 3D printing can also be used by terrorists to print gun and bomb parts that would be hard to spot by authorities. Again, other aspects of terrorism will be covered in upcoming segments of this book.

The British Military Searches for its Identity

Experienced in counter-terrorism, the British military nevertheless has an identity problem, and it is not clear what role it is to play in the coming decade. Despite limited resources, the British military is enacting some military modernization efforts. They are getting into the directed energy game by developing a defensive laser program. The British Ministry of Defense spent $162 million in 2020 for three new proofs

---

[273] Berman, Ilan. 2019. "Technology is Making Terrorists More Effective—And Harder to Thwart." *The National Interest*. Feb. 22, 2019.

of concept to demonstrate laser capabilities.[274] The lasers will be used to take out drones and incoming missiles. However, the new systems will not be ready for field testing until 2023 and are not expected to be deployed to frontline troops for up to ten years. British procurement needs to iterate faster on this project as other countries have leapt ahead in directed energy technology.

The British military does have what they are calling a "Transformation Fund." This $80.7 million fund is dedicated to three areas. According to Sian Grzeszczyk of Forces.net, the following items will be pursued by the UK:

"New systems: Army vehicles will be fitted with remote control capability so they can be sent ahead of manned vehicles and used to test the strength of enemy defenses. New autonomous logistics vehicles: they would be pre-programmed to deliver vital supplies to troops in conflict zones and help remove soldiers from dangerous resupply tasks so they can focus on combat roles. New mini drones: these would be lighter and considerably smaller than those used at the moment. These would be aimed to be used across all battlefields from counter insurgency to disaster relief."[275]

The British Ministry of Defense has recognized the value of 3D printing as well. The Defense Science and Technology Laboratory is working on 3D-printed explosives.[276] Explosives under this type of additive manufacturing will create explosive charges on demand. This will reduce the difficulty of transporting and storing explosives. The laboratory has ponied up over $12 million for the project. Since 2018, British

---

274 Chuler, Andrew. 2020. "British Defense Secretary Says, 'Tough Choices' Are Coming Due on Spending." *Defense News*. Dec. 11, 2020.

275 Grzeszczyk, Sian. 2019. "'Revolutionizing': £66m Investment Confirmed For Future Military Technology." *Forces Net*. March 5, 2019.

276 Petsch, Michael. 2020. "UK Defense Agency Plans to 3D Print High Explosives." *3D Printing Industry*. March 16, 2020.

Army engineers have used 3D printing during a deployment in South Sudan to make industrial strength plastic for construction of a hospital.

When it comes to aiding NATO in a future conflict with Russia, the British military could come up short in at least one metric. According to the think tank Royal United Services Institute in 2019, the British lack the artillery pieces to go toe to toe with Russia. In fact, the Royal United Services Institute warned that the Russians could overwhelm the British in a shooting conflict. "The UK's ground forces are comprehensively outgunned and outranged, leaving enemy artillery free to prosecute fire missions with impunity. This must ultimately fix and suppress British guns and maneuver elements, and thereby lead to the defeat of UK units," according to the report.[277]

Israel Sprints Ahead with New Technology

Israel always has to worry about getting outgunned and outmanned in the Middle East. That is why it relies on technological breakthroughs for military needs. Like other countries, Israel is developing solid-state lasers for defense purposes. Israeli lasers will be used for eliminating drones, aircraft, missiles, rockets and other incoming projectiles. Directed energy will be used in conjunction with Israel's vaunted Iron Dome missile defense system. According to the Missile Defense Advocacy Alliance, "The system uses a high-energy fiber optic laser to destroy airborne objects within four to five seconds of firing. Current power levels of the lasers are in the tens of kilowatts and are expected to increase for greater destructive capability."[278]

Israel has other innovative systems and weapons. It has a mine-clearing system called the "Tzefa Shirion" that is a missile with a long chain attached. When it hits the ground, it explodes mines and clears roads

---

[277] Chuter, Andrew. 2019. "British Army Needs Bigger Guns, Study Finds." *Defense News*. Nov. 27, 2019.

[278] "Iron Beam Quick Facts." Missile Defense Advocacy Alliance.

almost 400 feet long. The "EyeBall" system allows Israel Defense Force soldiers to see and hear inside rooms and look for the enemy without actually being inside. The eyeball is a small ball that soldiers throw inside a room without entering. Eyeball is about the size of a tennis ball and has a next-generation infrared camera that allows soldiers to know if a terrorist or hostages are in the room before entering.[279]

The Spike LR II is Israel's next-generation missile that has a range of 3.4 miles and weighs 28 pounds. Do not be fooled by its small size because the Spike LR II packs a punch. According to the *Jerusalem Post*, it can attack "vehicles, helicopters, ships and ground launchers, and has advanced electro-optic seekers which include capabilities of a smart target tracker with artificial intelligence features."[280]

A game-changer for Israeli Air Force is the new American F-35 fighter that has been integrated and adapted to Israeli standards. The fighter jet is stealthy and able to fly undetected and can outmaneuver S-300 missile defenders in Iran if needed. The Israeli Air Force has ordered 33 F-35s from Lockheed Martin.

The United States and United Kingdom have much work cut out for them in terms of future weapons systems and arms procurement. China and Russia are leaping ahead as near-peer competitors. President Joe Biden must work with a progressive House of Representatives to keep defense funding at a level that can support hypersonic weapons, lasers, and 5G weapons. North Korea is always dangerous. Israel must compete with Iran and be on guard from extremist terror. All countries are caught up in realist international theory with self-help and security-dilemmas as competitors increase the level of power.

---

[279] Axe, David. 2009. "What's Wrong with Israel's EyeBall Bot?" *Wired*. July 20, 2009.

[280] Ahronheim, Anna. 2017. "Israeli Defense Company Unveils 5th-generation Spike Missile." *Jerusalem Post*. May 29, 2017.

CHAPTER SIX

QUANTUM COMPUTING, DRONES, AND ROBOTICS

The F-22 streaks across the night sky over hostile air space. Suddenly, out pops 12 "gremlin" battle drones that buzz downward to deliver certain doom to the enemy. The pilot smiles and relaxes for a moment. "That's one less thing to worry about." But if the pilot is taking a brief break from combat, who or what is controlling the drones?

It is a quantum computer blazing with activity and supervising a fleet of the autonomous gremlin recoverable drones launched from a flight of F-22s. This is one potential technology development that the U.S. Air Force covets with quantum computing.

Some of these new-fangled quantum computers are already operating to verify and validate aircraft software for American defense contractors such as Lockheed Martin.[281] It takes a human several months to debug code from an F-16 – a quantum computer can do this in seconds.

The key difference between quantum computing and conventional computing is the use of the quantum bit or "qubit." Classical bits can only hold a binary value of 0 or 1, but a qubit can hold a combination of

[281] Leopold, George. 2016. "Quantum Leaps Needed for New Computer Approach." *Defense Systems*. Dec. 9, 2016.

0 and 1 at the same time. This makes their computing power formidable and faster. The other big difference is that quantum computing is much more energy efficient, and as problems that need computational power evolve and require more energy consumption, this is a great advantage.

And those recoverable gremlin drones launched from the U.S. stealth fighters? They should be deployed in the next couple of years, according to DARPA. "U.S. Air Force F-22s and F-35s will soon launch and control recoverable attack drones from the cockpit of the plane to expand air-combat operations, test enemy air defenses, conduct long-range intelligence, surveillance, reconnaissance, and even deliver weapons," the defense think tank said.[282] Quantum computers are a natural fit for this system.

On the ground, quantum computers are giving cyber security a needed boost. A startup backed by Jeff Bezos called D-Wave released its 2000Q rig to fight cyber-crime last year.[283] Information security could be transformed as well. According to software engineering analyst Adrian Bridgwater, "Perhaps the most compelling near-term impact of quantum is the role of security 'distribution functions' that use quantum effects, providing us with a powerful mechanism for sharing cryptographic keys between remote parties with a high degree of implicit security."[284]

Better security for cryptography and encryption is good news for sensitive and classified systems, that in turn, could boost hopes for improvements to radar and sonar for the military. Quantum computing could also help motherships that deploy drones when the drones are

---

282 Osborn, Kris. 2018. "F-22s and F-35s Will Launch Recoverable Gremlins Attack Drones." *Warrior Maven*. May 10, 2018.

283 Newman, Lily Hay. 2017. "Quantum Computers Versus Hackers, Round One. Fight!" *Wired*. Jan. 27, 2017.

284 Bridgwater, Adrian, 2017. "Five Ways Quantum Computing Will Change Cybersecurity Forever." *Raconteur*. Dec. 17, 2017.

recovered in mid-air after their mission. A C-130 cargo plane, for example, could serve as the mothership or flying aircraft carrier to launch swarming drones. This is currently happening when the C-130 carries the X-61A Gremlins Air Vehicle drones. The Gremlins were successfully tested in 2020 when a Gremlin drone flew from the C-130. The program began development by DARPA in 2018. It will only improve in the future as the C-130 gets better at recovering the drones and then launching them again.

The U.S. Army is developing swarming drones through its program "Cluster UAS Smart Munition for Missile Deployment." These so-called "slaughter bots" or small drones would come out of a missile warhead. The drone swarm would then autonomously look for enemy vehicles such as tanks and armored personnel vehicles and destroy them with an explosively formed penetrator. The munitions shoot a high-speed slug that pierces armor plating.

Artificial Intelligence and Unmanned Flight Create a New Wingman

How about when fighter pilots get a new wingman that is unmanned? That is where the XQ-58A Valkyrie comes in. I mentioned the Valkyrie before, but did not include its artificial intelligence aspect. The Valkyrie is the air force's latest unmanned combat air project that incorporates artificial intelligence. The Valkyrie has an internal brain that is called "Skyborg." *Breaking Defense* describes Skyborg as an artificial brain that will "provide data, such as telemetry, flight plans and weather, that a manned wingman's aircraft normally would provide."[285] The Valkyrie, as of 2020, now known as the Skyborg program, can fly out ahead of the formation and can also track enemy targets for its manned wingmen. This allows safer stand-off missile launches from its manned brethren.

---

[285] Hitchens, Theresa. 2020. "Valkyrie Back In The Air With Successful Flight Test." *Breaking Defense.* Jan. 14, 2020.

The Valkyrie is a stealthy aircraft and hard to track on radar. But it is expendable if shot down and this lessens the chance that a live pilot gets taken prisoner after ejecting. It is also less expensive than a $80 million manned fighter. It is launched from a shipping container so that makes the launcher highly mobile. This container-launch means that the Valkyrie does not need a runway, so one could imagine all the possibilities for deployment on a battlefield because existing military trucks can carry it from one location to another. The Valkyrie is then recovered by parachute, again not needing a runway. It can carry four bombs internally and the aircraft has a range of at least 2,000 miles.

The Human Mind Can Control a Drone

Some drones do not even need an artificial intelligence brain on board – they can be controlled by the human mind. The Pentagon has been working on this audacious goal since 2019 with six research teams trying to figure out how military personnel can use a non-invasive brain-computer interface to control singular drones or swarms of drones. This interface would be wearable. DARPA's Next-Generation Nonsurgical Neurotechnology program is heading up the project. The research teams at various universities have different ideas on how to solve the problem. One team is using ultra-sound and electrical signals while another is utilizing near-infrared light to get the job done.

What if drones are used to kill other drones? So-called "soft kill" systems rely on electronic jamming and counter-measures to "spoof" enemy drones. The U.S. Navy and Marine Corps has its Light Marine Air Defense Integrated System that sits on wheels and is strapped down on the deck of amphibious assault ships. The jammer is placed on a couple of tactical all-terrain vehicles, so it is highly mobile. This system is for defeating hobby drones and ultralight aircraft that would drop explosives onto ships. The radar targets low-signature targets that would be missed by conventional radar and then another pod distributes the electronic counter measures that disrupts the link from an enemy drone and its remote pilot. The system could have a laser on board in the future to target unfriendly drones and remove them from the battle space. In the summer of 2019, an Iranian drone was taken down by the Light Marine Air Defense Integrated System. The drone was flying over the USS Boxer amphibious assault ship in the Strait of Hormuz. The enemy fixed-wing drone came within 1,000 meters of the ship before it was "soft killed" by the jamming system. Marines from the 22nd and 13th Marine Expeditionary Units engaging in land warfare have also deployed with the Light Marine Air Defense Integrated System.

Drone on Drone Warfare Will Engage Hard-to-Kill Targets

That is one way to knock out a drone. Other solutions involve drone-on-drone warfare in which the killer drone uses kinetic force to destroy an enemy unmanned aircraft. These are known as "hard kill" drones. Hard kill drones bang into other drones to annihilate them. Tech startup Anduril is confident its hard kill solution is better than soft kill systems. "Anduril's quad-copter Interceptor uses its own onboard electro-optical and infrared sensors to spot, track, and, as the name implies, intercept the target. An operator on the ground can watch the feed through a hand-held controller and then gives the final order to attack the threat."[286]

In order to be successful, these systems must identify drones and classify them into friendly or hostile categories. Northrop Grumman has an anti-drone system that can identify friend or foe called the Sophisticated Counter Unmanned Systems Weapon Radio Frequency. This is used in conjunction with a U.S. Army Stryker armored personnel carrier. The Stryker is equipped with a chain gun to take out the hostile drones. This system was tested successfully at Fort Sill, Oklahoma in early 2020.

---

[286] Terithick, Joseph. 2019. "The U.S. Military Is Buying These Small Interceptor Drones To Knock Down Other Drones." *The Warzone*. Oct. 4, 2019.

The U.S. Marine Corps is searching for man-portable solutions to counter drones. Some of these systems use lasers and one even fires a net at approaching drones. However, the marines are moving away from man-portable systems because they create too much added weight for its ground personnel. The Marine Corps would rather have a system that is mounted on HUMVEEs or other personnel carriers that is laser-based. Or they would like to have drones that can kill another drone. These systems could be kinetic or electronic-based attack.

Land warfare fighters from the army and marine corps still need drones for intelligence, surveillance, and reconnaissance. And these are often man-portable. The army has purchased the portable and pocket-sized helicopter reconnaissance drone called the Black Hornet as part of the Soldier Borne Sensor program. The army and marine corps have been using the Black Hornet since 2016, but each iteration of the system has improved its capabilities. The Black Hornet can fit inside a soldier's or marine's hand as it weighs only 18 grams. The newer version made available in 2019 was larger and slightly heavier with a sturdier frame. Even though the drones are pocket-sized they offer comparable intelligence, surveillance, and reconnaissance capabilities as much larger airplane-sized unmanned aerial systems.

Swarming Drones on the Attack

Swarming drones are the future of unmanned warfare and they are already being used. In 2018, at Russia's Khmeimim airbase in western Syria, a swarm of 13 drones equipped with explosives were launched from non-state extremists toward the airbase. The Russians were able to fight them off by shooting down seven and jamming six of the swarming drones, but it was a red flag for future warfare. Swarming drones were also reportedly used against Saudi oil facilities in 2019.

Swarming drones are thought to be given a GPS coordinate for the attack. [287]And then the idea is to overwhelm enemy defenses by

[287] Safi, Michael. 2019. "Are Drone Swarms the Future of Aerial Warfare?"

sheer numbers, speed, and lack of prior warning. In the Khmeimim attack, Russian radar was able to spot the swarm early and engage targets successfully, but in the future, swarming drones will be faster, stealthier, and smarter. Future swarms will likely have numerous different GPS coordinates during the attack to make it more difficult to shoot them down. They may also be equipped with electronic counter-measures or even weapons that can engage and neutralize air defenses. The most frightening aspects of swarming drones is their potential ability to deliver a payload of nuclear, biological, and chemical weapons.[288] The drones would not have to be that accurate with their targeting. However, the swarm could communicate with each other for better targeting. And the swarm would only need to have one drone that hits the target even if all the other drones fail in their mission. Nuclear, biological, chemical weapons delivered by drones should keep many personnel in the unmanned community up at night.

New Unmanned Platforms Enter the Battlespace

Unmanned ships are entering the U.S. Naval fleet. DARPA and the navy are designing a ship that will never have a soul aboard. The NOMARS program stands for "No Manning Required Ship." According to DARPA, "By removing the human element from all ship design considerations, NOMARS will demonstrate significant advantages, to include size, cost (procurement, operations, and sustainment), at-sea reliability, survivability to sea-state, survivability to adversary actions (stealth considerations, resistance to tampering, etc.), and hydrodynamic efficiency (hull optimization without consideration for crew safety or comfort)."[289]

---

[288] Kallenburn, Zachary and Phillip C. Bleek. 2019. "Drones of Mass Destruction: Drone Swarms and the Future of Nuclear, Chemical, and Biological Weapons." *War on the Rocks*. Feb. 14, 2019.

[289] Avicola, Gregory. "No Manning Required Ship." DARPA.

This concept keeps the stand-off launch strategy and tactical doctrine intact. The unmanned ship can forge ahead of the main battle group, launch its missiles, and withdraw. If the unmanned ship is destroyed, no personnel are lost. The downside of the unmanned ship is maintenance. Maintenance requires, at the bare minimum, a human touch and some living soul there to identify, diagnose, and address maintenance problems. NOMARS is a concept, but in 2020, the navy will get two new large, unmanned surface vessels called Overlords. The existing Sea Hunter medium undersea vehicle developed by DARPA and the navy has been around since 2016. It has a 10,000 nautical mile range which means it can go across the Pacific from San Diego to Guam. The Sea Hunter operates with carrier strike groups. It needs no crew for navigation and steering. The Sea Hunter mission will be a floating radar and sensor craft to help identify foes at sea.

The navy is also pursuing undersea unmanned vehicles such as the Orca Extra Large Unmanned Undersea Vehicle (XLUUV) and the Large Diameter Unmanned Undersea Vehicle (LDUUV). They both can be utilized for attack purposes or for intelligence gathering. The idea for these crafts is to be able to operate for 70 days submerged. They will be integrated into the fleet of other submarines and manned ships. The drone is 80-feet long and 50-tons with a range of 6,500 nautical miles.

Naval aviation should not be forgotten because the navy also has an unmanned fighter plane. The EA-18G Growler, as described in a previous chapter, is an electronic warfare airplane that has an unmanned twin. Unmanned versions of this airframe were tested successfully in 2020. A manned Growler controlled two unmanned twins in flight. This is a surprise because it was believed the navy had been only working on an unmanned tanker. The unmanned Growler, according to *Popular Mechanics*, "carries both a jamming pod designed to interfere with enemy radars and communications, preventing enemy air defenses from acquiring inbound aircraft and coordinating their attacks. The Growler also carries HARM anti-radar missiles, which detect the probing beams of enemy air defense radars and follow them to their source, and acts to finally destroy them. Without radars to guide anti-aircraft systems, many types of air defense missiles become unusable in combat."[290]

The United States should invest in systems that could destroy enemy ICBMs with a two-stage booster rocket most likely fired from the Global Hawk that can fly at 40,000 feet. The technology is not there yet, but it could be a new, exciting, and cheap way to conduct missile defense.

What about shape-shifting drones? The U.S. Army's Research Laboratory in conjunction with Texas A&M University are working on a project that considers the type of flight needed for drones in order for them to change shape during flight. Drones need to fly fast and then loiter around a target for intelligence, surveillance, and reconnaissance. The problem is that different wings are needed for each aspect of a mission. Longer wings are better for loitering while shorter wings are needed to fly fast to a target. That is why researchers are looking for ways to make a drone change its wing shape during flight.

The future of drone warfare will continue to be targeted assassinations of terrorists and other nonstate actors engaging in nefarious activity that challenges U.S. international security. Since 9/11, American armed drones have depended on the Hellfire missile which was originally developed for the Apache attack helicopter to "plink" enemy main battle tanks. Hellfire missiles launched from drones have been particularly effective at targeting terrorists moving in vehicles or hiding in houses. The future may lie into changes to the Hellfire missile when it is engaging soft targets moving in the open for targeted assassinations. Reported Hellfire modifications of a so-called "ninja" missile have been covered in the mainstream press in 2020. The ninja missile is known as the R9X as well that uses "six swords" instead of an explosive warhead.

---

[290] "The Navy's Surprise Unmanned Fighter Is a Glimpse of War's Near Future."

The R9X has been launched against al-Qaeda and ISIS figures so far with investigators finding evidence of missile parts after explosion that have the R9X nomenclature stamped on the rocket.

China's Drone Program Creates a 'Sharp Sword'

Unsurprisingly, America's number one near peer competitor China is leaping ahead with its various drone programs. First, China's new aircraft carriers, the Liaoning and Shandong, are in service with a third to come online in the mid-2020s. These carriers are busy in the East and South China Sea protecting sea lanes and their various territorial claims on rocks and reefs in those bodies of water. The Liaoning and Shandong are also patrolling near Taiwan to remind the Taiwanese that China can always conduct a show of force. The Chinese want to remind Taiwan that reunification is around the corner and this will continue to be the case in the future.

China's new naval drone designed to be launched off aircraft carriers is in business. The Gongji-11 "Sharp Sword" is a flying wing with a stealthy exhaust system. The Gongji-11 can make deep strike operations and also serve as an aerial targeting supplier for missiles in the Chinese arsenal. The next newfangled Chinese drone is the WZ-8 rocket-propelled supersonic aircraft. The WZ-8 is launched out of the air by a bigger airplane and its job is intelligence, surveillance, and reconnaissance to give information and bomb-damage assessment for potential naval attacks on American shipping.

Smaller medium altitude long-endurance drones are enjoying a renaissance in the Chinese fleet. These are drones with a ceiling of 27,000 feet that can fly up to 24 hours or longer.[291] They are propeller-driven and are similar to the American Predator and Reaper drones. The BZK-005 Sea Eagle (for the Chinese Navy) and Giant Eagle (for the Chinese Air Force) has an electro-optic turret as its main radar. Larger medium

---

[291] Joe, Rick. 2019. "China's Growing High-end Military Drone Force." *The Diplomat*. Nov. 27, 2019.

altitude long-endurance drones include the GJ-1 and GJ-2. These drones can launch air-to-ground anti-tank missiles.[292] The GJ-2 is larger and has a synthetic aperture radar.

The next class of Chinese drones are the High Altitude Long-Endurance models. These have a high ceiling of up to 59,000 feet. These drones are usually jet powered and are similar to the American Global Hawk strategic drone that can fly from continent to continent. They are known as WZ-7s but have other monikers such as the Soaring Dragon or EA-03.[293] Finally, the Divine Eagle is the other High Altitude Long-Endurance drone. This is one of the most advanced drones in the fleet since it can reportedly conduct airborne early warning duties and direct air traffic ahead of naval flotillas.[294]

The Chinese do not have as many drones as the United States, but their fleet is diverse and robust. There are many capabilities that rival the quality of American drones. Unlike the United States, the Chinese drones are not battle-tested. They also are likely not fully integrated with troops on the ground. It is not clear if they communicate with only the various service-branches of the Chinese military or if they are in touch with intelligence services of the Ministry of State Security. The American Central Intelligence Agency has its own drones, so it can be argued that the United States has a more developed drone program, but China is right on the heels of American innovation in drone operations and technology. However, the United States still has the edge in drone propulsion technology.

China also has undersea drones which it deployed to the Indian Ocean beginning in 2020. 12 un-crewed underwater vehicles were gathering intelligence during a two-month period. The Sea Wing drone is designed to glide underneath the waters. It is shaped like an aerial drone

---

[292] *Ibid.*

[293] *Ibid.*

[294] *Ibid.*

for better aerodynamics, yet this is a ship that can loiter below sea for months. Curiously, these drones do not have a power source. They glide below and on top of water in a chain of events that consist of inflating and deflating a "balloon-like device filled with pressurized oil. At the same time, they have large wings so they can glide forward though the water. This allows them to run for extremely long periods of time, travelling vast distances."[295]

China is most proud of another unmanned underwater vehicle it calls the HSU-001. This craft is also used for intelligence, surveillance, and reconnaissance. Instead of a glide vehicle that looks like an aircraft, this vessel looks like a conventional submarine. The HSU-001 will be used in the East and South China Sea where Beijing has military installations on its land claims in various rocks and reefs. This is an important development for the People's Liberation Army Navy. The PLAN is staking its reputation on keeping up with the United States in the East and South China Seas. The HSU-001 can also be used to spy on U.S. allies such as Japan and South Korea.

Do not forget future potential conflict between China and Taiwan. Unmanned amphibious attack ships are entering into the PLAN. This development poses a direct threat to Taiwan. The 36-foot long "Marine Lizard" drone ship can go 50 knots an hour. Then when it gets near land it deploys tank-like tracked vehicles enabling it to move over ground. The unmanned amphibious ship is armed with missile-launchers that can hit targets in air, on sea, and on land. It has a range of 745 miles – plenty of range to attack Taiwan from the mainland because the Taiwan Strait is only 110 miles wide. The Marine Lizard is controlled by satellites and it goes 12 miles an hour on land, not extremely fast, but quick enough to advance into Taiwan's costal defenses. It can autonomously avoid obstacles as it travels.

---

[295] Sutton, H. I. 2020. "China Deployed 12 Underwater Drones In Indian Ocean." *Forbes*. March 22, 2020.

Another bonus unmanned system that the Chinese could deploy in a future conflict with Taiwan is a four-wheel drive truck that can launch two types of swarming drones. The truck, built by Yanjing Auto, can go up to 77 miles per hour.[296] The truck has 12-tubes that can launch drones. "Four of the tubes launch smaller SULA30 drones, which are scouts with over an hour of flight time. The remaining eight tubes will hold larger SULA89 drones, which can carry over four pounds of explosives and crash into targets at a speed of over 110 mph."[297] This truck is an extremely interesting amalgam of different technologies. It has obvious advantages in land warfare. It is difficult to foresee a scenario in which the Taiwanese Army could react quickly enough to counteract such a fast-moving truck that can take the fight to the enemy with two different types of drones. The scout drones can fly far ahead to predict enemy activity. Then the attack drones can destroy targets in a stand-off manner. After launch, the truck has the speed and maneuverability to leave the area of operations, move to a new location, recover its drones, and then re-launch another salvo.

Russia Is Not to Be Outdone With Their Drone Program

Another near-peer competitor has made great strides in its quest for unmanned vehicles. Russia is developing several drone programs to stand up to the United States and NATO. Russia has one of the most advanced drones in the world. Dubbed the "Okhotnik" ("Hunter"), it can fly up to 600 miles per hour. The Okhotnik has a flying wing design and is one of the largest drones in the world weighing in at 20 tons, which is heavier than some fighter aircraft. The flying wing is stealthy due to its shape and low silhouette. The Okhotnik has some artificial intelligence capabilities giving it autonomous ability on how to conduct its own

---

296 Atherton, Kelsey. 2019. "This Chinese Truck Can Launch a Salvo of Drones." *C4ISR* Net. May 14, 2019.

297 *Ibid.*

targeting maneuvers and protocols. This means that it does not require a full-time link to a human operator and is at an advantage when it is confronted with electronic countermeasures. The Okhotnik can engage in deep strike with a range of 3,700 miles and attack with munitions or serve as an airborne early warning craft.

Russia is also developing smaller, swarming "suicide drones" to overwhelm enemy targets. ZALA Lancet is the moniker for the suicide drones which operate by colliding into a target and exploding. The system has a range of 25 miles with a light weight of only 88 pounds. The ZALA Lancet can autonomously find its own target. It does not have to directly hit its target; it can explode just feet away and destroy what it seeks.

Russia has around 4,000 military drones, ranking it third behind the United States and China. Unlike China, Russia has war experience having used its drones in the Syrian civil war. There have been 23,000 Russian drone flights lasting 140,000 hours over Syria. Weighing in at only 9-pounds, the Eleron-3 lightweight unmanned aerial vehicle has been the workhorse for the Russians in Syria. The Eleron-3 utilizes satellite guidance to help intelligence, surveillance, and reconnaissance – information that assists friendly forces in Syria. The largest drone the Russians fly over Syria is the Forpost-R. The Forpost-R is also for reconnaissance and is based on an Israeli model. It weighs over 1,000 pounds with an endurance time of 18 hours. The Russians have plans to add weapons to the Forpost-Rs once they are fully updated with modern reconnaissance capabilities. Russia has another copycat Reaper drone called the Orion. The Orion could be sold for export and it has a strike radius of 155 miles. Two Russian drones in development – the Korsar and the Carnivora – can reportedly hunt enemy drones.

The Russians are struggling to field the Altius, but this drone is a dandy and look out when it becomes operational. It is a High-Altitude Long Endurance unmanned aerial vehicle that could transfer 2.5 tons of cargo, including weapons, up to 6,000 miles. Look for this craft to come into service in 2022.

The most dangerous drone planned for the Russian military is the Poseidon, which is slated to come into service in 2027. While many years away in development, the weapon is chilling. It is an undersea drone launched from a submarine that is equipped with a nuclear warhead of up to two megatons. The drone will be powered by nuclear-propulsion so it will not have to worry about running out of fuel – it will have unlimited range. The Poseidon has already been nicknamed the "Doomsday Drone." It can traverse the North Atlantic autonomously. Russia eventually wants 30 Poseidons on duty that can be launched in the Atlantic at U.S. targets. The Kremlin believes the Poseidon will be much more difficult to eliminate than land-based ICBM launchers.

Iran Threatens the Middle East With Its Drones

While the Russians grow their drone arsenal, the Iranians are also advancing their various unmanned programs. The Iranians first rely on copies of American drones such as the RQ-170 Sentinel stealth drone and the American MQ-1 Predator. In 2019, the Iranians tested 50 copycat Sentinel and Predator drones in a wargame conducted by the Islamic Revolutionary Guard Corps. The test was a weaponized strike at a target on Bani Farur Island in the Persian Gulf. Some of the drones flew around 600 miles from Iranian bases.

There have been at least two incidents of Iranian drones flying close to U.S. naval shipping. In 2019, an Iranian unmanned vehicle flew within 1,000 yards of the USS Boxer in the Persian Gulf as it steamed toward the Strait of Hormuz. The Americans claimed they shot it down while the Iranians denied any drone had been destroyed and said they produced three hours of surveillance video of U.S. naval vessels in the area. In 2018, an Iranian copycat Sentinel flew from Syria to Israel. The Israelis destroyed the drone, and in retaliation, conducted air strikes on Iranian air defense sites. Then the Iranians shot down an Israeli F-16, which stoked a possible war in the region. In 2016, an Iranian drone buzzed over American and French aircraft carriers. It was for reconnaissance purposes, but it showed the world that Iranian drones had the reach and wherewithal to fly over allied shipping. The Iranians claimed they had "precise" images of the carriers and other ships in the strike group.[298]

Iran's command structure always remains vigilant and boastful about their drone program since it began in the 1980s. *The National Interest* quoted Rear Admiral Hossein Khanzadi, the head of Iran's Navy, in 2019. "Our drones have significant ranges and have no limitations in communication links. We have a complete archive of images of American vessels approaching from far distances ... an immense archive of the day to day and even moment to moment movements of American forces, whether in the Persian Gulf or Oman sea."[299]

The Iranians also have indigenous unmanned craft like the Ababeel series of drones that can be armed or used for reconnaissance purposes. The Ababeel-S is probably the most advanced reconnaissance drone with a ceiling of 14,000 feet and with a modern collection of surveillance gear. The Ababeel-3 can fly 93 miles and is a hybrid reconnaissance-attack drone that can conduct bomb-damage assessment – a valuable capability since the Iranians have a powerful ballistic and cruise missile inventory. The Ababeel-T can be armed with strike munitions. The Shahed-129 has a range of 1,200 miles and The Karrar is an offensive attack drone that entered into service in 2010. The Karrar can reportedly be used as a "kamikaze" drone.[300] The Iranians are probably known most for their Mohajer remotely-piloted vehicles that fly at 130 miles per hour with a 31-mile range. The first Mohajer was used in the

---

[298] "Unarmed Iranian Drone Takes 'Precise' Photos of US Ship, State Media Reports." *Associated Press*. Jan. 29, 2016.

[299] Bakeer, Ali. 2019. "Iran's Drones: A Big Threat to the U.S. Military In a War?" *The National Interest*. Sept. 15, 2019.

[300] Frantzman, Seth J. "Iran Shows Off Drones that Can Reach Israel, Threat Increases." *Jerusalem Post*. April 19, 2020.

Iran-Iraq war in the 1980s. Now there is the Mohajer-6. This generation of unmanned vehicles can be equipped with Qaem missiles or bombs.

Seth J. Frantzman, executive director of the Middle East Center for Reporting and Analysis, said in 2020 that "Last year [Iran] began using a new drone unit within the Islamic Revolutionary Guard Corps. It has exported drone technology to Hezbollah in Lebanon and the Houthi rebels in Yemen. Iranian drones have been used by the Houthis frequently against Saudi Arabia's armed forces and against airports and infrastructure."[301]

The Iranians reportedly used a drone swarm during their 2019 attacks of the Saudi Aramco oil infrastructure in Abqaiq and Khurais. Frantzman called Iran a "drone superpower."[302] Bottom line, Iran's drone program can reach Israel and American naval forces in the Middle East.

Iran is also adept at destroying drones in flight. In 2019, an Iranian missile defense battery took out an American Global Hawk drone. This craft is the crown jewel of the U.S. drone fleet. It costs $100 million and weighs 12 tons. The Iranians have downed other U.S. drones over the last decade. They hacked into a Lockheed Martin RQ-170 Sentinel and put it down in 2011. In 2012, the Iranians took possession of a Boeing Insitu ScanEagle.

Secretive North Korean Drones Attempt to Dominate the Skies

Another rogue state, North Korea, is taking its cues from the Iranians when it comes to using drones for asymmetric warfare. North Korea cannot match the United States and South Korea in the skies, so it is looking for ways to mitigate this advantage. Drones are cheap and they are often cloaked as anonymous, so their flight offers plausible deniability.

---

[301] Rogers, James. 2020. "Drone superpower? Iran's Arsenal of Unmanned Aerial Vehicles should Not Be Underestimated, Expert Warns." *Fox News*. Jan. 8, 2020.

[302] *Ibid.*

If a drone is shot down or if it is discovered by the media, Kim Jong Un can say that North Korea had nothing to do with it. For example, in 2017, South Korea said it shot down a small reconnaissance drone thought to be from the North. It was reportedly spying on the American Terminal High Altitude Area Defense (THAAD) anti-missile system in Seongju. There have been other drone transgressions by the North over the Demilitarized Zone during the last decade. More troubling is the revelation by a South Korean think tank that the DPRK reportedly has 1,000 drones which could carry weapons of mass destruction in their payloads to drop over South Korea.[303] Again, one of the reasons for equipping drones with biological or chemical warfare agents is that the North has an inferior air force compared to South Korean and United States aerial assets, which include the deployment of the F-35 Lightning stealth fighter.

Business Insider revealed that the DPRK has been reported to "possess around 25 chemical agents, including six nerve agents like sarin and VX," according to a 2016 report from the Korea Institute for Defense Analyses. Additionally, the country is estimated to have 13 types of pathogens, like anthrax and clostridium botulinum, which can be weaponized for a biological attack."[304]

Terrorists Have Drones Too

While the North Koreans are working on making a chemical/biological capability to the drone force, terror groups are also using drones for asymmetric warfare. Drones have proliferated beyond nation states. State-sponsors of terror are also making drones a key part of their proxy war play book. Iran has helped Hezbollah in Lebanon and Houthi Rebels in Yemen become drone masters. Nigeria, Pakistan, and Turkey

---

[303] Choi, David. 2017. "North Korea Reportedly Has a Fleet of 1,000 Drones It can Use for Chemical Attacks." *Business Insider*. March 30, 2017.

[304] *Ibid.*

have used drones in combat. ISIS has deployed drones in Syria. ISIS made its first successful drone attack in 2016 killing two peshmerga fighters in a strike over northern Iraq. A drone with explosives in its payload tried to assassinate Venezuela's premier Nicolas Maduro in 2018. Since commercial drones can be bought off the shelf, terrorists can use the store-bought or Internet-bought remotely-piloted aircraft as part of their arsenal. They develop their own with off the shelf parts and a drone hobbyist working for a terror group can quickly become a drone expert.

It is within the realm of plausibility that a terror group could launch an attack on the American homeland with a chemical or biological agent. Or artificial intelligence can be used to create a killer robot drone that acts intelligently to conduct targeted assassinations against American political leaders. Swarming drones launched by terrorists could overwhelm bodyguards and security personnel. So-called "slaughter drones" could ravage a group of citizens at large events in stadiums and arenas.

Analyst Jacob Ware, writing in *War on the Rocks*, believes that countering this threat should be of paramount concern. "Western states could strengthen their defenses against drones and weaponized artificial intelligence. This might involve strengthening current counter-drone and anti-AI capabilities, improving training for local law enforcement, and establishing plans for mitigating drone or autonomous weapons incidents."[305]

Israel is a Leader in Drone Technology

The Israelis must use counter-drone warfare against Hezbollah. With Iranian assistance and hardware, Hezbollah has deployed unmanned craft since 2004 when it sent a reconnaissance drone into Israeli air space. Hezbollah leader Hassan Nasrallah has declared that his terror group could launch drones filled with explosives into Israel for years.

---

[305] Ware, Jacob. 2019. "Terrorist Groups, Artificial Intelligence, and Killer Drones." *War on the Rocks*. Sept. 24, 2019.

In 2012, Hezbollah conducted its most ambitious flight to the nuclear weapons complex at Dimona. Israel shot down the drone, but it could have delivered valuable intelligence on Israeli nuclear infrastructure to the terror group. By 2013, Hezbollah had an estimated 200 drones.[306] By 2014, Hezbollah was using its drone fleets to assist the Assad regime in the Syrian civil war. A conflict with Israel would surely have drone-on-drone warfare featuring the Israeli drone program versus Hezbollah's program.

While not as advanced and heavy in numbers as Hezbollah, Hamas also has military drones. One flew over Israeli air space in 2019 and dropped a bomb that did minor damage to an Israel Defense Forces jeep.

In the future, drones could be used by Western militaries to implement facial recognition software to identify terrorist assassination targets using extensive data bases owned by NATO members. Facial recognition from drones is already available from private companies such as FA6. According to the firm's web site, "The FA6 Drone uses a face recognition software which identifies criminals, missing people, and civilians from a drone's camera. FA6 drones run in real time and can also process recorded videos. The capability to identify people from the air automatically provides a unique value which cannot be achieved otherwise. FA6 Drones allows you to collect personal information and find your target in the crowd."[307]

Israel faces threats from Hezbollah and Hamas on a daily basis and since it resides in such a dangerous neighborhood, the Israelis have been global leaders in developing unmanned aerial systems for decades. Israel's Tadrian Mastiff is seen as the world's first military drone. It was deployed in 1973 and provided real-time video intelligence for ground forces to help them see over the horizon. An early Israeli drone flew in

---

306 Kais, Roi. 2013. "Hezbollah Has Fleet of 200 Iranian-made UAVs." *Y Net News*. Nov. 25, 2013.

307 https://www.face-six.com/)

1982 during the Lebanon War. The Zahavan "Scout" was a crude reconnaissance drone, but it worked well and could fly for several hours, and even though human pilots of the Israeli Air Force were skeptical, the country continued to invent even better drones. Later in the 1980s the Israelis brought the AAI RQ-2 Pioneer into service that started mass use of tactical drones. Since then, Israel has built and exported hundreds of drones. Now they have strategic drones that can reach Iran. By 2005, the drone industry was worth $1.5 billion. Seven years later there were another $4.6 billion in sales of drone exports that go to Europe and Asia.[308]

Dozens of Israeli startups currently introduce new drones on a monthly basis and there are about 100 different varieties. Now Israeli drones are connected by satellite GPS and can be launched by a couple of soldiers with catapults and then recovered and relaunched in as little as 30 minutes. These new Israeli tactical reconnaissance drones can fly up to six hours at 15,000 feet with a range of over 100 miles. Multiple drone launches are enabled by a system called UVision's Hero-400 multi-canister launcher. The multiple-tube launcher can be mounted on a vehicle. These drones are called "loitering munitions," which are otherwise known as slaughter bots or suicide/kamikaze drones.[309] Israeli mini-drones are now able to fly with more than just a camera for reconnaissance. They are equipped with thermal sensors and are carrying a small number of explosives for targeted assassinations. UVision is leading the way for these tiny deadly drones with payloads of as little as a few ounces or a few pounds of explosives. These drones can find enemy combatants who are hiding behind walls or structures. They can fly into a window and then angle downwards to attack and eliminate an adversary.

The manned Israeli Air Force, so prominent in previous wars, has taken a backseat to drones. Now, an astonishing 80 percent of Israeli

---

[308] Frantzman, Seth J. "How Israel Became a Leader in Drone Technology." *The Jerusalem Post.* July 13, 2019.

[309] *Ibid.*

Air Force flight operations are unmanned, and they are used daily in a number of roles.[310] This is a monumental shift in doctrine and technology. Entire manned squadrons are being replaced by drones. Israel's strategic unmanned aerial vehicle, similar to the U.S. Global Hawk, is called the Heron. The Heron is a long endurance high altitude drone weighing in at nearly 12,000 pounds with a ceiling of 45,000 feet. A large compartment gives it a choice of all kinds of different payloads for sensors and other targeting mechanisms. Most people are familiar with how drones are flown. Usually, one pilot in a remote location controls the stick and rudders and then another person controls weapons, radars, cameras, or cannons. The Heron is almost autonomous. It just requires the pilot to press a button and then it takes off and lands automatically by computer.[311] Of course, the Heron still has a pilot and payload operator mid-flight, but automation is advancing in an upward trend of new technology.

Other vertical take-off and landing drones do not need runways and can be launched from a number of different types of locations like trucks and boats. The technology is constantly evolving because drone startups in Israel have employees who are often combat veterans from the military. These personnel know just what a drone needs in terms of flight capabilities, sensors, and weapons. The industry is constantly evolving. New drone pilots in the military have grown up with the Internet and video games that makes them easier to train when it comes to remotely-piloted vehicles.

Israel has killer drones too. The Drone Dome has advanced sensors, optics, and jamming counter-measures that allow enemy drones to be frozen or dropped from the sky. The Drone Dome can also shoot down enemy drones with a laser. It was tested in 2020 taking out a three-drone

---

[310] Egozi, Arie. 2019. "Exclusive: Drones Now Dominate Israeli Flying Operations." *Breaking Defense*. Sept. 27, 2019.

[311] *Ibid.*

enemy swarm. Other anti-drone systems are extremely innovative. The DROM Done Defense Systems can be mounted stationary on the ground or in a vehicle. The DROM can identify a drone two miles away. Its radio frequency system picks up the enemy communications link. Then once identified, the operator of the system signals the DROM to take the enemy drone out of the sky. The system can even identify where the enemy drone is being controlled so the shot-down drone lands away from the enemy so they cannot recover it.

The SMASH 2000 system is mounted on a soldier's rifle. The system works on drones flying about 300 feet away. According to the *Jerusalem Post*, "The soldier selects and locks onto the target. The moment the trigger is squeezed, the system calculates the target's movement and predicts its next location using advanced image processing and algorithms. SMASH 2000 prevents the bullet from being fired until the target is precisely in its crosshairs.[312] D-Fend Solutions is another system that "hijacks" enemy drones and lands them before they can shoot video or launch weapons.

Israeli killer drones made a deadly appearance in the 2020 "brush-fire" war between Azerbaijan and Armenia in the disputed region of Nagorno-Karabakh. "Kamikaze drones purchased from Israel have been used to devastating effect by Azerbaijan. "These small craft, also known as loitering munitions, are able to surveil targets including tanks, artillery installations or troops before blowing themselves up."[313]

Britain Focuses on Mini-Drones and Swarms

The British are also forging ahead with their various drone programs and funding them fully. Britain's Ministry of Defense is pouring money into

---

[312] Ahronheim, Anna. 2019. "How Can Israel Stop Hamas Drones Infiltrating the Gaza Strip?" *The Jerusalem Post*. Sept. 8, 2019.

[313] "Azerbaijan's Turkish and Israeli Drones Are Wiping Out Tanks, Artillery, and Soldiers as the Armenians Lose Ground in the Disputed Territory of Nagorno-Karabakh." Syrian Observatory for Human Rights. Oct. 26, 2020.

a fleet of mini-drones. The price tag for the investment is $44 million. This expenditure was called a Transformation Fund by UK's Minister of Defense Gavin Williamson in 2019. The reconnaissance drones will fit in a soldier's hand and weigh as little as 7 ounces.

Equally exciting is the new Royal Air Force's Protector drone. The Protector can be used for intelligence, surveillance, reconnaissance, and target acquisition purposes. With a loiter time of 40 hours, it also has offensive characteristics that can drop several laser-guided bombs or launch 18 precision-guided missiles.[314] The drone is satellite-linked and can take off and land anywhere in the world and also deploy its armaments around the globe. The Protector does not need a sophisticated ground control station. It can reportedly be controlled with only two personnel with a laptop.[315] It got permission to fly over Europe and could conceivably conduct reconnaissance operations over Ukraine to monitor that conflict. 16 Protectors are on the way for the British. However, the Protector was two years behind schedule as of 2019.

The Royal Navy is not being forsaken when it comes to unmanned vehicle development. Detonating and disabling undersea mines is inherently dangerous for human crews. That is why the British are bringing in to service an unmanned mine-sweeper. Called ARCIMS, "the self-driving launch can tow three smaller boats, each carrying acoustic, magnetic and electrical devices that can trigger naval mines at a distance," according to *The Maritime Executive*.[316]

The British have plans for drone swarms in so-called "swarm squadrons." The BBC interviewed Paul Scharre from the Center for a New American Security think tank in 2019. "If you imagine a football match,

---

[314] Osborne, Simon. 2019. "RAF Unveils Deadly New Protector Done Armed with 'Game-Changing Technology'" *Daily Express*. Aug. 22, 2019.

[315] *Ibid*.

[316] "Autonomous Minesweeper Set for "Live" Operations." *The Maritime Executive*. Jan. 14, 2020.

a coach isn't going to tell the players from the sidelines exactly where to run and what to do," he said. "Players are going to figure that out on their own. Similarly, the robot agents need to coordinate among each other what actions to take."[317]

Drones and robots are similar. Most people associate drones with remotely-piloted vehicles whether they operate in the sky, on the ground, or in water. There is a "air-land-sea" component to drones. They were originally called unmanned aerial vehicles, then unmanned aerial systems, and later known as remotely-piloted vehicles. Drones are becoming "smarter" and more autonomous, but many require at least one human operator. More and more drones have some automated features, especially when it comes to take off and landing for aerial drones. Robots, on the other hand, are programmed to be more automated than drones and can conduct a series of complex movements and actions without the help of humans.

Robots Lean Into Logistics Support and Combat

The distinction between drones and robots is beginning to blur. DARPA, the is developing a system with a university in New York to use video gamers' brain waves to train the artificial intelligence of robot autonomous swarms. Researchers at the University of Buffalo have developed a strategy game that 25 individuals play to produce brain wave data. This data then is used to train the AI. The plan is for swarms of up to 250 air and ground drones to be inspired by gamers. This has ethical ramifications. How well screened are the individual gamers? They could be hyper-aggressive and allow the swarms to cease their ability to identify friend or foe. It would be important then for the gamers to have ethical and sound moral compasses to make sure the swarming drones do not attack everything they see.

---

[317] McMullan, Thomas. 2019. "How Swarming Drones Will Change Warfare. *BBC.* March 16, 2019.

Perhaps killer drones are not the answer. When I was in the U.S. Army, I had three different jobs or military occupational specialties during the time I was in the service. I originally enlisted as a public affairs specialist or military journalist. As an officer cadet, I served in a field artillery unit, and finally, I became on infantry officer. While in the field artillery unit, I gained experience on the M109 Paladin self-propelled howitzer. Often mistaken for a "tank," the Paladin is a tracked vehicle, but it has a long "tube" to launch shells up to 19 miles. Now with a longer tube and rocket-boosted shells, the Paladin can fire up to 39 miles, which is a remarkable distance. One thing a Paladin must have is a steady supply of 155-millimeter shells. These projectiles weigh 100 pounds each and they must be manually carried by soldiers several different times before they are loaded into the Paladin. I have moved my share of these shells and it was a task that got old quickly.

Now robots are coming to the rescue. The army is creating a program for a robot to take over this chore. Six companies are competing for a contract for "Field Artillery Autonomous Supply." The Army Futures Command is in charge of the program and will pick a winner. This will allow the Paladin to go from firing four shells a minute to 10. The eventual logistics robot will be able to move shells from the rear echelon into the M992 ammo hauler and then transport them from the ammo hauler to the Paladin. A robot may even be able to load the projectiles directly into the breach of the gun.

Logistics robots make more sense in terms of ethics. They are not "killer robots." Soldiers do not have to worry as much about logistics robots over-riding their controls and causing unethical mischief. This is a key aspect, and one could imagine numerous jobs that a logistics robot could do for the military, especially when it comes to loading and unloading ammunition, ordinance, food, and water.

You probably associate robots with four-legged animal bots that look like they could teeter, fall down, and break into pieces on rough terrain. Many are slow too. This is beginning to change in the civilian world and the militaries of various countries will take notice because advances in robotics are happening worldwide. Some are still shaped like four-legged animals, but their dexterity and agility have improved significantly. The Massachusetts Institute of Technology's DARPA-funded cheetah robot can jump over fences at a gallop and run 28.3 miles per hour. "PETMAN" (Protection Ensemble Test Mannequin) from Boston Dynamics is a Terminator-like humanoid. It can squat and do simple exercises. It is currently used for testing human uniforms, but its developers have greater things in store for PETMAN. The Department of Defense is interested in using PETMAN as a "chemical sniffer" to search for and root out chemical and biological weapons.

Also from Boston Dynamics is logistical robot "Handle," which has two wheels and can adroitly pick up a box from one location and quickly stack it on a pallet. University of Michigan's robot MABEL is a humanoid that can run like a person. The Institute for Human and Machine Cognition's (IHMC) robot called Planar Elliptical Runner – can run on a treadmill quickly – and that means faster than a human. IHMC also has "HexRunner" that can go faster than MIT's cheetah. It clocks in at 32.2 miles per hour.

These speedy robots have numerous military applications, whether for rear echelon logistics endeavors to forward echelon battlefield tasks. The bi-ped or two-legged robots could run out ahead of infantry units and check for improvised explosive devices and land mines. They could work with overhead drones and check houses and other hiding places and send that real-time intelligence back to the unit. And of course, they could eventually be armed to create killer bots.

The U.S. Air Force is moving ahead with its "optionally piloted aircraft" concept. This means that robot pilots will be available in order to make an aircraft fly without a live pilot. The system is called "Robopilot," and it was hatched by the air force Research Laboratory. The idea is to convert manned flight into unmanned flight without having to build a new drone. It uses existing aircraft. Already, the air force has a robot pilot that can fly a Cessna airplane.

According to the air force Research Laboratory, "The system 'grabs' the yoke, pushes on the rudders and brakes, controls the throttle, flips the appropriate switches and reads the dashboard gauges the same way a pilot does. At the same time, the system uses sensors, like GPS and an Inertial Measurement Unit, for situational awareness and information gathering. A computer analyses these details to make decisions on how to best control the flight."[318]

The U.S. Navy is developing a robot submarine software system that would enable Orca unmanned subs to attack and sink enemy shipping without a human on board. Known as CLAWS, the unmanned sub algorithmic system would use artificial intelligence and smart sensors to make Orca robot subs autonomous.

DARPA also has a separate program to create a fleet of manta-ray shaped robotic submarines. Manta-ray is expected to be done by the end of 2021. The idea behind manta-ray is that it will stay out to sea while other manned submarines have to come in for maintenance. That way the numbers of submarines at any given time will remain constant.

The navy also is working on a robotic surface vessel that would protect ships anchored at harbor called the Common Unmanned Surface Vehicle. The craft is 39 feet long and can steam at 35-knots. The "robo-boat" can sail for 20 hours at a time.[319] It is designed to be autonomous, but a human can take over controls at any time. Humans also control the robo-boat's .50 caliber machine gun.

The British are also investing in robots. The Royal Navy spent around $95 million on robotics and autonomous vehicles in 2019. The "NavyX" program is meant to harness all the Royal Navy's human

---

[318] "US Air Force Unveils Robot Pilot." *Flight Safety Australia*. Aug. 21, 2019.

[319] Mizokami, Kyle. 2020. "The U.S. Navy's New Robo-Boat Has No People, But It Does Have a Very Big Gun." *Popular Mechanics*. Feb. 19, 2020.

capital brainpower to help the initiative with its various robotics concepts. For example, the Royal Navy wants to keep developing its autonomous mine-clearing crafts to maturity. They also want to use NavyX to build high technology accelerators to borrow from practices of civilian startup culture.

The British Army is testing a robot tank for infantry support. The robot tank can be outfitted with a machine gun or it can serve as a medevac on the battlefield or in the rear for logistics. Dubbed "Titan Sentry and Strike," the mini-robot tank is 6.5 feet wide and 3 feet tall. It can go 20 miles per hour. The British are also considering buying a mini-robot tank that is wheeled instead of tracked. This robot tank is more focused on IED detection and logistics.

Russia is not as concerned with the ethical ramifications of robot killer-soldiers and the Kremlin has moved forward on making so-called "robot brothers" to supplement regular Russian infantry troops. Russia has its own version of DARPA for advanced military concepts. These scientists are taking the lead on robot brothers because they move faster and make split-second decisions on target acquisition on the battlefield. The Russians are also making robotic mini-tanks and robots that can identify IEDs in urban combat.

China has its own killer robots. These are tracked vehicles meant to fight out in front while manned forces stay back. The killer robots, dubbed Sharp Claw I, weigh 265 pounds, and are equipped with "machine guns, night vision, missile loaders, and camera sensors," according to the *National Interest* in 2020.[320] The "thigh-high" war robots from the Chinese military can go six miles per hour, and are reportedly semi-autonomous at this time, but in the future, they could likely become fully-autonomous.

Obviously, humans who design killer robots must be ethically aware of what they are doing. Authoritarian countries such as China,

---

[320] Osborn, Kris. 2020. "Robot vs. Robot War? Now China Has Semi-Autonomous Fighting Ground Robots." *The National Interest*. June 15, 2020.

Russia, and Iran, including totalitarian countries like North Korea, have a culture that is more communal than the individual liberties enjoyed by Western countries. This makes ethical decisions different. As I will explain in future chapters on cyberwar and artificial intelligence, training of drone operators should include sections on ethics and morality, especially when it comes to targeted assassinations.

CHAPTER SEVEN

CYBERWAR, INTERNET, AND INSECURE COMPUTING

It was an alarming thought. The U.S. Army's Paladin self-propelled howitzer required a critical startup phase before operations of the system could ensue. Syncing the clock and other connections to Global Positioning Systems was paramount. Without GPS, digital connectivity, targeting, radio communication, and tracking would not be possible. No GPS equaled no fire mission. I immediately made an observation when I understood the ramifications of this. "What would happen," I asked the crew, "if the GPS is jammed or hacked and the Paladin could not sync to GPS?" Nobody said anything. They had never thought about this scenario. I asked that question over 20 years ago and it is still relevant today and in the future.

Now the army is worried about this danger too. The army calls a non-functioning GPS and other electronic challenges a "Degraded, Denied, and Disrupted Space Operating Environment." The Russians excel at making adversaries' major end items like tanks and howitzers get degraded, denied, and disrupted through jamming and electronic countermeasures. It is asymmetric warfare at its finest. The Russians, in a shooting war with the United States, would likely attempt to hack and jam GPS satellites. China is also adept at electronic and cyberwarfare as it pertains to denying adversaries connections to satellites.

Cyber warfare is still a human struggle, despite the heightened state of technology. It is part of the sociological operating environment. Humans still push the buttons and make mistakes. Humans have good cyber hygiene or bad cyber hygiene, and humans are still the weakest link on the cyber kill chain. Moreover, cyber offense and defense creates bureaucracies which are an important aspect of sociology.

Cyberwar, war fought in the "Fifth Domain," according to the World Economic Forum, "is best understood to refer to an act of aggression, committed through a digital network, meant to cause damage in the real world, either to civilian or military targets, in order to force a sovereign state to act or refrain from acting."[321] This is distinct from cyber-crime, propaganda, cyber activism from hactivists, and cyber vandalism. This is instead grey or ambiguous warfare that is hard to discern. It is difficult to tell whether it is coming from state actors who seek to wage war with computers and the Internet or if it is part of traditional combat that includes airplanes, tanks, ships, missiles, rockets, and infantry fighters. Some analysts do not place terrorism under the rubric of cyber warfare, but this is incorrect. Terrorism is often an act of war, even if it falls short of a cyber "Pearl Harbor" or Armageddon attack, since many terror groups do not have the knowhow or talent for such a large-scale incident. Cyber war is often thought of a way to "soften the battlefield" before a kinetic attack – cyber strikes against radars, sensors, anti-aircraft systems networks, and computer attacks that come before the traditional use of military assets.

Cyberwar is made up of assaults against sovereign states to minimize their power to wage traditional combat. It is usually cyber conflict between two sovereign states. For example, a cyber-attack comes from

---

[321] Dobrygowski, Daniel. 2018. "What Would a Cyberwar Look Like?" World Economic Forum. April 25, 2018.

a country that hits another state's military air base that compromises its electric power and neutralizes its ability to fight by grounding aircraft. Can cyberwar be as destructive as a physical attack in which military personnel or civilians die? Steve Ranger of ZDNet says that cyberwar is a cyber-attack that results in "damage, death, and destruction."[322]

What if No-one Dies During a Cyber War?

Sometimes a cyber-attack will bypass the military defenses of a country to attack the banking and financial system, for example, and this is difficult to classify as an act of war since it is not likely that someone dies. Since cyber war includes state actors, it is difficult to tell if an attack is carried out by non-state actors or proxies affiliated with sovereign states. Another difficulty is that there is no international law that defines what cyber war is, but cyber and international law experts are trying to remedy this. They have developed the so-called "Tallin Manual" to organize their thoughts on what constitutes a cyber act of war. "The manual consists of a set of guidelines – 154 rules – which set out how the lawyers think international law can be applied to cyberwarfare, covering everything from the use of cyber mercenaries to the targeting of medical units' computer systems."[323]

The idea is that by making the law around cyberwarfare clearer, there is less risk of an attack escalating, because escalation often occurs when the rules are not clear, and leaders overreact.[324] The Tallin 2.0 manual really tries to unpack what it means to have a cyber-attack that violates international law and norms because there are so many cyber-attacks during peace time. After all, there will be 6 billion people on the

---

[322] Ranger, Steve. 2019. "What Is Cyberwar? Everything You Need to Know About the Frightening Future of Digital Conflict." *ZD Net*. Dec. 4, 2019.

[323] *Ibid.*

[324] *Ibid.*

Internet by 2022, according to *Cybercrime Magazine*.[325] That is a lot of people who could be victims of cyber intrusions. To put that in perspective, in 2018, there were 3 billion users of the Internet, which worked out to be 51-percent of the total global population.

One of the earliest times cyberwar was used in print was in 1993 in a report from the RAND Corporation that was ahead of its time.[326] It noted that war would soon be fought in the information space or the World Wide Web as it was called then. The authors believed that cyberwar would be the new blitzkrieg of modern warfare. They claimed that it would be malign groups made up of nonstate actors such as cartels, terrorists, and other transnational criminals that would instigate new weapons of mass destruction. Clausewitz' notion of the fog of war would move from the physical and traditional battlefield to the digital domain. And this would be comprised of offensive types of cyber battles, not just defensive maneuvers to protect infrastructure. President Bill Clinton noted in a 2001 speech that hackers would target critical systems. Later Russia, North Korea, China, and Iran would either commit acts themselves or have cyber criminals from those countries enacting nefarious cyber deeds.

Can U.S. Cyber Command Come to the Rescue?

Leaping forward to the 21st century, the U.S. Cyber Command, now a unified combatant command, is improving its capabilities for defensive and offensive cyber acts. It is attempting to get its numbers of cyber personnel to over 6,000 and to establish over 130 teams for various actions withing the realm of the command. For offense, there is a cyber combat mission force and for defense there is a cyber protection force. Some observers think this separate force could create a Cold War-like

---

[325] Morgan, Steve. 2019. "Humans On The Internet Will Triple From 2015 To 2022 And Hit 6 Billion." *Cybercrime Magazine*. July 18, 2019.

[326] Arguilla, John and David Ronfeldt. 1993. "Cyberwar is Coming!" Rand Corporation.

arms race, in which companies stockpile weapons, and simple attacks can mushroom into much bigger stakes.[327] One potential positive development would be cyber-deterrence in which sovereign state actors are afraid of launching attacks because of what could happen in retaliation. The United States military, NATO, and the European Union are attempting to fashion such an elevation of potential responses. These entities and organizations are using cyber wargames between hundreds of participants to fashion a strategic deterrent. Some analysts seek to elevate U.S. Cyber Command into information warfare, which will be discussed in the next chapter.

John Davis, chief security officer for Palo Alto Networks, quoted on the web site *Fifth Domain*, said, "Enemies have learned that the integrated use of not just cyber capabilities but the combination of disinformation, denial capabilities, the psycho-social aspect of weaponizing social media, which provides an enormous platform ... to sow division and doubt."[328]

Cyber War Enters Outer Space

This brings our attention to cyberwarfare and space. Iran is also jumping into the fight when it comes to jamming GPS satellites. In 2019, the Iranians have attempted to block and interfere with the GPS of U.S. Naval shipping in the Persian Gulf and the Strait of Hormuz. The Iranians have GPS jammers in that area of operations on Abu Musa Island. The Iranians also attempted to spoof U.S. Naval bridge-to-bridge communications. The Russians could be up to the same thing, but their target is fighter planes. The Israelis reported in 2019 that airplanes flying over Syria had strange things happen with their GPS systems in which the wrong location was displayed, or the GPS just stopped

---

327 "What Is Cyberwar?"

328 Pomerleau, Mark, 2019. "What the Future Holds for Cyber Command." *Fifth Domain*. July 25, 2019.

working altogether. A researcher from the University of Texas, Todd Humphreys, has tracked the location of where the jamming is coming from. He uses sensors from the International Space Station to determine the strongest signal.[329] Humphreys said the jamming signals are coming from Russia's Khmeimim Air Base, which is on the western coast of Syria. Humphreys has also spotted GPS jamming signals coming from the Black Sea around Russia's borders and from near the Kremlin. What if the target is U.S. F-35s and F-22s? It is plausible the Russians have plans to jam the GPS of those airplanes. Russia also uses jammers on cell phone towers to potentially fool the location apparatus on incoming ballistic missiles, so it would have an advantage in potential nuclear conflict.

The U.S. Army is responding to this cat and mouse game by first focusing on protecting the GPS of its ground forces in Germany. *Breaking Defense* reported in 2019 that "the US Army is rushing jam-resistant GPS kits to the 2nd Cavalry Regiment in Germany by the end of the year. The service is already evaluating proposals for an upgraded second-generation version that will include an Inertial Navigation System (INS) as a fallback for times when GPS is completely unreachable."[330]

Land and sea military forces are cognizant of threats to GPS. But the new U.S. Space Force should make the cyber security of space its number one priority. Space holds the most of the world's vulnerabilities for the protection of critical infrastructure on the ground. Most cybersecurity efforts are focused on terrestrial earth. It is time for Space Force to step into this void and first protect GPS systems from spoofing because spoofing is considered a cyber-attack. As Greg Falco of Harvard's Belfer Center described it, "There are multiple ways to spoof a GPS satellite.

---

[329] Cross, Judah Ari. 2019. "GPS Jamming Affecting Israel Comes from Russian Base in Syria: US Researcher." *The Times of Israel*. June 28, 2019.

[330] Freedberg, Sydney J. "Army Fields Anti-Jam GPS In Germany This Fall." *Breaking Defense*. June 6, 2019.

One mechanism to do so is by compromising the satellite receiver and altering the output signal from the satellite. Another opportunity is via a false data injection attack where an adversary uses a GPS signal simulator (whose success will be limited because it cannot always trick the receiver) or uses a software-defined spoofer."[331]

U.S. Space Force should ensure all transmissions to space are encrypted, that includes communication with satellites, as Falco recommended. Falco also favors developing new norms and standards for cyber security in space. He also says it is necessary to identify the correct cyber security specialist and make him or her cognizant that the correct aspects of space communications are secure, this includes building a space cyber security culture with all workers.[332]

Space Force should be able to handle these reforms. The bottom line is that Space Force must protect all U.S. satellites from cyber-attack from Russia and China because the future of cyber warfare will be prosecuted in space. U.S. satellites can not only be spoofed but they can also be hijacked, be disrupted, or have its telemetry confounded – all dangerous scenarios for Space Force. The Chinese are surprisingly heavy-handed when it comes to space warfare since they successfully tested a missile against a satellite target in 2013 and in 2018. They are usually more subtle when it comes to warfare in general because the Chinese have not fought a war since 1979 when it battled Vietnam. China is also developing quantum computing, and this makes their code breaking capabilities excel and allow for the potential of breaking into a satellite through cryptography.

Now China has its own space force. In 2015, China's People's Liberation Army established the Strategic Support Force, which encompassed space, cyber, and electronic warfare activities. China understands

---

[331] Falco, Gregory. 2018. "Job One for Space Force: Space Asset Cybersecurity." Belfer Center, Harvard University. July 12, 2018.

[332] *Ibid.*

that space, satellites, and cyber war are related. As Elsa Kania wrote in a report from think tank CNA in 2018, the Chinese believe, "Whoever is the strongman of military space will be the ruler of the battlefield; whoever has the advantage of space has the power of the initiative..."[333]

Space Force is developing its first offensive weapon, and this is a communications jammer that will interfere when enemy countries talk to their own satellites. Say the U.S. adversary has a satellite that provided early warning of a U.S. attack, Space Force would make this communication void. Space Force also keeps track of space junk, provides early warning for enemy missile launch, and works with private space companies such as SpaceEx and Blue Origin.

Sometimes hackers go after the information in military networks. P.W. Singer and Allan Friedman explained that a cyber intrusion on a network could send "false reports via its own devices."[334] The authors continued, "Inside a foe's communication networks, one can disrupt or even disable command and control, keeping commanders from sending out orders, units from talking to each other, or even individual weapons systems from sharing needed information."[335] This attack could affect the "trust" of the information coming from networks and instigate confusion and a lackluster response to a conventional kinetic attack from airplanes, naval ships, and tanks.[336]

How Does a Government Classify a Cyber Attack?

The future of offensive and defensive cyber warfare is the problem of recognition, attribution, and proportionate response. How does a

---

333 Kania, Elsa. 2018. "China Has a 'Space Force.' What Are Its Lessons for the Pentagon?" *Defense One*. Sept. 29, 2018.

334 Singer, P.W. and Alan Friedman. 2014. *Cybersecurity and Cyberwar: What Everyone Needs to Know*. New York: Oxford University Press.

335 *Ibid*, pg. 129

336 *Ibid*.

government first identify and classify an attack? In offensive cyber warfare, there is the classic case of Stuxnet, a cyber weapon used by the United States and Israel, most likely in 2009. Stuxnet was in development for an estimated four years before it was hatched. What if Israel and the United States suffered a Stuxnet-like attack from Iran? It would perhaps take the same amount of time to recognize and identify the attack. Then figure out it came from Iran and execute a decision loop to devise a way to respond. The Israelis and the Americans would probably not agree on the path forward. The same problems afflict cyber defense. Who did it? Is the first question. It is often not clear if a cyber breach can be attributed to a state actor. Often the culprit in an attack is a group loosely-affiliated with a nation-state. This allows governments to have plausible deniability. The usual suspects in an offensive cyber breach are Russia, China, Iran, and North Korea, but it can be argued that hackers in all those countries may not be tied to the government. The second group of questions is what to do about it? And what is the correct proportionate response?

Sometimes the answer is to log and describe a cyber-attack and refrain from attacking the perpetrator in response. The Obama administration opted for this tactic and overall strategy because it did not want to give away its cyber offensive capabilities, although it did have "ace in the hole" attacks planned for when diplomacy did not work. For example, the Obama administration had cyber-attacks in mind for the Iranian government if its negotiations for the nuclear deal with Iran failed. The plan was called "Nitro Zeus." The Trump administration was more public about announcing and instigating cyber-attacks against rival nation states. When Iran downed a U.S. drone, some of his national security team members wanted a kinetic attack in response, Trump publicly called for a cyber-attack against Iran, claiming that he saved Iranian lives by not conducting a bombing. Later, the Trump administration gave the permission to U.S. Cyber Command to conduct attacks without presidential approval. The Biden administration will likely take the same tack as the Obama administration.

One problem in all of this is that other countries – Iran, China, Russia, and North Korea – are getting "cyber-war" experience and the United States is not getting the same amount of experience. These rogue countries will take the lessons learned and fuse them into war fighting doctrine, while the United States is more in the mode of knowledge-collection and norms-building to excel in identifying, classifying, and thwarting attacks. All of these aspects are important, but it appears that reprobate countries are more likely to engage in cyber warfare.

When an Attack is a Perfect Storm

While the U.S. cyber defenses were focused on protecting the 2020 election from outside intrusion, the United States was hit with a different type of attack that amounted to a perfect cyber storm. In late December of 2020, it was revealed that software maker SolarWinds became the victim of a huge cyber intrusion. SolarWinds said 18,000 customers were compromised by the breach. This list of victims included the U.S. Department of Energy and the National Nuclear Security Administration, the Department of Homeland Security, the Department of State, and the Department of the Treasury.

Hackers thought to be from Russia and backed by the Russian government, most likely foreign intelligence agency SVR, were reportedly behind the intrusion. This may have started in March of 2020. The Russians are believed to have inserted malware into SolarWinds Orion IT monitoring system software via a Trojan Horse style attack. U.S. governments downloaded the malware-infected software through a routine update. This created a backdoor for the hackers. Observers and policy makers immediately began to speculate on whether this was an attack or an intrusion and pondered what the appropriate response should have been. But it is clear the Russians found a large gap in American cyber defenses.

The United Kingdom must deal with cyber-attacks as well. The British Army's 13th Signal Regiment, as of 2020, has responsibility for protecting the military and coordinating responses to cyber intrusions. It will work together with the Royal Navy and the Royal Air Force. But the 13th Signal Regiment must deal with the challenges of identifying and classifying attacks and developing a proportionate response.

Greg Austin, Senior Fellow for the Cyber, Space, and Future Conflict Program at the think tank IISS, used an analogy when it comes to identifying an attack and classifying it. "A hammer is a tool – it can be used for making things. But a hammer can also kill people. And code is the same: it can be a tool for making things and it can be a weapon that kills people."[337]

The U.S. Department of Homeland Security has its Cybersecurity and Infrastructure Security Agency (CISA), which is a defensive program that excels at "risk advising." It shares details of cyber-attacks and threats that are passed to the Department of Homeland Security from other government agencies and the private sector. The problem with cyber risk advising is that it requires another organization to share what happens during a cyber-attack. Many companies in the private sector are not willing to share the details of a cyber-attack because of embarrassment, legal liability, and trade secrets. So, aspects of the United States cyber strategy are focused on defense instead of cyber offensive operations. This applies to protecting critical infrastructure as well.

Cyber expert Michael Myers, writing in *The Hill*, agrees. "The dilemma is as wide as it is deep," Myers wrote. "The majority of the nation's critical infrastructure is privately owned and operated. This leaves assessment, oversight, and compliance enforcement a challenge for the federal government. Some critical infrastructure sectors may be more inclined to share with DHS (and the public) their cyber shortcomings than others."[338]

---

337 Stacey, Ed. 2020. "The Future of Cyber Warfare – An Interview with Greg Austin." *Strife Blog*. April 26, 2020.

338 Myers, Michael. 2018. "Our Critical Infrastructure Is Not Ready for Cyber Warfare." *The Hill*. Feb. 14, 2018.

How Blockchain Can Alter the Balance

The future of cyber warfare could be defended in the realm of blockchain. Most associate blockchain with cryptocurrencies, but blockchain has other applications. I defined blockchain in a previous chapter but allow me to revisit it and flesh it out as it pertains to cyber security. Blockchain "blocks" are digital ledger storage units that keep digital pieces of information. Each block has a cryptographic hash or unique identifying code that links the two blocks, and they form a chain. The chain can be a public or private database. A network of computers vet new data entries. Thus, data is stored in a peer-to-peer network and it is not centralized. Data blocks can also be encrypted for additional security. This makes for a good cyber defense since the information is not a part of a centralized vulnerability and contributes to a way to manage data integrity.

According to David Schatsky, Managing Director at Deloitte U.S., "The (blockchain) technology provides a way of recording transactions or any digital interaction in a way that is secure, transparent, highly resistant to outages, auditable, and efficient."[339] The data in a blockchain is traceable. Each time there is a new transaction on the chain, it is digitally notated, and time stamped. This allows organizations to have assurance that the data is authentic and real. The data also has no "single point of failure" which is another advantage when a cyber defense system fights a distributed denial of service attack. "With blockchain, there is not a single, definitive account of events that can be manipulated. Instead, a hacker would need to manipulate every copy of the blockchain on the network. This is what is meant by blockchain being a 'distributed' ledger."[340]

---

[339] Picini, Eric and Larry Kehoe. "Blockchain and Cyber Security. Let's Discuss." Deloitte.

[340] Conway, Luke. 2020. "Blockchain explained: Investopedia." Nov. 17, 2020.

Virtual Reality for Cyber Analysts Has Advantages

The future of cyber warfare can also be defended in the realm of virtual reality and augmented reality. Both domains can train a cyber security analyst to improve reactions to cyber-attacks. A 3D virtual reality and augmented reality environment can serve as a "heads up display" to help the analyst see and identify multiple threats at once. It allows a different combination of tools to be used. For example, the display could pull up different documents such as from Microsoft Word or Excel files into the virtual or augmented environment. The virtual environment can also combine systems into the heads-up display, so threat analysts see the safety of networks, mobile phones, servers, and storage. Through this environment, an analyst sees an attack develop in real time.

The future of the Internet itself will likely be without a monitor, keyboard, and a mouse. Users will mostly conduct activity on the Internet with virtual and augmented reality tools.[341] This includes the spoken word as well as search that will be voice activated – a scenario that is already taking place with chatbots such as Apple's Siri. Foreign languages will be automatically translated so virtual reality and augmented reality users can communicate in real time.

Artificial Intelligence Can Be the Difference-Maker

Future cyber security systems can also use artificial intelligence to predict the next attack. The Intelligence Advanced Research Projects Activity (IARPA) in the United States is working on such a concept. The IARPA program is called Cyberattack Automated Unconventional Sensor Environment, or CAUSE, and it has a three-year development phase. The program has several partners led by BAE Systems, StratumPoint, Digital Operatives LLC, and the University of Maryland – Charles River Analytics, Leidos, and the University of Southern California.

---

[341] Blitz, Matt. 2019. "What Will the Internet Be Like in the Next 50 Years?" *Popular Mechanics*. Nov. 1, 2019.

The web site *Fanatical Futures* interviewed a project leader. "We are focusing on the human aspect of prediction versus detection," said Anne Taylor, technology group director at BAE who said the company is "applying human behavioral, cyber-attack, and social theories to publicly available information — such as posts on social media — to develop a network of unconventional sensors that can monitor a range of different activities that could indicate the early formulation of an attack."[342]

Other cyber experts agree. Attila Tomaschek, Cybersecurity Researcher at ProPrivacy, said in an interview with *Disruptor Daily*, that "The future of cybersecurity will have a heavy focus on using artificial intelligence to secure devices and systems in the increasingly connected world. With the internet of things and connected devices proliferating at such an incredible rate, the ways in which we leave ourselves exposed to potential cyber-attacks are also increasing."[343]

Artificial Intelligence can also be used by malign actors for offensive attacks that create opportunities for cyber breaches. Take, for example, the notorious and dangerous Emotet trojan. Emotet is a spam phishing attack that targets emails. But this is not an outdated brute force attack. It is subtle. It can insert itself into existing email conversations by providing context of the communication and send phishing emails that fake the target out into clicking and allowing the malware to flood in. The worry is that hackers who utilize the Emotet trojan can use artificial intelligence to make the attack more believable. As the World Economic Forum described it, "This would mean that an AI-powered Emotet trojan could create and insert entirely customized, more believable phishing emails. Crucially, it would be able to send these out at

---

342 Griffin, Matthew. 2016. "US Government Unveils CAUSE, a Program to Predict Cyber-attacks Before They Happen." 311 Institute. Oct. 16, 2016.

343 Mire, Sam. 2019. "What's The Future of Cybersecurity? 39 Experts Share Their Insights." *Disruptor Daily*. June 26, 2019.

scale, which would allow criminals to increase the yield of their operations enormously."[344]

Joshua Davis, Director of Channels at Circadence, said, "The future of cybersecurity is going to include humans working alongside automated assistants, where artificial intelligence and machine learning assist in operations."

AI-fueled cyber-attacks will be able to impersonate your peer that you are emailing by mimicking your friend's writing style through natural language processing. It will be easy for you to mistake a tainted email loaded with malware from legitimate communication.[345] AI-fueled attacks will also "hang out" and "study" the people and data sets that are most vulnerable. Machine learning will allow the attacker to automatically learn the optimum time to strike and find the most valuable data to steal. As the World Economic Forum noted, "Not only will AI-driven attacks be much more tailored and consequently more effective, but their ability also to understand context means they will be even harder to detect. Traditional security controls will be impotent against this new threat, as they can only spot predictable, pre-modelled activity."[346]

Marty Wachocki, Lead Developer and Partner at Propel Technology said, "The future of Cybersecurity is definitely AI. There are new tools and software coming out on a constant basis now that are able to automatically adapt and detect new types of malicious activity, intrusions, attacks, etc."[347]

Steve Tcherchian, Chief Product Officer, XYPRO Technology Corporation, chimed in. "Automation and machine learning have catapulted us beyond the limitations of human skill. But what AI can

---

[344] Dixon, William and Nicole Eagan. 2019. "3 Ways AI Will Change the Nature of Cyber-attacks." World Economic Forum. June 19, 2019.

[345] *Ibid.*

[346] *Ibid.*

[347] "What's The Future of Cybersecurity? 39 Experts Share Their Insights."

promise will change and evolve our understanding for the next few years as we continue to understand its capabilities and gaps. Machines fighting machines or machines fighting humans made for great blockbuster movies 25 years ago, and that may be a reality at some point."[348]

The future of cyber warfare is also in the mobile phone realm. Israeli cyber intelligence firm features Pegasus – a brand of cyber offense that targets mobile phone users. Pegasus can gain access to Android and iOS operating systems to steal files, photos, texts, and emails. Pegasus can also spy on a phone user by monitoring the phones' still and video cameras.

The Internet of Military Things Can Be Hacked Too

You have heard of the Internet of Things, how about the Internet of Military Things, in which more and more defense infrastructure is connected via the web? Sensors and radar are examples of intelligence, surveillance, and reconnaissance "things" that are Internet-connected. Military computer processors, transmitters, and data storage are other examples. The Internet of Military Things has implications for cyber security. One way to mitigate risk is to "air gap" at least one computer on a network. Air gap means that there is a gap or physical isolation point between a local area network and a computer on the Internet. But as more and more "military things" are Internet-connected, the risk of a cyber breach goes up. Sometimes "things" are unsecure such as web cameras, microphones, and memory sticks. These can be taken on a remote control "journey" that overwhelms defenses when web cams and microphones are taken over. This has happened to the person-to-person video communication tool Zoom. As of 2020, the U.S. Department of Defense has approved Zoom for military personnel communicating in a non-classified environment or for the exchange of non-classified communication. But Zoom introduces risk and human error that can lead

---

[348] *Ibid.*

to problems as the service had security and encryption issues in 2020. Meanwhile, humans are the weakest link on the cyber kill chain, so time will tell if military personnel can exhibit proper cyber hygiene to mitigate security risk while using Zoom.

Defense Contractors Succumb to Ransomware Attacks

The future of cyber intrusions in the military are ransomware attacks on defense contractors. This happened in 2020 when defense contractor Communications and Power Industries (CPI) was attacked by ransomware and the ransom was $500,000. CPI is a contractor for the DOD and DARPA. The attack was described as when "a 'domain admin' — a user with the highest level of privileges on the network — clicked on a malicious link while they were logged in, which triggered the file-encrypting malware. Because the thousands of computers on the network were on the same, unsegmented domain, the ransomware quickly spread to every CPI office, including its on-site backups."[349]

Defense contractors have also fallen victim to "watering hole" attacks. This happens when a group of users visit the same web site from a work computer. Think of a watering hole that animals use out in the wild – that is the analogy. When hackers use a watering hole site, it is often fake and loaded with malware. It may be a site that looks exactly like a news channel such as CNN. Visitors hit the fake site and take the malware back to their network. The malware is able to make a botnet and the infected computer becomes a "slave" to the botnet. Then the botnet vacuums up all files such as sensitive and classified Microsoft Word and Excel files. One could imagine how damaging a watering hole attack is. And victims rarely know they have been breached.

---

[349] Whittaker, Zack. 2020. "Defense Contractor CPI Knocked Offline by Ransomware Attack." *TechCrunch*. March 5, 2020.

Cyber Attacks Can Diminish the Chance of a Shooting War

While much of analysis of cyber-war focuses on the goals of causing damage and reducing the risk of extreme harm, sometimes a cyber-attack can de-escalate a tense diplomatic or intelligence situation. The example would be the conflict between Iranian proxy Hezbollah and Israel. Hezbollah is usually attempting to draw Israel into an armed conflict. Israel often seeks to have an "off-ramp" to avoid kinetic operations. According to the Atlantic Council, "While kinetic options could escalate conflict and draw the ire of the international community, cyber operations can provide de-escalatory alternatives under challenging operational circumstances like southern Lebanon and Syria, where Hezbollah has embedded caches of increasingly sophisticated munitions deep within civilian population centers."[350]

In 2020, Israel responded to a reported cyber-attack on its water supply computers and infrastructure with its own attack on Iran's Natanz nuclear facility that caused fires and at least one explosion. The exchange of cyber tit-for-tat was reported by Kuwaiti newspaper *Al-Jarida*.[351]

This runs contrary to our view of warfare – that war is often a tit-for-tat group of battle tactics that ends up becoming a shooting war. The cyber-realm allows the adversaries to use less than deadly force. However, cyber-attacks on critical infrastructure could involve loss of life. Cyber-attacks to a health system or hospital could put patients in jeopardy. Ransomware against hospital record systems have placed a freeze on healthcare activity. If a doctor or nurse cannot see a patient's health records, there could be a number of victims.

Another danger would be a critical infrastructure attack on a nation's water system. Countries in desert and water insecure environments such

---

350 Handler, Simon. 2019. "The Zero-day War? How Cyber Is Reshaping the Future of the Most Combustible Conflicts." Atlantic Council. Oct. 28, 2019.

351 Frantzman, Seth J. 2020. "Arabic Media: Israeli Cyberattack Struck Natanz Nuclear Facility." Jerusalem Post. July 3, 2020.

as Israel would be placed at risk. Indeed, Israel said Iran conducted this type of cyber-attack against them in 2020. Then the Israelis responded by conducting a retaliatory attack on Iran's maritime trading infrastructure in the Strait of Hormuz. *Foreign Policy* magazine says that this stage of cyber conflict between the two nation-states has entered a public phase, which is different than the hyper-secret nature of cyber-attacks that one usually expects when analyzing cyber conflicts.[352]

As *Foreign Policy*'s Gil Baram and Kevin Lim wrote in 2020, "State-sponsored cyber-operations have long been defined by secrecy, even as they have become more important as routine instruments of statecraft in the pursuit of power, influence, and security. Their covert character is not limited to deniability but inherent in the anonymous nature of the technological medium itself."[353]

The authors believe that these Middle East cyber-attacks are going against civilian targets rather than just military targets, which is a significant departure. Also, Israel is coming out of a secretive closet to show that it will retaliate immediately, and it does not care if its cyber capabilities are shared in public.

Is this a type of mutual assured destruction between Iran and Israel with both countries playing a public game to one-up one another? My inclination is that Iran does not care whether the cyber-fight is done in secret or in public. It is satisfied with showing off its skills or not displaying its capabilities. On the Israeli side, since it is a democracy, it may want to show cyber retaliation to its citizens as a matter of transparency or for showing that the money plowed into cyber capabilities is worth the investment. Israeli Prime Minister Benjamin Netanyahu is also aware of wanting to look tough against the Iranians. Netanyahu is

---

[352] Baram, Gil and Kevjin Lim. 2020. "Israel and Iran Just Showed Us the Future of Cyberwar With Their Unusual Attacks." *Foreign Policy*. June 5, 2020.

[353] *Ibid.*

not shy about notifying the public of cyber offensive attacks against Iran and showing the public that he will protect the homeland.

Iran, while only nominally a democracy, does have a parliament and a popularly-elected prime minister, but in many ways, it is a sham democracy. The elected officials have public profiles and want to also show a toughness when it comes to facing and attacking Israel, whether conventionally or in the cyber domain.

Cyberwar and the Attribution Problem is a Huge Challenge

When it comes to attacks and potential attacks from Iran targeting the United States, Congress and the DOD is struggling with the attribution problem and how to identify and classify cyber-attacks. This makes it difficult to devise an overarching strategy for Iran because each malign event has to be treated separately and the response is then ad hoc and case-by-case. This is dangerous because the Iranians can then believe that certain attacks will not receive a proportionate response that is connected to pre-ordained U.S. strategy, operations, and attacks. Members of Congress thus ask the Pentagon to define what type of cyber-attack is an act of war deserving of a kinetic response. An example of this type of red line would be an Iranian attack on critical infrastructure – that would constitute a response. Would it be a cyber-attack from the U.S. or a kinetic traditional military attack such as an air strike? This remains the question. The situation can also be reversed. In 2019, when the Iranians shot down an American Global Hawk strategic drone – one that cost over $130 million – most of President Trump's national security team recommended and braced for an air strike against the Iranian air defense system. Trump instead gave the approval for U.S. Cyber Command to deliver an offensive cyber strike. It is not clear if Iran responded in kind with their own cyber-attack, but analyst Bruce Sussman said they did.[354]

---

[354] Sussman, Bruce. 2019. "Cyber War vs. Traditional War: The Difference Is Fading." *SecureWorld*. Dec. 27, 2019.

This is where norms and definitions make this situation murky. Was this tit-for-tat situation an example of cyber-war or was it Trump choosing one less deadly option from other violent options?

Sussman interviewed U.S. Air Force retired Colonel Cedric Leighton about Iran. "Although the Iranians are primarily regionally focused, they are also going after the United States. If tensions continue to increase with Iran, we can expect more cyber events to originate from Iran and from the IRGC cyber army."[355]

Sussman noted that analysis of warfare used to be focused on the physical realm – how many soldiers, ships, aircraft, and tanks an adversary's military has. Now this distinction is blurred and the sooner the United States and the United Kingdom accept this reality, the better they will be able to prosecute a cyberwar.

Russian Cyberwarfare Is One of a Kind

While Iran has a more concrete strategy when it comes to cyberwar, that is, to keep it as a separate domain from traditional military attacks, Russia certainly has a unique approach to cyber warfare. According to Michael Connell and Sarah Vogler of the think tank CNA, Russia is locked in an ongoing struggle inside the state and outside the state for superiority in information warfare.[356] So the Internet and free flow of information is looked at as both a threat and opportunity. Interestingly, unlike the West, Russian military intellectuals usually do not use the terms cyber and cyber warfare like Westerners do. Cyber operations are considered a part of information warfare, which is a larger concept that includes "computer networks, electronic warfare, psychological operations, and information operations."[357]

The Kremlin believes that information warfare is part of an

---

[355] *Ibid.*

[356] Connell, Michael. 2017. "Russia's Approach to Cyber Warfare." CNA.org. March, 2017.

[357] *Ibid.*

unending constant battle for supremacy. They will continue to perpetuate cyber offensive operations, not thinking they are remarkable, but the West will consider each cyber intrusion attributed to the Russians as a big deal. So, to the Russians, an offensive cyber operation is another normal day at the office for them, while the West will have self-righteous indignation about a cyber intrusion that they attribute to Russia.

The Russian military in the past few years has resisted the notion that they are responsible for offensive cyber missions, but the Kremlin has specifically directed the military to incorporate offensive and defensive cyber operations in their doctrine and in their tactics, techniques, and procedures throughout its armed forces.[358] Hacktivists and cybercriminal syndicates have been a central feature of Russian offensive cyber operations, because they are anonymous, and they give Putin plausible deniability. These operations from non-military personnel will likely be taken over by the FSB (Federal Security Service) or other Russian intelligence and government security organs such as the GRU and SVR.[359]

Cyber is thus a component of Information Warfare. The Russians do not usually use "cyber warfare" in their own language unless they are referring to another country's use of the term. The word they use is "informatization."[360] Cyber is considered a mechanism for enabling the state to dominate the information landscape, which is regarded as a "warfare domain,"[361] Cyber then is part of the whole war effort and just one of many tools. This blurring of the doctrinal definitions goes back to the Soviet Union. Information warfare is usually first used before military force, and therefore the Russians do not have to risk blood and treasure or endanger troops on the ground. It also allows them to achieve political objectives without using military force. Cyber is

---

[358] *Ibid.*

[359] *Ibid.*

[360] *Ibid.*

[361] *Ibid.*

"used as information warfare to disorganize governance, organize anti-government protests, delude adversaries, influence public opinion and reduce an opponents' will to resist," according to Russia analyst Mark Galeotti.[362] Just like artillery is used to "prep the battlefield" before a conventional military attack, the Russians believe that information operations are used first in a similar way to soften the adversary before combat starts.

The Russians, like hackers around the world, are going to get better at cyber dirty deeds. Mark Herschberg, CTO of Averon, said, "We'll continue to see the democratization of hacking. It used to belong only to those with specialized technical skills. With the growing communities on the dark web advanced hacking techniques have become productized, packaged, and sold. Hacking tools have supply chains as sophisticated as any industry."[363]

Russia, Iran, China, and North Korea each have their own vision of cyberwar, but all combatants in each country would be excited about the following attack. Singer and Friedman described a frightening scenario, "But if the computers on robotic weapons systems are compromised, they could be 'persuaded' to do the opposite of what their owners intended. This creates a whole new type of combat, where the goal may not be to destroy the enemy's tanks but to hack into his computer networks and make his tanks drive around in circles or even attack each other."[364]

China's strategy in the military realm is one of asymmetric action against Western powers such as the United States. The goal would be to use cyberwar against American military might to render the Americans

---

[362] Galeotti, Mark. "The 'Gerasimov Doctrine and Russian Non-Linear War." *In Moscow's Shadows Blog.*

[363] "What's The Future of Cybersecurity? 39 Experts Share Their Insights."

[364] *Cybersecurity and Cyberwar: What Everyone Needs to Know*, pg. 130

combat-ineffective. This is network and electronic warfare against U.S. cyber infrastructure.

As Joel Brenner, former inspector general of the National Security Agency described it, "They would target the communication and control nodes and so lead us to distrust our own systems and undermine our decision making, operations and morale. Electricity, transportation, and financial networks would be punched out. Blindness and paralysis would follow."[365]

Cyber Diplomacy Needs Norms and Rules of the Road

Cyberwar will also become more democratized as developing countries see how a small number of resources can make them adept at cyberwarfare versus how much money and resources are required for conventional warfare. Cyber diplomacy will increasingly enter the picture in the future. Governmental and non-governmental organizations are working to establish rules of the road in the cyber space. This is difficult because not everyone agrees on definitions and norms of what constitutes cyberwar. Cyber diplomats are also attempting to make certain hacks a war crime that would punish actors caught in cyber raids against institutions such as hospitals that could result in a loss of life. Microsoft has even called for a "Cyber Geneva Convention" administered by the United Nation or the G20 to establish what constitutes a cyber-crime against humanity.

What are the ethics of cyber offense? What does it mean to go too far in an attack perpetuated by the United States or allies like the United Kingdom?

Cyber warfare is ultimately a human activity. Human actions, particularly errors in cyber hygiene, lead to successful cyber-attacks. Evil humans create evil attacks. But how to extinguish the good guys from

---

[365] Brenner, Joel. 2011. *Glass Houses: Privacy, Secrecy, and Cyber Insecurity in a Transparent World*, pg. 135-6. New York: Penguin Group.

the bad guys if both groups are perpetuating cyber-attacks? One human's cyber terrorist is another human's cyber freedom fighter. It comes down to the humanity of future warfare. Cyber warfare training must include teaching modules on ethics, so operators contemplating offensive cyber actions think twice about attacks that could endanger lives.

CHAPTER EIGHT

INFORMATION WARFARE

It was a bizarre and frightening text. The Ukrainian soldier had checked his phone and did not know what to believe. His parents had received their own text that he had been killed in action and they were obviously scared and upset. But who sent the text? Pro-Russian separatists, likely with help from their Russian masters, had somehow achieved access to the soldier's contacts and found his parent's number. Then the separatists texted them with the fake message. Other soldiers received the same message. When the separatists noticed how many cell phones became active, they found the location and sent an artillery strike to that area of operations.

The pro-Russian separatists have been engaging in information war by sending numerous texts to Ukrainian regular and national guard soldiers since 2014. How did they find the soldiers' location and phone numbers? They used an electrometer, a device that measures electrical differences in extremely low voltages, perfect for spying on cell phone activity. The separatists also fly drones to conduct electromagnetic reconnaissance. The *Associated Press* described it as spying "through cell site simulators, surveillance tools long used by U.S. law enforcement to track suspects' cellphones. Photos, video, leaked documents and other clues gathered by

Ukrainian journalists suggest the equipment may have been supplied by the Kremlin."[366]

The threatening texts include messages such as your commander is running away; you should run away; you are losing your pay and money; you are surrounded and abandoned; and you can live if you retreat. This is another example of sociology in warfare through manipulation of information to move large groups of people. The separatists are also combining information warfare with psychological operations, although now they are electronic – instead of dumping paper leaflets on the enemy side – practices that are traditional in psychological operations. These tactics definitely have a human touch combined with a frightening use of technology.

The United States and NATO forces on the European continent will have to deal with this type of information warfare if there is a conflict with Russia. And they are not experienced waging information warfare over phones or unmanned aerial vehicles that can scope out electronic signatures.

Headquarters units will have to find a way to refrain from having numerous antennas in one location. These antenna farms can be spied on with their location revealed by using electrometers. And soldiers from the United States and NATO may have their GPS jammed – a practice that has been described in this book.

Information warfare, as defined by the Federation of American Scientists, is "the application of destructive force on a large scale against information assets and systems, against the computers and networks that support the four critical infrastructures (the power grid, communications, financial, and transportation).[367]

---

[366] "Sinister Text Messages Reveal High-tech Front in Ukraine War." *Voice Of America*. May 11, 2017.

[367] Lewis, Brian C. "Information Warfare." FAS.org.

Information Warfare or Information Operations can also be defined as the dissemination of various media by a variety of means to attain political or military objectives.[368] Various media includes propaganda, news, and disinformation. According to the Congressional Research Service, information warfare campaigns can include spreading false or altered information to create confusion or revealing damaging personal information against a targeted country, group, or individual.[369] Russian information operations are often just a way for the government to tell lies and create falsehoods that sow doubt in people's minds. Information operations are considered grey or hybrid warfare. During the Cold War, influential diplomat George Kennan described information operations as "employment of all the means at a nation's command, short of war, to achieve its national objectives. Such operations are both overt and covert. They range from such overt actions as political alliances, economic measures, and 'white' propaganda to such covert operations as clandestine support of 'friendly' foreign elements, 'black' psychological warfare and even encouragement of underground resistance in hostile states."[370]

Other Countries and Terrorists Practice Information Operations

Along with Russia, China has historically used information warfare to create a strategic advantage. Currently, it has targeted the United States through American academia recruiting faculty members to share their research and locating Confucius Institutes that communicate pro-China cultural aspects to students. Recently, it has attempted to control the narrative of the coronavirus and Covid-19, by blaming the virus spread on the U.S. Army.

---

[368] Theohary, Catherine A. 2018. "Information Warfare: Issues for Congress." Congressional Research Service. March 5, 2018.

[369] *Ibid.*

[370] *Ibid.*

North Korea is a master at internal propaganda and "purple rhetoric" to the outside world. Purple rhetoric is when the North Koreans use words that are completely over the top, such as calling the United States "capitalist pig dogs" and threatening nuclear war. Kim Jong Un's sister Kim Yo Jong convinced many Western media outlets that she was a rising diplomatic star at the 2018 Winter Olympics in South Korea. The North Koreans considered her display of public diplomacy an information operations propaganda win.

According to the Congressional Research Service, Iran's "information operations target and discredit dissenters and adversaries, both domestic and foreign—to include journalists, online media activists, and human rights defenders—and limiting or prohibiting attempts by protesters to coordinate and organize."[371]

ISIS at one point had mobile television stations they used to indoctrinate new members with propaganda that looked like a Western television news program. They had news vans pull into towns and set up large screens so a crowd could watch the show.

The widespread use of information warfare by American and Western adversaries, has some observers calling for the U.S. Cyber Command be broadened to become the U.S. Information Warfare Command. This would enable friendly forces to adapt to the 21st century way of conducting war – encompassing historical precedent and future aspirations – to go from dropping leaflets to moving toward the digital realm of information warfare. This would also allow U.S. Psychological Operations and Civil Affairs to be continually co-located at the army Special Operations Command at Fort Bragg and the new proposed U.S. Information Warfare Command.

One of the difficulties of information warfare is getting people and entities to agree on what it is and how it will define warfare in the

---

[371] *Ibid.*

future. There are many domains associated with information warfare as Lt. Gen. Stephen G. Fogarty, Army Cyber Command's commanding general, pointed out in a conference in 2019. "With the growing threat within the cyber and information domains, the army is already looking into better ways to leverage its signal, cyber, information and psychological operations, electronic warfare, intelligence, and public affairs capabilities," Fogarty said.[372]

Information warfare has become an "all of the above" proposition. The United States, the United Kingdom, and NATO allies must define it and prioritize the different aspects of it. Nevertheless, Western intelligence and espionage will likely stay in their silos in the future and will not be part of information warfare even though it probably should be. Public affairs should be separate because it is more like media relations and should not be part of a targeted information or propaganda campaign. Psychological operations should be part of information warfare as should electronic warfare, jamming, spoofing, and countermeasures. That leaves the cyber-domain, and it will likely fall under the information warfare construct in the future.

Brian David Johnson, a futurist at Arizona State University, said at the same conference noted above that "the increase in cyber capabilities by non-state actors and near-peer competitors means the U.S. military must prepare for conflict within the physical, cognitive, and digital domains."[373] This means that information warfare becomes ambiguous and grey – in a murky region that makes it difficult to define. This is why many observers believe that information warfare can be called grey, ambiguous, and hybrid as well. Hybrid warfare was covered in the beginning of this book, but it combines information warfare with the physical or human domain – kinetic and traditional. This indeed is the future of

---

[372] Suits, Devon. 2019. "Growing Concern Over Information Warfare Continues to Shape Military." *Army News Service*. Dec. 5, 2019.

[373] *Ibid.*

warfare and it is happening now, prosecuted most effectively by Russia along with Israel and Hamas.

Classic Information Warfare Is Between Israel and Hamas

One example of blatant information warfare was perpetuated by Hamas against Israel in 2017. Fake accounts set up by Hamas operatives pretended to be Israeli women linked with Israeli soldiers on Facebook. The fake accounts gathered sensitive information via Facebook messaging while Israeli soldiers thought they were communicating with "attractive" women in Israel and overseas. After friending each other on Facebook, Hamas operatives convinced the soldiers to download a separate mobile chat application that enabled the terrorists to steal sensitive information such as contacts and images. This is the 21st century version of the "honeypot trap" by dangling attractive females to an intelligence target. Like many soldiers, the Israelis had taken photos of where they were stationed, unwittingly supplying Hamas with valuable intelligence. The Israel Defense Forces have tried to restrict social media use by military personnel, but this has proved difficult since Israel has a draft beginning when people are 18-years-old who are avid consumers of social media.

Hamas has used grey-zone warfare against the Israelis by combining information operations with kinetic activities such as rocket attacks and tunneling to move arms and material for terror acts, in order to change the facts on the ground without using combatants. Cyber activities are also part of the grey-zone warfare. As conflict analyst Omer Dostri noted, "The purpose of this kind of warfare is to achieve political, economic, and security advantages by acting below the threshold of war with vague military, diplomatic, cybernetic, and information tools thereby trying to prevent the rival from responding with force."[374]

---

[374] Dostri, Omer. 2020. "The Reemergence of Gray-Zone Warfare in Modern Conflicts: Israel's Struggle against Hamas's Indirect Approach." *Military Review*. Jan.-Feb. 2020.

Hamas also works to force Israeli media to write and present articles and newscasts that dissuade Israel to fight back against Hamas. Hamas has utilized social media to get the international community to side with its cause by highlighting civilian casualties that happen when Israel uses drone strikes and traditional air strikes from aircraft that cause collateral damage. In turn, the IDF social media also highlights civilian casualties caused by Hamas rocket attacks. In 2012, both sides used Twitter often. In a visual propaganda study by University of Kansas, scholar Hyunjin Seo found that "Images posted by Hamas often resorted to the emotional propaganda frame to increase effects of their messages. Hamas frequently tweeted pictures of sobbing parents or relatives in front of babies and children killed or injured by Israeli airstrikes. Hamas also posted an image contrasting an Israeli girl sleeping on a comfortable bed holding a teddy bear with Palestinian children killed and laid in a hospital bed. The caption for the photo read, 'That's the way children all over the world sleep. That is the way our children sleep forever.'"[375]

Grey-zone warfare and information operations are a cheap option for Hamas compared to costly force-on-force pitched battles against Israel. Sometimes grey-zone warfare results in a kinetic response. In 2019, Israel responded to a Hamas cyber-attack with an air strike. The Israelis claimed they found a building where Hamas had cyber operatives conducting attacks against the IDF. The Israelis said they removed the physical structure of "HamasCyberHQ.exe" from the battlefield. This set back Hamas cyber operations for a number of months until Hamas could revert to the status quo with a new center for cyber-attacks against Israel. This, of course, would be easy since the Internet is ubiquitous, and a new cyber center could be set up immediately by Hamas. The Israeli attack was thus symbolic and used as a deterrent against the terror group,

---

[375] Seo, Hyunjin. 2014. "Visual Propaganda in the Age of Social Media: Twitter Images during 2012 Israeli-Hamas Conflict. *Visual Communication Quarterly*, Vol. 21: Issue 3, Pp. 150-161.

but it is interesting that Israel would scale up a kinetic attack after they were the victim of an information warfare attack. Look for this to be the future of information warfare in Israel and the Gaza Strip.

One of the most insidious information warfare attacks conducted by Hamas happened in 2001. A Palestinian woman named Amna Muna used a chat virtual meeting on the Israeli "ICQ" instant messaging service to lure an Israeli teenager to a location in Ramallah, in the West Bank, where he was ambushed and killed by Hamas operatives.

Information Warfare is Second Nature to Russia

Like Hamas and Israel, Russia has battled hard in the information warfare space against various enemies. Russia learned much from interventions in Chechnya and Georgia on how to control information that was coming out of those conflicts. Russia found that both Chechnya and Georgia initially controlled the information narrative as Moscow struggled to deliver its pro-Russian message to its own public and the rest of the world. The Chechen militants lost the information battle after they made spectacular terror attacks against Russian civilians that killed hundreds, even children. In Georgia, Russia also met its match as both sides tried to accuse each other of war crimes, and both tried to defend their intentions during and after the five-day war. In the Chechen wars and during interventions in Georgia and Syria, Russia allowed embedded reporters to offer the Russian point of view from the front. In the Ukraine, the Ukrainian government has been a worthy adversary against Russia when it comes to information warfare through the media, especially when it comes to blaming Russia for violent attacks in the Donbass region.

As a result, the Russian government has attempted to control the domestic media environment at all times by treating issues as a form of warfare that they learned during the military interventions. Thus, information operations are constantly on a war footing inside Russia. Domestic policy journalists often follow the party line drawn up by

Putin's political party United Russia. They rarely cover stories having to do with political opposition. Russia is trying to form a closed Internet similar to China's closed Internet. This allows the government to control the narrative that it wants and control the information that suppresses internal dissent. One example of Internet repression is that Internet cafes require users to provide their cell phone number so individuals can be tracked if they use sites that the government does not approve of.

Russia is still connected to the global Internet and it has Russian-language versions of Facebook and Google and then they have VK and Yandex as social media platforms. All sites that could possibly create any political risk for Putin are monitored closely by a sophisticated tool called SORM which records all Internet activity and is a powerful means for discovering and controlling online dissent. Those online repressive measures are for the domestic side of Russian politics. It is obviously much more difficult to control the Internet outside of Russia and thus control the message. So overseas, Russia has decided to control information using government-sponsored television and multimedia outlets RT and Sputnik. The Russian government uses official and unofficial social media channels to disseminate messages and combines these with statements by Russian government officials who usually enjoy having plausible deniability during military operations in Ukraine and Syria. Even though this propaganda is usually not believed by people outside of Russia and its allies, Russians are able to sow reasonable doubt and uncertainty. This creates a grey area in which the Russian government is difficult to pin down on their role in whatever event the Kremlin is attempting to monitor or influence. Examples of this are denials that the so-called "Green Men" operating in Ukraine were Russia military personnel. Russia decided to use this kind of information operations before the start of the annexation of Crimea.

Before the Euromaidan revolution, Russia began discrediting and slandering the European Union and NATO. The government decided that one way to influence ties to the EU was to target conservative and religious Ukrainians and send them the message that the EU was going to push LGBTQ rights on them against their will. Another large part of Russian information operations and propaganda is the use of trolls or pro-Russia online agitators that are either run by humans or remote-controlled Internet political bots. A political bot is an automated account set up to make posts without human intervention usually with a made-up screen name and fake photo. Atlantic Council's Digital Forensic Research Lab described the political bot process using the terms "shepherds, sheepdogs and electric sheep."[376]

Political Operations Using Bots and Human Trolls Difficult to Counter

Political operations utilizing bots start off with a number of "shepherd" accounts run by human users with large followings. Connected to the shepherd account are the "sheepdog" accounts. These are also human-run, and they are meant to retweet, like, and repost the original political signal.[377] Then the bots act as "electronic sheep, mindlessly re-posting content."[378] Political bots, according to the Atlantic Council, can post over 46,000 Tweets on an issue in less than four hours.[379] This all makes it look like there is a fake large-scale social movement going on, often called astroturf. Once this takes place, journalists from RT and Sputnik report on it, so if there is a disinformation campaign, it will look legitimate when reported by RT and Sputnik. They simply have to do a screen shot of the social media and show all the tweets, likes, and re-tweets. Sometimes the purpose is to create a fake hashtag trend on Twitter to make it look like there is a legitimate interest around a trend. These trolls

---

[376] Nimmo, Ben. 2017. "Why Bot Makers Dream of Electric Sheep." Atlantic Council. June 22, 2017.

[377] *Ibid.*

[378] *Ibid.*

[379] *Ibid.*

and bots are used to amplify a positive message about the Russian government or to amplify a message of denial.

To discredit western sources or to send propaganda messages to Russian "compatriot" speakers who are watching Russian television news and who want to do further research on the Internet, human trolls often post, like, or re-tweet on social media. They also prefer hanging out in "comments" sections on online news sites and attempt to hijack the comments toward a Pro-Russian message to create uncertainty. Russian trolls are particularly good at creating a plausible alternative story line that is very believable to Russian speakers who live outside Russia. They masquerade as real people and will convincingly interact with existing groups and commenters to spread their message and disguise the true identity of the account-holder. This is what State Department technology adviser Matt Chessen called computational propaganda done by machine-driven communication tools.[380] Computational propaganda is defined by the Oxford Internet Institute as the "use of algorithms, automation, and human curation to purposefully distribute misleading information over social media networks."[381]

In 2015, the *Guardian* newspaper identified a Russia "troll house" in St. Petersburg, which at the time was seen as the headquarters of Russia's troll army, the Internet Research Agency.[382] These trolls were being paid by reaching their quota of posts each day. If employees did not meet their quota of posts they were fined, according to former workers interviewed for the story. They were paid around $800 a month to create an online persona that sometimes made "normal" posts about non-controversial

---

[380] Chessen, Matt. 2017. "Understanding the Psychology Behind Computational Propaganda." *Can Public Diplomacy Survive the Internet?* May 2017.

[381] Woolley, Samuel C. and Phillip N. Howard, 2017. "Computational Propaganda Worldwide: Executive Summary." Oxford Internet Institute. June 19, 2017.

[382] Walker, Shawn. 2015. "The Russian Troll Factory at the Heart of the Meddling Allegations." *The Guardian*. April 2, 2015.

topics. At certain times they attacked the Ukrainian government as fascist or corrupt.[383] Each morning the human trolls would receive the "messages of the day" and were told to make their efforts conform to the message of the day.[384] They worked in teams of three, so one would post a complaint and then the other two would jump in and comment on the pro-Kremlin message of the day.[385]

Other trolls worked on "comedy sites" to make fun of American and Ukrainian political figures. Many of these comic sites had racist imagery of President Obama.[386] The main rules were to never post anything bad about the ethnic Russian areas of Ukraine and to never post anything good about the Ukrainian government. Facebook said on October 30, in 2016, that 126 million Americans may have seen Russian-linked political posts.[387] Facebook said that "Russia-based operatives published 80,000 posts on the social network over a two-year period in an effort to sway U.S. politics."[388] These were from Russia's top troll farm – the Internet Research Agency.[389] Facebook said this may have reached around half of the voting age population in the United States. Twitter said it had found 2,752 accounts linked to Russian operatives.[390] Google said it had found evidence that Russian linked accounts tried to influence the U.S. election with ads, although the spending was not a lot – around $5,000. Google found a separate $53,000 worth of ads with political material that were purchased from Russian internet addresses,

---

383 *Ibid.*

384 *Ibid.*

385 *Ibid.*

386 *Ibid.*

387 Ingram, David. 2017. "Facebook Says 126 Million Americans May Have Seen Russia-linked Political Posts." *Reuters*. Oct. 30, 2017.

388 *Ibid.*

389 *Ibid.*

390 *Ibid.*

building addresses, or with rubles.[391] It was not clear whether any of those were connected to the Russian government, and they may have been purchased by Russian citizens. The Russians used three of the most popular web properties in the world, headquartered in the U.S., against the U.S. to undermine American democracy.

This all falls under the rubric of "disinformation" and "computational propaganda." Disinformation, according to Alina Polyakova, then at the Brookings Institute, is "more than 'fake news' – it is a strategy primarily deployed by the Kremlin, amplified by Russian-affiliated social media accounts, organizations and media outlets, and supported by data theft. It is not random. It has an intent and aim that goes beyond U.S. elections and elections in general."[392] Polyakova believes that the Russians conduct disinformation attacks every day against Ukraine.[393]

Russian Government Are Still Using Compromising Material on People It Does Not Like

Russia also uses disinformation campaigns to discredit individuals it despises; this goes back to the days of the KGB and the Cold War. The KGB was always incredibly good at blackmail by collecting embarrassing and compromising information on targeted individuals. So, this is an important concept to know about Russian disinformation campaigns. It is called "Kompromat," which is a contraction of the phrase "compromising materials"

According to Levi Maxey of the *Cipher Brief*, the objective of Kompromat is to smear reputations of political opponents to discredit

[391] *Ibid.*

[392] Polyakova, Alina. 2017. "Why Talk About Disinformation Now?" Atlantic Council. June 21, 2017.

[393] *Ibid.*

their voices.[394] "The goal is to intimidate and pressure would-be critics through personal and salacious images, videos and documents – both real and doctored – with threats of disclosure for those that don't fall in line...and send a message of deterrence to anyone considering getting in the Kremlin's way," Maxey wrote.[395]

Moscow leverages Russian-sponsored media when distributing Kompromat: both traditional outlets such as RT and Sputnik – and even unwitting foreign media – and it leverages social media through Kremlin-paid trolling organizations such as the Internet Research Agency. Kompromat only needs to create a sense of doubt – or rather the mere possibility of truth – to have the desired effects. There is no need, or even necessarily a desire, to prove the outrageous claims.[396]

If operations fail to undermine or coerce those targeted, they are merely left by the wayside with little to no blowback for the perpetrators, as kompromat is often nonattributable or at the very least, plausibly deniable, according to the *Cipher Brief*.[397] Putin is always interested in having plausible deniability as I have discussed before. As the indictments have made clear, the U.S. Office of the Director of National Intelligence released its report on Russian activities during the 2016 elections.[398] The report said that the CIA, the FBI, and the NSA have "high confidence" that Putin ordered an influence campaign in 2016 aimed at the presidential election in order to "undermine public faith in the US democratic process, denigrate Hillary Clinton, and harm her electability

394 Maxey, Levi. 2018. "Inside the Competitive, Corrupt World of Russian Intelligence." *The Cipher Brief*. April 20, 2018.

395 *Ibid.*

396 *Ibid.*

397 *Ibid.*

398 "Assessing Russian Activities and Intentions in Recent US Elections." Office of the Director of National Intelligence. Jan. 6, 2017.

and potential presidency."[399] U.S. Office of the Director of National Intelligence believes the Russians were behind the spear-phishing attack on the Democratic National Committee and Clinton's campaign chairman John Podesta. The Russians also infiltrated the email accounts of Democrat staff members for the Clinton campaign, the DNC and other Democrat organizations, according to the report. Russians also reportedly tried to breach the Republican National Committee, but they were not successful.[400] The Russians then allegedly turned over the emails to Wikileaks for dissemination, according to the ODNI report. Russian intelligence also accessed elements of multiple state or local electoral boards. Election-related networks, including web sites, in 21 states were potentially targeted by Russian cyber actors.[401]

Russia Targets Voting Integrity in United States

There have not been many investigations into the 21 states that were targeted at the local level, but there were some strange things happening at local American polling places in 2016. Most of it was attributed to a software provider called VR Systems that had been penetrated by Russian hackers months before election day.[402] VR Systems provides back-office software used by election precincts. Most precincts use thick binders of voter records when people come into vote to show their voter registration cards or identification. VR Systems replaced these "poll books" with applications that run on laptops and tablets. Election campaign precincts in Durham, North Carolina used devices with VR Systems software and election officials believe this is why Durham had all kinds

[399] *Ibid.*

[400] *Ibid.*

[401] *Ibid.*

[402] Zetter, Kim. 2019. "Software Vendor May Have Opened a Gap for Hackers in 2016 Swing State." *Politico*. June 5, 2019.

of difficulty on election day, according to the *New York Times*.[403] Chaos ensued. Some people were turned away from the polls, others were sent from one polling place to another, some were told they had already voted. Election officials had similar complaints from precincts in states that ran the same software that they believed had been hacked and tampered with by the Russians. Other counties in North Carolina, Virginia, Georgia, and Arizona complained of things going haywire with their devices running VR Systems software.[404]

Russia has been conducting information warfare against the United States for many years. A Russian information operations campaign dubbed "Secondary Infektion" spent six years forging documents and setting up fake social media accounts to sow discord in America and other Western countries.[405] The operation used Twitter, Facebook, YouTube, and Reddit to influence elections by coming up with bogus articles, blog posts, and tweets from politicians and Trump cabinet officials and allies such as Senator Marco Rubio and Secretary of State Mike Pompeo. Over the years, Secondary Infektion posted malign content in seven languages across 300 Internet properties. One method the group used was to stoke tensions between white Americans and African-Americans. This was before the death of George Floyd who died in police custody in 2020 resulting in global protests. Secondary Infektion came up with a phony nonprofit called the Black Defense Foundation and posted a blog calling for a full political separation between whites and blacks.[406]

As the German Marshall Fund's Brad Hanlon wrote, "Kremlin accounts are not creating new disputes between groups, but rather

---

403 *Ibid.*

404 *Ibid.*

405 Newman, Lily Hay. 2020. "The Russian Disinformation Operation You Never Heard About." *Wired*. June 16, 2020.

406 *Ibid.*

inserting themselves into existing fractures in American society in an attempt to push people further from compromise."[407]

China Wages Information Warfare

China is constantly perpetuating information warfare against Taiwan, which it considers a wayward province and not a sovereign nation. Like the Russians, China has troll factories that spread misinformation. They also have loyalists in Taiwan who do not accept that the Taiwanese should have their own sovereign country. So, these people, who include opinion influencers, are constantly agitating for the Chinese point of view. These individuals are made up of politicians and those that work as public relations and public affairs professionals, and lobbyists. The influence operations are usually conducted prior to elections, especially during voting for the premiership, in which the Chinese want political leadership that is friendly to Beijing and leaders who do not want independence for Taiwan.

Like Russia, the Chinese always have what Henry Kissinger called a "prickly sense of sovereignty." They are sensitive and obviously concerned about democracy promotion and advancement in Hong Kong. Hong Kong has also been ground zero for Chinese information warfare. The Chinese use state-run media to make the protesters seems like they are being paid to protest. They take photos and video and change the context and meaning of the media. For example, a person from Hong Kong could be shown shopping with a wad of cash in her hands, and Chinese media could say she was being a paid operative as a part of fake "astroturf" instead of legitimate and organic protests bubbling up from the grass roots. They also label the protesters as terrorists.[408] Thus, China

---

[407] Hanlon, Brad. 2018. "It's Not Just Facebook: Countering Russia's Social Media Offensive." Alliance for Securing Democracy. April 11, 2018.

[408] Myers, Steven Lee and Paul Mozer. "China's Information War Is Trying to Turn Its Citizens Against Hong Kong Protesters." *The Independent*. Aug. 14, 2019.

uses propaganda as warfare because to paraphrase ancient Chinese military strategist Sun Zu, it is better to subdue the enemy without actually fighting in a physical manner. Beijing also depends on its great Internet firewall to cut off access to Western social media and to censor what is on Chinese social media. This creates a misinformation effect that makes Hong Kong demonstrators seem less legitimate and burns the image of protesters into citizens of the mainland as miscreant troublemakers.

Iran Flexes Its Muscles with Information Warfare

The Iranians target Western social media, particularly Facebook, to sow division in American elections. The Atlantic Council's Digital Forensic Research Lab found that the Iranians were using malign Facebook and Twitter pages and posts to favor Democrats over Republicans in the 2018 midterm Congressional elections to undermine President Trump's political power.[409] Most of these pages and accounts were ultimately removed by Facebook and Twitter, but not before they weaved their devious web. About a third of the pages on Facebook had been active since 2014. Two accounts went back as far as 2010.[410] The posts were in at least eight different languages which shows ambition and global reach on behalf of the Iranians. Many of the pages also targeted Israel and Saudi Arabia.

As the Atlantic Council concluded as reported by *The Cyber Edge*, "the Digital Forensics Research Lab research showed that Iran relies on artificial amplification to get traction for its information operations. Some of the Iran-linked pages the lab analyzed generated high levels of organic traffic; others had less organic-looking engagement levels and likely relied on artificial amplification to reach their target audiences, including bots and inorganic engagement farms. The artificial

---

[409] Barojian, Donara. 2019. "Eight Takeaways From Iranian Information Operations." *The Cyber Edge*. April 1, 2019.

[410] *Ibid.*

amplification was not limited to one social network and appeared to have been used on both Twitter and Facebook."[411]

In 2018, *Reuters* found that Iran had an information operation that used 70 web sites in 15 countries to disseminate pro-Iranian propaganda. The sites were visited by about 500,000 people a month and then amplified on social media accounts that had more than a million members.[412]

North Korea Wages Information War Too

North Korea is also a talented player in the disinformation game. Operatives from North Korea often use cyber methods to hack into journalists' accounts to spread misinformation and propaganda in South Korea. The Foundation for the Defense of Democracies in 2020 quoted a South Korean think tank that "North Korea employs 7,000 agents engaged in propaganda and information warfare."[413] North Korea also uses information operations against its own citizens. Even though some people in the North are getting smart phones, the state monitors and censors all activity.

We have entered a period of Forever War, not necessarily kinetic with bullets and missiles flying, but warfare in the information sphere that is constantly evolving, used by nation states and non-state actors. It is becoming more and more difficult to spot and to act against. As data analyst Renee DiResta pointed out after Congressional testimony in 2018, "We should anticipate an increase in the misuse of less resourced social platforms, and an increase in the use of peer-to-peer encrypted

---

411 *Ibid.*

412 Stubbs, Jack and Christopher Bing. 2018. "Special Report: How Iran Spreads Disinformation Around the World." *Reuters*. Nov. 30, 2018.

413 Ha, Matthew. 2020. "North Korea Turns to Cyber Disinformation Attacks Amid Global Coronavirus Outbreak." Foundation for the Defense of Democracies. April 11, 2020.

messaging services. Future campaigns will be compounded by the use of witting or unwitting people through whom state actors will filter their propaganda. And we should anticipate the incorporation of new technologies, such as videos ("deep fakes") and audio produced by AI, to supplement these operations, making it increasingly difficult for people to trust what they see."[414]

Deep Fakes Become a Problem

DARPA is trying to fight deep fakes. Deep fakes are fake synthetic videos that can mimic a human voice and facial expressions that are on video. They are named for the deep learning techniques they use to exploit artificial intelligence. The danger of deep fakes is that they can spread like wildfire on today's social media platforms. Many deep fakes are compelling for people who often trust what they see on the web. Deep fakes can also do still photo manipulation. DARPA's Media Forensics unit is attempting to combat forged and spoofed video. Sometimes deep fakes can be used for entertainment purposes, but DARPA is concerned about international security because deep fakes can be utilized for information warfare and propaganda purposes. DARPA's Media Forensics unit brings together researchers from around the country. These scientists are building a smart platform that will identify deep fakes or any type of photos and video that is being manipulated for malign purposes. The platform will sniff out information on how deep fakes are performed. The issue is challenging because the bad guys are using their own artificial intelligence and neural network software to change video and photographs for the wrong reasons. It is relatively easy to get one's hands on the deep fake software. People use "FakeApp," an application that is readily available to users who know how to deploy programs on TensorFlow, Google's open-source artificial intelligence framework.

---

[414] DiResta, Renee. 2018. "The Information War Is On. Are We Ready For It?" *Wired*. Aug. 3, 2018.

Images, of course, have been manipulated for a long time. The Soviet Union intelligence organs used to change photos for blackmail purposes. It is easy and straightforward to change an image on Adobe Photoshop. It is not just the Russians perpetrating these activities. The Qatari government has been the victim of deep fakes that hold Qatar in a damaging light to stir unrest in the Middle East.

In 2019, DARPA modified their program to get more input from the public and private sector. The Semantic Forensics program, a next-generation procurement format based on Media Forensics, will look at fake images, audio, and video. Computers will be used to spot fakes by ferreting out semantic errors which are a giveaway for deep fakes. These telltale signals can also solve the attribution problem that will tell analysts who, what, and where the deep fake is produced. People who make deep fakes will always have the first mover advantage in the same way a zero-day computer virus or spear phishing technique is unveiled and used by bad actors. So, protection from deep fakes must be defensive in nature. This gives an advantage to the individuals and groups who are operating video, audio, and photo deep fakes for nefarious reasons. Fortunately, defensive programs against deep fakes can usually spot shadows, light, and blinking patterns, or they at least attempt to do so. But despite the advances, deep fakes pose a pernicious threat. The Intelligence Advanced Research Projects Activity (IARPA) is also offering funds to supply a contest on best ways to defend against deep fakes.

The Washington Post interviewed Hany Farid, a computer-science professor and digital-forensics expert at the University of California at Berkeley in 2019. Farid believes playing defense has its drawbacks and can be overwhelming to fight back. "We are outgunned. The number of people working on the video-synthesis side, as opposed to the detector side, is 100 to 1," said Farid.[415]

---

[415] Harwell, Drew. 2018. "Top AI Researchers Race to Detect 'Deepfake' Videos: 'We Are Outgunned.'" *Washington Post*. June 12, 2019.

The U.S. Army has a biometric video, audio, and photo database that is being used to compare deep fakes in order to determine authenticity. These databases can identify media that is produced by bad actors and has all video, audio, and photos having to do with intelligence and defense. This includes terrorists and those who have been apprehended on the battlefield during the global war on terror.

Mass Media Is a Part of Information Warfare

Aside from modern databases, sometimes media coverage is the information warfare that makes the difference in warfare. Historically, information warfare used to, and still can, convince the general public that war is not worth it, and it is time to sue for peace. Therefore, media coverage is information that affects warfare.[416] Clifton Morgan borrowed heavily from Clausewitz in arriving at a definition of war. Since war is not an "independent thing," and that it is part of the political discourse, "An understanding of war cannot be based solely on a definition of war, which can only isolate the set of wars from the set of non-wars. Rather it is necessary to appreciate conceptually how war fits into a broader context."[417]

Morgan broke down the literature of war definitions into two camps—the case for war as bargaining and the case for war as force.[418] Scholars such as Thomas Schelling[419] and Henry Kissinger[420] argued that a limited form of war will eventually lead to a settlement or agreement

---

[416] Morgan, Clifton 1990. "The Concept of War: Its Impact on Research and Policy." *Peace and Change*. Vol. 15 (October): pp. 413-41.

[417] *Ibid*, pg. 419

[418] *Ibid.*

[419] Schelling, Thomas. 1983. "Conservatism, Not Interventionism: Trends in Foreign Policy Opinion 1974-1982." In *International Systems Structure and American Foreign Policy*.

[420] Kissinger, Henry. 1957. *Nuclear Weapons and Foreign Policy*. New York: Harper.

between the two parties.[421] Morgan wrote, "According to this conceptualization, war is an instrument of, and inseparable from, bargaining."[422] The opposing view of war sees force as the prime means of achieving a political outcome. Or war may be fought as bargaining or as force, as Clausewitz described," War can be of two kinds...to overthrow the enemy—to render him politically helpless or militarily impotent, thus forcing him to sign whatever peace we please, or merely to occupy some of his frontier districts so that we can annex them or use them for bargaining at the peace negotiations."[423]

The different viewpoints on the conceptualization of war are important because policy makers wrestle with these notions as they attempt to shape policy, set agendas, and transmit their intentions in the media. This is where disconnect occurs—policy uncertainty, elite dissensus, framing, agenda setting, manufactures consent, and policy media-interaction arise from competing concepts of how war is defined in the media. Disparate concepts of war give rise to the push-pull theories of the media shaping policy.

The concept of casualties in warfare is an excellent example of this type of disconnect in the conceptualization of war in the media, as explained by opinion data collected by Daniel Byman and Matthew Waxman.[424]

"The data indicated that support for coercive operations is likely to erode as casualties rise, particularly when vital interests are not at stake, when the public views victory as unlikely, and when the non-administration elite do not support the policy."[425] Further study in war cover-

---

[421] Morgan, Clifton. 1990.

[422] *Ibid*, pg. 424.

[423] *Ibid*, pg. 429.

[424] Byman, Daniel and Matthew Waxman. 2002. *The Dynamics of Coercion: American Foreign Policy and the Limits of Military Might.* New York: Cambridge University Press

[425] *Ibid.*

age by the media would appear to support many of the categories of theory on how the media affects policy. And this fear of casualties can be a good rule of thumb to apply to the problems of modern war in the post-Vietnam era.

Often political leaders prefer the less costly measures of high-tech weapons and the use of technological rather than human capital. Erik Gartzke wrote on the U.S. cruise missile strike on Iraq in 1996, "Fear of casualties, particularly so close to an election, was thought to have led administration officials to choose the costly pilot-less weapons." And a similar thought process reportedly inspired actions in the former Yugoslavia, "In the Bosnia and Kosovo crises, NATO leaders restricted military action to air strikes and cruise missile attacks, apparently to limit casualties"[426]

These fears of high casualties go hand in hand with fears of the protracted struggle. This ties the length of war with the erosion of public support. D.S. Bennett and A.C. Stam pointed out that after 18 months of war, democracies must respond to public opinion.[427] And often this public opinion is centered on whether to intervene at all in humanitarian causes. Michael Mandelbaum believed the question of intervention is a conceptual one, and to paraphrase, he asked, do some groups deserve to have support in building a new country? And if one decides to help that country, what is the best way to do it?[428]

These questions are more modern forms of the questions asked in opinion studies conducted after the Vietnam War. As Bruce Russett and Miroslav Nincic observed, "public opinion is now much less favorably

---

[426] Gartzke, Erik. 2002. *The Dynamics of Coercion: American Foreign Policy and the Limits of Military Might.* New York: Cambridge University Press.

[427] Bennett, D.S. and A.C. Stam. 2002. "The Declining Advantages of Democracy: A Combined Model of War, Outcomes, and Duration." *Journal of Conflict Resolution.* Vol. 42: pp. 344-366.

[428] Mandelbaum, Michael. 1994. "The Reluctance to Intervene." *Foreign Policy.* Vol: 95, Summer 1994: pg. 16.

disposed toward the use of American military force abroad than at any time since the beginning of the Cold War.[429] Russett and Nincic also found that the public is highly selective when it comes to choosing where the United States should send forces, and that this phenomenon has to do with geographic proximity to the U.S. "The public willingness to employ American forces also depends strongly on the nature of the threat. Depending on the country threatened, between two and four times as many people would use American troops to defend against an external attack as against an indigenous insurgency."[430]

John Mueller found in a comparative study of public opinion data from the Vietnam and Korean wars that "In each war, support is projected to have started at much the same level and then every time American casualties increased by a factor of 10 (i.e., from 100 to 1,000 or from 10,000 to 100,000), support for the war dropped by about 15 percentage points."[431]

Intervention, the Vietnam Syndrome, and fear of casualties were not the only trend in public opinion and foreign policy in the late 70's and early 80's. Researchers such as William Schneider found that from 1974 to 1982; public opinion began to slide toward a more conservative rather than interventionist or isolationist profile.[432] Schneider pointed toward events such as the Iran hostage crisis and the Soviet invasion of Afghanistan and credited them for working to "revive the national will."[433]

---

[429] Russett, Bruce and Miroslav Nincic. 1976. "American Opinion on the Use of Military Force Abroad." *Political Science Quarterly*. Vol. 91: (Autumn, 1976): pg. 411.

[430] *Ibid*, pg. 430

[431] Mueller, John. 1971. "Trends in Popular Support of the Wars in Korea and Vietnam. *The American Political Science Review*. Vol. 65: (June 1971): pp. 358-375.

[432] Schneider, William. 1982. "Conservatism, Not Interventionism: Trends in Foreign Policy Opinion 1974-1982." *International Systems Structure and American Foreign Policy*.

[433] *Ibid*, pg. 35.

Schneider, through data collected from the National Opinion Research Center, was able to construct a model based on disagreement on foreign policy issues. He found that "internationalists," those better-educated Americans who paid more attention to foreign affairs and preferred a more active U.S. engagement in international affairs, split into two camps.[434] Conservative internationalists "pictured the world primarily in East-West terms: democracy versus totalitarianism, capitalism versus communism, freedom versus repression."[435] Liberal internationalists emphasized economic and humanitarian problems over security issues and rejected a hegemonic role for the United States. They wanted leaders to think in global terms: the scarcity of natural resources, environmental and oceanic pollution, and international economic inequality. [436]

Both sides sought to put more morality back into the Kissinger notions of balance of power and national interest foreign policy. These two sides, however, do not cover the full spectrum of American foreign policy opinion in the 70's. "Non-internationalists, who comprised almost half of the American public in the 1974 study, do not share this moralism. They are suspicious of international involvements of any kind... unless a clear and compelling issue of national interest or national security is at stake. If we are directly threatened or if our interest *is* involved in any important way, this group wants swift, decisive action but not long-term involvement."[437] The significance of this group is clear to the politically-savvy; this group is the swing vote that "swings left and right unpredictably in response to its current fears and concerns."[438] For example, noninterventionists support a strong military in general, but fear long military interventions in cases like Vietnam, Iraq, and Afghanistan.

---

[434] *Ibid.*

[435] *Ibid*, pg. 40.

[436] *Ibid.*

[437] *Ibid*, pg. 42.

[438] *Ibid.*

Noninterventionists can swing and support conservatives on some issues like the military, but also support the liberals in terms of taming American intervention.[439]

Thus, information warfare can force a government to swing both ways depending on the media coverage. An adversary who is adept at disseminating media coverage has the advantage in information warfare.

Information Warfare Can Prepare the Conventional Battlefield

The Western way of war trains participants to think of the beginning of battle as the point in time when the shooting starts. But information warfare presages battle. It "softens" the battlefield or tilts the battlefield in one direction or another depending on when and how information is used. Sometimes this can be an Internet meme that spreads disinformation. Sometimes it is election meddling that aims to destabilize and foment divides in society along ethnic, racial, and class boundaries. The Russian interference in the 2016 U.S. general election is a case in point. Russia's Internet Research Agency worked 24-7 to undermine American's beliefs in peaceful practices, outcomes, and non-violent transfers of power when elections are held. As long as there is freedom of speech, it is difficult to police such behavior. Facebook and Twitter often try to eliminate memes, disinformation pages, and accounts as much as possible, but this is a fleeting effort. Some are calling this memetic warfare.

Major Jessica Dawson, research lead for information warfare and an assistant professor at the Army Cyber Institute, said, "When we think about memetic warfare, what's really happening is we're taking these sorts of deep-seeded emotional stories and we're collapsing them down into a picture, usually it's something that has a very, very quick emotional

---

[439] *Ibid.*

punch," she said. "They're collapsing these narratives down into images that are often not attributed, that's one of the things about memes is they really aren't, someone usually isn't signing them, going 'I'm the artist.' There [are] these really emotional punches that are shared very, very quickly, they're self-replicating in a lot of ways because you see it, you react and then you immediately pass it on."[440]

So, it is not just military personnel who participate in information warfare, it could be any digital citizen who clicks "like" or "retweet" in that critical five minutes between when one sees a meme or post, processes it, and interacts with it to map the battlefield, even when the participants are non-combatants. This is what makes information warfare so powerful, and this is the sociology of war – when combatants and non-combatants interact on the Internet and social media.

[440] Pomerleau, Mark. 2020. "Memes, the Pandemic and the New Tactics of Information Warfare." *C4ISR Net*. July 23, 2020.

CHAPTER NINE

ARTIFICIAL INTELLIGENCE ON THE BATTLEFIELD

Artificial intelligence can be scary and from a sociological perspective, it is becoming a threat to humans. I know this fear factor in an up close and personal manner. My tech startup GovBrain predicted world events using artificial intelligence, machine learning, and natural language processing. My view of successful startups is that you should be blown away by your technology and blown away by the demand for this technology. During the seven-year life cycle of GovBrain we had both. GovBrain software and machine intelligence could predict the stock market, predict the outcome of elections, and could spot early indicators of geopolitical events. In 2017, for example, GovBrain correctly predicted the winners in head of state elections in South Korea, Iran, Japan, France, the United Kingdom, and the Commonwealth of Virginia. The software routinely made minute-by-minute financial market predictions on numerous individual equities, bonds, currencies, and commodities for seven years. It made early warning detections on the Iranian-backed Houthi rebels drone attack on two Saudi Arabia oil facilities in 2019, among many other predictions of geopolitical events. The uncanny nature of the software prediction sent up alarm signals to me as AI has also sent out alarming messages to many others.

Let me first define artificial intelligence using the construct from the Congressional Research Service in 2020.[441] Artificial intelligence is, "performance of tasks under varying and unpredictable circumstances without significant human oversight, or that can learn from experience and improve performance when exposed to data sets."[442] This "solves tasks requiring human-like perception, cognition, planning, learning, communication or physical learning."[443]

What if the GovBrain AI software ever got in the wrong hands? Would it be misused and abused for malign purposes by our current and future customers? This means that not only would the artificial intelligence software need to be trained by a moral, ethical, and virtuous person, it must be also trained by the same high-integrity person. How do we maintain control over the machine intelligence?

Humans Controlling Artificial Intelligence

This is really the main theme of this chapter and this ethical human aspect of artificial intelligence is part of the sociology of warfare in the modern age. I am operating under the assumption that the current state of the art in artificial intelligence is that of a 12-year-old. So, this "age" or level of maturity makes it easier to train the machine or software in some ways, but more difficult to train the machine intelligence in others. And it is somewhat easier to train in a virtuous manner where the trainer is the "hero" and the ultimate arbiter concerning the behavior of the machine. I also believe that there are plenty of examples of much more sophisticated AI and I will explain how to maintain control in those environments in the latter parts of this chapter. Keeping it simple helps control the machine.

---

[441] "Artificial Intelligence and National Security." Congressional Research Service. Nov. 10, 2020.

[442] *Ibid*, pg. 1.

[443] *Ibid*.

The first aspect of building a machine-learning or AI application is to adhere to basic and simple principles in mathematical and statistical modeling known as parsimony, elegance, and maximizing aspects of Occam's Razor. Those principles are intuitively appealing to people experienced in technology. So, in applied computer science, creating fewer and more efficient lines of code is preferable to making a hairball of software development code. Einstein's $E=MC^2$ was parsimonious and elegant and adhered to Occam's Razor because it was a short equation with few variables in the model. His model explained much behavior in the universe concerning mass and energy. So, we want just a few variables that explain a lot of behavior. Some theoretical computer scientists remember working on search problems and they encountered the "Counting Problem," which lends itself to what is called a "parsimonious reduction." Going back to basic data science; in a linear regression model, one is looking for data, when plotted, that has an advantageous level of "goodness of fit." So, R^2 is the measurement we want that is between 0 and 1 and we are looking for something over 0.5 that shows the model is able to explain a lot of variability, which is desirable.

Now let me discuss what I mean by controlling the 12-year-old. Remember, my assumption about the current state of artificial intelligence is on the level of a 12-year-old: sometimes scary; sometimes not – perhaps about 50 percent scary. One wants the machine to only conduct a simple chore or task, but to have that one task include broader uses. You remember the principle of a manufacturing assembly line that can be shut off when any employee is concerned about something like safety of quality control? You want to be able to shut down the assembly line when it comes to training the artificial intelligence too, as I have pointed out in a previous chapter. So, the scientist is always in control. That is the biggest fear – when the scientist is not in control. Those of us who work in the field have to be responsible and ethically and morally strong. And make sure you can shut off the assembly line and make "human" corrections at the appropriate time, especially when the 12-year-old becomes a teenager and beyond.

This brings us to intelligent machines and artificial intelligence software that affects warfare. Technology on the scale of a 12-year-old can be dangerous if it is not "raised" by ethical humans. Some areas that are affected by machine intelligence and artificial intelligence and building future applications are combat platforms, cyber defense, logistics and re-supply, target acquisition, combat medicine, simulation and training, and situational awareness. All of these require human trainers to be ethically and morally sound. We also have to be on the look-out for rogue countries who have different ethics and morality than the West.

China and Russia Could Leave the West in the Dust

Artificial intelligence will require a profound re-imagining of future warfare. There is a fear that the United States and other Western militaries and NATO members will be left behind due to advances in technology by China and Russia. Vladimir Putin has said that the country that rules in artificial intelligence "will be the ruler of the world."[444]

Sociology plays into this. Russia and China have a collectivist culture that favors a mobilization of their militaries to develop wartime technology. The United States has an individualistic culture that favors innovation and technological advancement. Both cultures and their sociological drivers will move toward an arms race of artificial intelligence, machine learning, neural networks, deep learning, and other facets of the technology.

---

[444] Davis, Zachary. 2019. "Artificial Intelligence on the Battlefield: An Initial Survey of Potential Implications of Deterrence, Stability, and Strategic Surprise." *Prism*. Vol. 8: No. 2: pp. 114-131.

General and Narrow AI in the Battlespace

The technology falls under two rubrics: narrow artificial intelligence and general artificial intelligence. "Narrow AI uses discrete problem-solving tools to perform specific narrow tasks. General AI encompasses technologies designed to mimic and recreate functions of the human brain."[445]

General AI is the panacea for warfare, but also dangerous to create because it could lead to a "Terminator"-like moment in which the AI is smarter than humans. Narrow AI has been achieved by game-playing in chess and the boardgame go. It is also close to making intelligent and "killer" robots a priority. As Zachary S. Davis, from the Lawrence Livermore National Laboratory, has pointed out, "For military applications with direct analogs in the civilian world, like logistics, planning, analysis, and transportation, AI-supported data analytics are already in use throughout the defense and intelligence communities."[446] As Davis has written, these AI advancements can have effects at the operational and strategic level of war. The tactical level would also be included in this rubric. In these levels of warfare, strategic is anything that affects warfare above the level of a division in the army up to the National Command Authority with the Joint Chiefs, the Department of Defense, and the White House. The operational level is anything above battalion-strength and the tactical level is anything battalion-strength and below.

Different Uses for AI in Defense

For example, at the strategic level, AI could help decision-making in deciding and planning for how large an effort a hypothetical war could be. At the operational level, AI could help deployment of troops in this hypothetical war, and at the tactical level, AI could enable super soldiers to be used in this hypothetical war. So, AI at its current iteration, according

---

[445] *Ibid*, pg. 2.

[446] *Ibid*, pg. 4.

to Davis, is that the operational level is better for war planning, modeling, simulations, and wargaming. At the strategic level, it could be used for planning a nuclear war or ballistic missile defense that pack strategic nuclear warheads.[447]

Ethical and sociological considerations abound. Policy makers may favor a way to limit the arms race of artificial intelligence because of ethical considerations. For example, should there be a ban on certain AI weapons? Because of the secretive nature of any weapons development by various countries, bans would probably be a bridge too far, but it is an understandable aspiration. The United Nations has written a report on the militarization of AI and stated that "certain uses of AI could also undermine international peace and security by raising concerns about safety and security of the technology, accelerating the pace of armed conflicts, or loosening human control over the means of war."[448] The UN would be the obvious arbiter regarding the regulation of wartime artificial intelligence.

The RAND Corporation recommended that "Department of Defense leaders work with the State Department to seek greater technical cooperation and policy alignment with allies and partners, while also exploring confidence-building and risk-reduction measures with China, Russia, and other states attempting to develop military AI."[449] RAND is also concerned with ethics of AI in warfare because malign cases of AI could increase the likelihood of war.

Numerous human tasks are being eclipsed by AI. Paul Maxwell of the Modern War Institute wrote in 2020 that "identifying a Russian T-90 battle tank in a satellite image, identifying high-value targets in

---

[447] *Ibid*, pg. 4.

[448] Sisson, Melanie et al. 2020. "The Militarization of Artificial Intelligence." United Nations Office for Disarmament Affairs. June 3, 2020.

[449] Morgan, Forrest et al. 2020. "Military Applications of Artificial Intelligence: Ethical Concerns in an Uncertain World." RAND Corporation.

a crowd using facial recognition, and translating text for open-source intelligence," are becoming more prevalent.[450]

The enemy has a vote in all this. You can be sure that there will be attempts at overcoming this AI and the execution of adversarial attacks from the other side. Maxwell calls these enemy responses "evasion, inference, poisoning, and extraction."[451]

Data and AI Lead to 'Speed War'

This execution has been going on since the advent of AI and the original moniker of "artificial intelligence" that appeared in print in 1956. But it was not until around 2017 that 90 percent of the world's data had been produced. Machine learning steps into this void as data is needed to train models for prediction and analytics. This notion is based on speed. Never before has the conflict decision-making calculus been so fast. This affects decision-making on nuclear weapons, which is a grave concern. Could AI foster a higher capability that leads to nuclear war? That is a future of the nuclear-triad that needs to be examined by the world's war fighters that have nuclear weapons. If humans are removed from the decision-tree then you have fundamental change in the way that nuclear war could be prosecuted.

This type of warfare is what I call "speed war." Fighting by months, weeks, days, hours, and minutes could be reduced down to seconds or even nano-seconds with artificial intelligence decision-making. Where does that leave the grand strategists and practitioners of operational art? I have established in this book that the future of warfare is still human and steeped in sociology. People matter. Nuclear strategists since John von Neumann, Edward Teller, and Henry Kissinger have always assumed a human trigger finger. War fighters, usually in the West, have institutional and cultural norms that place a taboo and ban on the first

---

[450] Maxwell, Paul. 2020. "Artificial Intelligence is the Future of Warfare (Just Not in the Way You Think." Modern War Institute. April 20, 2020.

[451] *Ibid.*

strike practice when it comes to the utilization of nuclear weapons. First launch in speed war could be affected by humans who train the AI, and this is where ethics comes into play. The most ethical humans must be used to train the machine learning, neural networks, and other aspects of AI to promote a safety factor in nuclear weapons strategy. Missile defense will also improve, most likely with the advent of improved lasers. Satellites will be threatened by missiles, especially those in low earth orbit. Again, there is further changing of the decision-making calculus that humans must use, especially when it includes machine intelligence.

So, speed war is still human. And this means that bad actors, those countries who are rogue and do not have the Western values of a no first-strike mentality, can produce AI by humans who do not have the same ethical and moral compass as those in the United States, the United Kingdom, and other democratic nuclear-powers. Some of this nuclear restraint or absence of nuclear restraint is sociological. Russia, China, Iran, and North Korea are more communal countries and authoritarian in the first place and not bound by the same sociological and moral trappings that the West has. They encourage the notion that survival of the state is paramount. Citizens of these countries are not as individualistic as Americans or Britons. This could lead to a different take on speed war when it comes to the potential use of nuclear weapons with AI robustness. Thus, speed war is more dangerous in those communal and authoritarian countries.

Once called the "Axis of Evil" during the George W. Bush administration, communal countries, especially those that are currently or formerly Communist, are a great danger in the speed war construct. And speed war is also a trait of conventional warfare using AI, machine learning, neural networks, and quantum computing. The decision, at least in the West, to place humans in harm's way, is often the biggest decision a political leader may make. In speed war, the decision is based on machine-generated data that is backed by humans but will not be made by a purely human calculus.

Therefore, there must be a defense against speed war that is perpetuated by rogue actors. Perhaps this is the best use of AI in the West – in the defense. Clausewitz devoted much of his military analysis and strategy on fighting in the defense. He would probably say today that speed war should be defended against by an amalgam of humans and computers – often called the human-computer hybrid by Peter Thiel – a concept that I have written about in previous chapters.[452] The human-computer hybrid is a huge part of speed war. In some way that is a good thing. It is smart, it is ingenious, and it is the pantheon of technology in warfare that is constantly evolving in the first place. Speed war may indeed be the pantheon of warfare (the best reserved building block) because that is the highest form of fighting without the constant evolution and iteration of conventional war.

Speed war could be the pinnacle of warfighting and while it is still aspirational, that may not be a good or bad thing as long as humans are in control. Humans could still lose control over the AI that is required for the prosecution of speed war. Hopefully, allies will be involved with speed war. International organizations and alliances such as NATO could slow down speed war and this could lead toward a more ethical and moral fight. But individual states such as Russia, China, North Korea, and Iran would not be bound by such ethical mores. Speed war could lead to a coalition of the willing collaborators that have liberal democracies to reduce the number of bad actors who are willing to use AI for nefarious purposes.

If it is true, as Sun Zu has written, that all war is primarily about deception, what does this mean for speed war and AI? Will there be trust in "The Machine?" Even in speed war, the hope is that humans will not be replaced in the kill chain. But deception is another matter. Drones can deceive, especially when they are networked with AI. Enemy radar

---

[452] Thiel, Peter. 2014. *Zero to One: Notes on Startups, or How to Build the Future.* New York: Penguin Random House.

can be jammed. AI can "think" about things that human beings cannot decipher – such as completely complicated mathematical equations. Deception is also about surprise and seizing the initiative, both concepts that AI can help with. And that would meet Sun Zu's approval.

The principles of warfare under speed war do not change that much. The United States, the United Kingdom, and Australia adhere to similar principles of war such as economy of force, security, and surprise. The United States differs in its dedication to mass, maneuver, and unity of command. Speed war AI assists in all of these principles. Humans will still be on the battlefield, but this time during speed war, there will be robots and these early type of war robots will need simple commands in order for the nascent AI to be carried out. Speed war necessitates that these robots eliminate or minimize fratricide, collateral damage, and civilian deaths. This is where speed war will be challenged because these types of negatives are inevitable in many forms of combat.

What is then the public perception of speed war? Employment and deployment of force in the Western world has a shelf life. During employment and deployment of force there is an initial honeymoon period called the "rally around the flag" syndrome. Then civilian support of the conflict usually depends on how long the operation is and how many casualties are involved. The inevitable damage caused by "blue on blue" fratricide or "green on blue" attacks and civilian deaths, and even war crimes due to speed war mistakes and the negative aspects of AI, will erode public confidence and support. Clausewitz would not approve since civilian support for the war is paramount in what the Prussian called for in "On War."

Napoleon Buonaparte understood the need for public approval too. Napoleon was quite the spin doctor. Even in his most unsuccessful battles, which were few, he always spun the news advantageously, especially when it came to the number of enemy and friendly casualties. He reduced or lowered the number of casualties to prove a point or to control the news cycle in Paris as it existed in his era.

But the public, as Napoleon and Clausewitz knew, needed a unity of command or someone responsible to blame when things go wrong. Speed war, with its dependence on AI, would be sometimes simple and sometimes difficult to find who to blame. Miscommunication in the fog of war is not eliminated in speed war. The people need to know who is in charge – humans, machines, or data? Hopefully, the answer will be humans.

What is more important – for AI systems to think and act like humans or for systems to act and think rationally? Speed war needs all of the above to be effective. For the war robots to be most successful, they will need to think rationally in order to increase the level of ethics and morality. These war robots will need to have intelligent and safe behavior.

U.S. Joint Artificial Intelligence Center Offers a Glimpse Into the Future

Fortunately, the U.S. military is already moving in an appropriate manner. The Pentagon's Joint Artificial Intelligence Center has 185 employees with a $1.3 billion yearly budget. It is focusing on joint warfighting operations and delivering automated AI-systems to the individual soldier, marine, airmen, or sailor. This is the essence of speed war. Various stakeholders and participants in the Pentagon's artificial intelligence systems are being sent to a Joint Artificial Intelligence Center "bootcamp" to learn principles of ethics. These personnel will be trained on AI ethics and morality with five principles in mind – responsible, ethical, traceable, reliable, and governable. This will create "responsible AI champions" across the Department of Defense.[453]

This is good news for AI development and speed war. It is critical to take a DOD-wide, robust, humanitarian, whole-of-government

---

[453] Barnett, Jackson. 2020. "JAIC Launches Pilot for Implementing New DOD AI Ethics Principles." *FedScoop*. April 1, 2020.

approach. Humans must win the battle for control of AI because weapons are becoming more dangerous. Brookings Institution defense analyst Michael O'Hanlon has chronicled this likelihood.[454] AI-enabled "smart, mobile mines" can destroy shipping. Iran could use them to block the Strait of Hormuz. Cluster munitions using loitering aerial devices along with the "Brilliant Anti-tank Weapon" could make tanks obsolete by enabling an adversary such as Russia or China the ability to destroy echelons of armor with one fell stroke. AI-enabled unmanned underwater vehicles could allow NATO to deny access to the Russian Navy's yearnings to project power in the Baltic Sea.

Speed war is a natural development from the concept of anti-access/area denial that defines warfare in the 21st century. It is better to have robots man the picket lines rather than humans to block areas in which you do not want the enemy to operate. Let the robots do the dirty and dangerous work. The world is watching, and the world needs ethical AI, especially when it comes to warfare. Speed war is an inevitable iteration that started centuries ago.

Napoleon was no stranger to speed war. He understood speed. His armies traveled quickly on roads that enabled them to double-time march faster than the armies of his heroes Julius Caesar and Alexander the Great. Napoleon was also a fast horseman using a whip and wearing out numerous horses as he incessantly inspected his troops and their offensive and defensive efforts. Despite his skills on horseback, he was not a trained cavalry officer. Adept at mathematics, he was chosen to be an artillerist, which at that time was the most prestigious branch of the French Army. Napoleon had an affinity and aptitude for mathematics, which he credited for developing his prowess as a strategist and statesman. It allowed him to have the mental acuity to compartmentalize different aspects of military strategy and operational art. Speed in

[454] O'Hanlon, Michael E. "The Role of AI in Future Warfare." Brookings Institute. Nov. 29, 2018.

decision-making and execution of his orders were principles he admired when leading troops. This led to the development of his genius on the battlefield.

AI and the 'Flash of Brilliance' Show Military Genius

Clausewitz called this mental capacity *coup d'oeil.*[455] *Coup d'oeil* is the "flash of brilliance" or "stroke of the eye" – a particular necessity for genius in military affairs. It is mental speed and a necessity for speed war. It also denotes a practice of taking advanced thoughts from a mastermind and translating them quickly into simple commands. Skipping ahead to the present day – it takes *coup d'oeil* for humans to train machines and analyze the data for artificial intelligence on the battlefield. *Coup d'oeil* should also lead to ethical and moral thinking during the training period. This mental acuity should also be present in political leaders as they ponder the question on whether to go to war in the first place. Clausewitz knew this was one of the most difficult decisions a leader could make, since war was so uncertain and very much a gamble. Napoleon considered simple luck to be a large factor in many of the victories he engineered in his career. Clausewitz knew that governments wagered blood and treasure in warfare, so the moral dimension of these heavy decisions weigh down policy makers. Napoleon, of course, was both a military and political leader, but his actions on and off the battlefield also showed that flash of genius over and over.

It can be argued that Western states are out of genius leaders and military cults of personality. I once brought up retired General and Secretary of Defense James Mattis in a course I was teaching on international security at The George Washington University Elliott School of International Affairs. One of the students, a former marine, said Mattis was a "god." And he repeated this many times. According to this student,

---

[455] Clausewitz, *On War.*

Mattis instituted a particular esprit de' corps, which Napoleon excelled at instilling in his men. In the U.S.-led wars in Iraq and Afghanistan, there are few generals or admirals that had that kind of following and few that had a stroke of genius. If one goes back to the first Gulf War during Operation Desert Storm to examine the leadership of Generals Norman Schwarzkopf and Barry McCaffery, it is difficult to see them pondering the use of artificial intelligence. McCaffery loved speed in the armored cavalry though and Schwarzkopf used deception well. Patton could be considered one of the most innovative generals who foresaw the advent of armored warfare, coupled with air assets. But that of course was between World War One and World War Two. I argue that *coup d'oeil* no longer exists in modern-day generals and admirals and that is a shame. Just how many flag officers can you name in the U.S. military since 9/11? Very few I would wager. Although perhaps having a general with the cult of personality of Patton would be dangerous in the 21st century. The American public is not clamoring for larger-than-life military leaders – someone like a Douglas MacArthur – for example, would not have quite the allure or success in this age.

Are we producing the kind of generals and admirals who can lead speed war and institute the major changes required in artificial intelligence development? The service academies are still primarily engineering schools. That is good because cadets can take classes or major in mathematics, physics, or computer science. Others major in the liberal arts, humanities, and social sciences, and they have a solid grounding in ethics and morality. This can be desirable too since speed war needs plenty of humanity, ethics, and morality. But many officers are still faceless and are not exactly comprised of the right stuff needed for *coup d'oeil.* Without the flash of brilliance, speed war and artificial intelligence development are more difficult to achieve.

I do not see many flag officers from other adversarial armies and navies displaying coup d'oeil either. Iran's Qasem Soleimani had a cult of personality. One could make a case for Valery Gerasimov from Russia who has a great intellect and has displayed many strokes of genius over the years. China has its share of military thinkers in various think tanks, but China has not experienced warfare since the invasion of Vietnam in 1979. A whole generation of Chinese generals and admirals have no military experience. Western generals, particularly in America and Britain, do have ample military experience, although is it enough experience for them to develop a flash of brilliance?

Computers Have Skills While Humans Have Rules

As M. L. Cummings from Chatham House has written, computers have skills while humans have rules, knowledge, and expertise – all in an uncertain and dangerous environment on the battlefield.[456] This means human commanders will still need knowledge and skills in AI as well. But training at the enlisted level – the first entry into the military – still teaches skills over knowledge. Robots can replace junior enlisted humans, but it will be difficult for machine intelligence to replace flag officers. So, training of humans is important. It is difficult to ascertain whether the Pentagon's Joint Artificial Intelligence Center contains junior enlisted and senior enlisted soldiers, sailors, airmen, and marines. They are the personnel that will actually prosecute the speed war.

Does artificial intelligence lend itself to the analysis of sociology in warfare? That depends on the growth of speed war. The military is a social group after all and sociologist C. Wright Mills made this distinction, although Mills believed in the advent of a military social elite with an appetite for power, he did not analyze the battlefield. Mills, along with Dwight Eisenhower, also contrived the notion of the military industrial complex and built that into a sociological phenomenon. The military industrial complex in the 21st century also includes the various think tanks, inside and outside the armed forces, and in academia. These are

---

[456] Cummings, M.L. 2017. "Artificial Intelligence and the Future of Warfare." Chatham House.

necessary for speed war and artificial intelligence. Think tankers have time to ponder and navel gaze – something that field commanders, pilots, and ship drivers do not have time to do. While military personnel with "muddy boots" often look down upon think tankers and academics, the thinkers' value in analyzing speed war, AI, and sociology is pronounced and significant.

Speed war and AI are social developments, especially when it comes to ethics and morality. Speed war and AI takes professionalism, esprit d 'corps, and a willingness to fight – all aspects of sociological analysis of the military. Speed war will still be human-controlled, and it should be.

My mentor and former commander in the army, Robert R. Leonhard, instilled speed war in me. Although this was not necessarily about the rise of AI, Leonhard was focused on armored maneuver warfare. In his well-received book, *Fighting By Minutes*, Leonhard "laid out the important time dimensions of warfighting: duration, frequency, sequence, and opportunity. He showed how the great captains of history turned the enemy's time flanks, preempted defenses, or manipulated the frequency of operations to their advantage. Leonhard likewise dissected the phenomenon of surprise in war, explaining how combat forces delay detection and hasten contact to overturn the enemy's perception of the fight."[457]

Fighting By Minutes struck a chord in me while I was just an army officer cadet. Leonhard later updated the work with a second edition in 2017 after he released *The Principles of War for the Information Age* in 2000, also highlighting aspects of future war.[458] Speed war is a natural outgrowth of these books and it modernizes the entire list of principles of war. Speed is defined by the *Armed Forces Journal* as "the rapid

---

[457] Leonhard, Robert R. 1994. *Fighting By Minutes: Time and the Art of War.* Westport, CT.: Praeger Publishers.

[458] Leonhard, Robert R. 2000. *Principles of War for the Information Age.* New York: Ballentine Books.

execution of all functions and operations related to war. Implied in speed are the current principles of offensive and maneuver. The practice of seizing the initiative, striking an enemy and striking him again before he has a chance to re-orient and act has proven successful time and time again. Speed enables a force to seize the initiative, deliver time-critical strikes and plan and decide on the fly."[459]

One can grasp quickly that AI is a force multiplier for speed. But does war even have a future, as Martin Van Crevald has asked?[460] Replying in the negative would undercut all the assertions I have made in this book, of course. But it is a fair question. Van Crevald pointed out that as history marches on, fewer people are involved in combat and fewer people are becoming casualties. He wonders if the better angels of our nature has led to what Emmanuel Kant called the advent of the perpetual peace argument that has reared its head again in the 21st century. I discussed the Endless War theme in previous chapters because it gets to the crux of sociology outside the military – namely how long will the public support a war? Which is also a Clausewitzian staple. People becoming "better" is what is needed for the ethics and morality of AI.

Neural Networks, Deep Learning, and Extremely Big Data Have Arrived

Often the learning associated with AI is "deep." Former U.S. Deputy Defense Secretary Robert Work "improved the foxhole" during his time at the Pentagon around 2017. Work wanted to integrate AI and machine learning in the military with a project he called "Maven." Project Maven featured neural networks and deep learning so Maven machine intelligence could learn as it matured. This is an excellent precursor of speed war. It had the appropriate amount of computer vision backed

---

459 Van Avery, Christopher. 2007. "12 New Principles of Warfare." *Armed Forces Journal.* July 1, 2007.

460 Van Crevald, Martin. 2017. *More on War*. Oxford: Oxford University Press.

by an elite gaggle of humans behind the scenes. This can add muscle to the arms race of AI that is not only in the military but in Big Tech from Silicon Valley on the civilian side.

DARPA is always in on the AI act with its Explainable Artificial Intelligence program. The idea of this program is to better understand the decisions made by AI machine intelligence. This is about speed too because the idea is for the AI to learn in real time which would help my notion of speed war. Sometimes the adversary must be understood. That is where the Naval Surface Warfare Center comes in. This battle lab is working on "applying advanced mathematical methodologies to better characterize the fragility of neural networks."[461]

Mathematical methodologies, indeed, because zettabytes are here to stay. What is a zettabyte you ask? Extremely big data. This is data that is made up of bytes that are ten to the twenty-first power or one followed by 21 zeros. By 2025, according to Peter Layton who was writing for the Royal Air Force, the world will produce 163 zettabytes of data.[462]

I could make a case that AI is needed in war fighting for that one big reason – data. Speed war will depend on the veracity of that data. We certainly have the volume, but is it useful? It is if the data is of high quality. Poor data, as Layton pointed out, makes AI "outputs dubious."[463]

What if every piece of data the Department of Defense produces is on a cloud, which is run by Microsoft? I am talking about the JEDI (Joint Enterprise Defense Infrastructure) cloud $10 billion contract that Microsoft Azure won over Amazon Web Services, which was an acrimonious battle between the two heavyweights. This could run the "Internet of military things," a concept I introduced earlier and created

---

[461] "The Rapid Rise of Neural Networks for Defense: A Cautionary Tale." 2018. Naval Science and Technology Future Force. Nov. 13, 2018.

[462] Lawton, Peter. 2018. "Algorithmic Warfare: Applying Artificial Intelligence to Warfighting." Air Power Development Center: Australian Department of Defense.

[463] *Ibid*, pg. 11

during lectures I gave at The George Washington University from 2016 through 2019. What if everything, including hardware, software, and human interactions was connected by the web and stored on JEDI? The cyber defense capabilities would need to be robust, to say the least. But one could see the advantages of having such a large footprint connection when it comes to prosecuting speed war.

Hyperactive Battlefields Feature Fighting in Uncertainty

Speed war will be fought on a "hyperactive battlefield," according to General John Murray.[464] This hyperactivity is a concept that the army Futures Command has coined. As Kris Osborn has reported, "a hyper-active battlefield is a chaotic, fast-moving mix of complex variables in need of instant analysis as lives...and combat victory...hang in a delicate balance of uncertainty."[465]

Uncertainty or fog of war, as Clausewitz called it, is a huge aspect of speed war. Battlefields have always had uncertainty. Napoleon relied on "luck" to navigate them, but he also was an intelligence enthusiast. Napoleon gathered his own intelligence – often personally interrogating prisoners of war. He also had his own soldiers discard their uniforms and dress as peasants to spy on the enemy. So, intelligence, surveillance, and reconnaissance has a long history on the battlefield. Sun Zu described it as well in the *Art of War*. I have shard the OODA loop in a previous chapter. OODA stands for Observe, Orient, Detect, and Act. The hyperactive battlefield, as Army Futures Command sees it, is about OODA and it requires warriors to "see first, decide first, and act first."[466]

This "data fusion" is an important aspect of speed war and the

---

[464] Osborn, Kris. "Future of War Will Be 'Hyperactive Battlefields': U.S. Army General." *The National Interest.* Jan. 30, 2021.

[465] Osborn, Kris. 2020. "Army Futures Commander Sees AI-Driven 'Hyperactive Battlefield" in Future War." *Fox News*. May 13, 2020.

[466] *Ibid.*

Internet of military things can aid in speed war prosecution and execution. This goes down to the junior enlisted warrior. The JEDI Cloud is enabling a "synthetic training environment."[467] Trainees in this environment will use virtual reality goggles. "The goggles can show the soldier anything from the direction to their objective, to exactly where their next shot will go, to virtual adversaries with realistic tactics they can fight against in training simulations."[468] I would venture to say that these goggles should collect data that would be uploaded into the cloud and stored to train AI and contribute to the Internet of military things.

While much of AI can be traced to the use by the individual soldier, the world is seeing an arms race develop among the United States, NATO allies, and rivals including Russia and China. Russia's Putin has said that "artificial intelligence is the future, not only for Russia but for all humankind... Whoever becomes the leader in this sphere will become the ruler of the world."[469]

Russia Has Many Axes to Grind

It is illustrative to examine some of the background on Russia's views on warfighting to better understand how the country views domination on the battlefield by use of technology. Why have relations between the United States and Russia have gone so bad over the years? The following list explains this:

- NATO enlargement encroaching on Russian borders, especially currently the threat of Ukraine and Georgia wanting to join NATO

---

[467] Freedberg, Sydney. 2020. "Army Targeting Environment, VR Training May Use Jedi Cloud." *Breaking Defense*. Jan. 24, 2020.

[468] *Ibid.*

[469] Simonite, Tom. 2017. "For Superpowers, Artificial Intelligence Fuels New Global Arms Race." *Wired*. Sept. 8, 2017.

- U.S. not giving enough monetary aid to Russia in critical years of 1991-2 and during the 90s
- U.S. and NATO bombing of Serbia in 1999
- Putin closing KGB and intelligence and military bases in Cuba and closing bases in Central Asia and U.S. not appreciating it
- Putin helping U.S. get overflight rights in Central Asia after 9/11 and U.S. not appreciating it
- U.S. support for certain pro-Western leaders in Georgia during Rose Revolution and in Ukraine in Orange Revolution
- Fear that after invasion of Iraq and intervention of Libya that the United States supported regime change in Russia too
- U.S. criticizing Russian human rights record
- U.S. supporting independence of Kosovo
- U.S. ignoring or not respecting Russia votes in UN Security Council
- U.S. missile defense systems in Poland and Romania
- Russia blaming the U.S. for the 2008 and 2009 financial crisis that caused much economic turmoil in Russia
- U.S. supporting Ukrainian shift to West, EU and NATO, and U.S. not appreciating that many Russians see Ukraine as part of Russia
- U.S. not recognizing many Russians see Crimea as part of Russia
- U.S. using economic sanctions
- U.S. not recognizing or respecting Russia as a great power

As you can see, Russia has a bone to pick with the United States, to state it mildly. Artificial intelligence can even the playing field and serve as asymmetric power against America. One of the ways that Russia has an advantage is the high level of esteem they place on intellectual thought in the science, technology, and mathematics fields. Anecdotally, I have witnessed the "educational chauvinism" that Russia believes in when it comes to mathematics. A friend I met when I represented the United

States at the 2006 NATO Young Leader's Summit was from Azerbaijan, but he was educated in Russia. He said he did an academic exchange program at America's respected higher-ed institution UCLA. My friend said the math courses at UCLA were absurdly easy compared to his assignments and work in Russia. He said American students could barely keep up with him in math.

This is an example of the intellectual quality of Russian thought. Russians, generally speaking, tend to be people who hold ideas and writing of literature in high esteem. The original revolutionaries in 1905 and 1917 were men and women of letters. Many of them only had the clothes on their backs. They had to get permission from the authorities to own a typewriter. The Tsarist internal police censured most writings, although they somehow allowed Karl Marx's Das Kapital to be translated into Russian and made available to the radicals (this turned out to be a mistake that led to revolution). Many people were full-time political agitators and revolutionaries for years. They were often expelled, arrested, and sent into exile to Siberia to work camps. It is difficult to imagine for us in 21st century America to draw comparisons. It would be like if you got expelled from school and your laptop and phone were taken away, your Internet access was taken away and all you could do would be to advocate for certain types of political points of view. The best you could get would be pamphlets and books that were illegal to possess. Could you do that? That is how committed the Russian revolutionaries were. They were people of ideas at a time when disseminating these ideas was dangerous. This intellectual courage makes them sometimes a more dangerous rival than China.

A New Cold War?

So, is the West or the United States in a "New Cold War" with the Russians? That phrase has sold a lot of books and titled a lot of articles. But the Cold War was an epic long-term, bipolar struggle between Communism and Democratic Capitalism. We have a multipolar world now with many different brands of authoritarianism, and frankly, somewhat of a reduction in the number of countries that can be called purely democratic capitalist. There are certainly many events that can be considered similar to Cold War crises: the 2008 Russian intervention in Georgia; the 2014 annexation of Crimea and intervention in Eastern Ukraine; and the 2016 election meddling in the United States.

In the future, we have artificial intelligence, and this will develop quickly because the Russians have a political system that lends itself to autocracy. This means the government can institute policies at the top, such as the growth of artificial intelligence; that will percolate down the lower level of the socio-economic pyramid. Political scientists have used various terms and concepts to describe how Russian government works. Russia has two over-arching political concepts that dominate government. "Power vertical" is where all power is stove-piped through the Kremlin and the federal government. This stands for order and stability in which the orders at the top are carried out below. In this case, an order from Putin to focus on artificial intelligence will be carried out for the most part. Another concept, called "manual control," means that instead of lower governmental systems functioning effectively to resolve issues, even relatively minor problems in terms of national interest rely on the personal authority of Putin for resolution. This also helps the development of artificial intelligence as Putin is taking a personal stake in the outcome. "Civilizationalism" is the belief that Russian culture, values, education, learning, religion, language, literature, and music is superior to the West. That Russia is exceptional, and the West is materialist, corrupt, individualistic, selfish, and rotten to its core. These chauvinistic beliefs mean that Russia would have an advantage in artificial intelligence development.

Russia has sought to emulate DARPA with its own defense think tank called the Advanced Research Foundation. This is comprised of 46 research laboratories. The laboratories are working on "image recognition, speech recognition, enabling control of autonomous military systems, as well as AI's support for weapons life-cycle"[470] There is also a Russian National Center for Artificial Intelligence. This is supposed to help the Kremlin win cyber wars and information operations. It also assists the Kremlin in maintaining a universal system of keeping the domestic population in line and putting down dissent through a network of 170,000 closed circuit cameras, some of which can utilize facial recognition AI.

Russia's experience in the Middle East, particularly deploying and employing troops in Syria, has been used as a laboratory for AI. Russia employed unmanned ground vehicles for navigating mine fields and unexploded ordinance that has proliferated on the Syrian battlefield since the civil war began. The Russians also deployed an unmanned combat vehicle that is based on a tank chassis for urban warfare. Russia is utilizing AI to send unmanned aerial vehicles to jam enemy communication signals. Margarita Konaev and Samuel Bendett, writing in *War on the Rocks*, said "the military today is experimenting with concepts like Glaz (The Eye) — a small camera and sensor package users launch from a flare gun, transmitting data to soldiers while it descends to the ground in a parachute. Russian soldiers presumably tested Glaz in Syria, and its very design lends it to be used in urban combat."[471]

Russia is also using AI-enabled software to protect its own intelligence, surveillance, and reconnaissance systems against cyber or electronic attacks. This shows how the Russians are participating in an AI-arms race or cat and mouse game with defense acquisition.

China Leads in STEM Fields

Like Russia, China has an exaggerated cultural chauvinism that believes it is further advanced than the West when it comes to science,

---

[470] Bendett, Samuel. 2019. "The Rise of Russia's Hi-Tech Military." American Foreign Policy Council. June 26, 2019.

[471] Konaev, Margarita and Samuel Bendett. 2019. "Russian AI-enabled Combat Is Coming to a City Near You?" *War on the Rocks*. July 31, 2019.

technology, engineering, and mathematics. And when it comes up short with the United States, it has no scruples. Espionage, whether in the human or cyber realm, is used to steal AI secrets, that is a well-established fact. China also emulates Russia in terms of controlling and spying on its own population. Their "Skynet" system is comprised of 570 million CCTV cameras across the country that track citizen activity.

Unlike in the Cold War, it could be now said that Russia and China are allies and this is a huge development in the future of warfare. Putin and Xi have met several times. They have consummated a major energy deal together. They consider themselves close friends. They often order the practice of joint military exercises. Both countries believe in the maximum level of sovereignty and do not believe in U.S. dominance in a unipolar world. They believe in multi-polarism. Both countries will continue to be the spoiler in the United Nations Security Council by vetoing actions they disagree with vis-a-vis the United States. This will aid China in its territorial claims in the East China and South China Seas. Russia had definitely pivoted to the East in a region dominated by China.

As noted energy and geopolitical analyst Daniel Yergin described it, "Moscow and Beijing are conjoined by their emphasis on 'absolute sovereignty,' their rejection of the 'universal' values and norms propounded by the West, their reliance on state-dominated economies, and their opposition to what they call the would-be 'hegemonic' position and 'unilateralism' of the United States."[472]

CCP General Secretary Xi Jinping is also an aficionado of artificial intelligence. He meets with AI scientists regularly and often makes speeches on the subject at various research centers and labs in China. Most of China's defense output when it comes to AI is on military

[472] Yergin, Daniel. 2020. *The New Map: Energy, Climate, and the Clash of Nations*. New York: Penguin Random House.

hardware such as robotic tanks and vehicles, autonomous drones, and remotely-piloted submarines.[473]

China sees the development of AI fitting into its "Assassin's Mace" concept in which the People's Liberation Army strikes in an asymmetric fashion against the enemy – think a missile strike against an aircraft carrier. Assassin's Mace can also include "the use of big data, the Internet of Things, or cloud computing integrated with next-generation weaponry."[474] China's Academy of Military Science is beginning to be the go-to laboratory for AI development in China. Individual researchers are working on machine intelligence that brings in the concept of "cognitive confrontation," which means that the PLA will achieve positive results on the battlefield in speed war with decisive supremacy in data, information, and awareness. Other scientists have focused on predicting the outcome of a battle before it happens – a notion called the "algorithmic game." Chinese machine intelligence is designed to overcome what Clausewitz called the "fog of war." China is thinking big with AI and grappling with solutions that deal with problems on the battlefield for "cognitive advantage, speed, early warning, and first-mover advantage."[475]

---

[473] Eastwood, Brent M. 2019. "A Smarter Battlefield? PLA Concepts for "Intelligent Operations" Begin to Take Shape." *China Brief.* Jamestown Foundation. Vol. 19: Issue 4, Feb. 15, 2019.

[474] *Ibid.*

[475] *Ibid.*

CONCLUSION

Speed war will require a new kind of soldier, marine, sailor, and airman. Fortunately, those who are joining the military now have grown up with the Internet and have honed their hand-eye skills with video games. New types of training will have to be emphasized and this could lead to gene editing for super soldiers, exoskeletons, and cyborgs. Humans, machines, and data leads to speed war and fighting by nanoseconds. Big data, machine learning, and artificial intelligence have also led to speed war.

Speed war is still more human than machine. This brings us to the main point of the book – that warfare is ultimately human, and humans make up the sociological operating environment of combat. The concept of Endless War is a part of this operating environment. As of this writing in 2021, there are around 2,500 troops in Afghanistan with peace efforts ebbing and flowing. There are approximately 2,500 American troops in Iraq and the United States still flies air missions over Syria and allows brigade combat teams into Syria. So far President Biden has not articulated a new strategy for America's longest war in Afghanistan and for South Asia and the Middle East in general. There appears to be no end-game. What does victory even look like? Over the last two decades, America has endured over 7,000 killed with 50,000 wounded and has spent at least $5.4 trillion in wars in Afghanistan and Iraq.[476]

---

[476] Paul, Rand. "Rand Paul: Why We Need to End the Forever Wars Now." *The National Interest*. Feb. 10, 2010.

And the warrior culture among Afghans is not likely to change. Peace in Afghanistan will require a demobilization and disarmament strategy that will probably not work because of the gun culture in the country. The Taliban will not want to disarm, and they will demand an Islamic emirate to be the law of the land. So, peace deals and power sharing agreements are a bridge too far anytime soon. Whatever side Afghans are on, they have been socialized into warfare over generations.

Transnational criminal organizations have also been socialized into a form of warfare that includes greed, power, money, and fear. Transnational organizations have created bureaucracies in a Weberian manner. They stick together because of micro-level solidarity. Charismatic leaders and narco-cultura are difficult for governments to mitigate. Often, when a government's police force eliminates a charismatic leader, more violence ensues as the cartel battles for turf and succession of power.

Now cartels are using technology such as drones and submarines to ship burgeoning amounts of narcotics. Elaborate tunnels for smuggling illegal drugs are becoming more common. Synthetic opioids such as fentanyl are bypassing border controls and can be delivered directly to users through postal systems. Mexican President Andres Manuel López Obrador has revealed that the state cannot win against narco-cartels and has proposed a so-called "hugs not drugs" program. This relies on fighting the relentless poverty with new social welfare constructs that target at-risk people to reduce the cartel's penchant for recruiting low-income people to enact the cartels' dirty deeds. Transnational gangs are global with criminal organizations thriving in Central America, South America, and Russia. These transnational gangs are also socialized into violence and hatred of authority figures.

The global gun trade has kept transnational criminal organizations in business for decades. Mexican cartels have the ideal geographical position to accumulate firearms from a country (United States) that has its own gun culture. In Africa, Libya has become the supplier of guns to many states on the continent. To circumvent this state of affairs, blockchain technology could be used to create databases that track the spread of firearms. This would aid law enforcement in reducing the spread and hunting down perpetrators of illegal arms sales.

While the transnational criminal organizations often target the developing world, climate change is a problem for all states. Numerous U.S. military installations are threatened. Sea level rising will affect bases on the coastlines. Natural disasters such as hurricanes and tornadoes will pit the personnel staffing the bases at risk. Water supplies could become contaminated. Huge numbers of refugees will require constantly changing operations plans and foment chaos. U.S. Naval forces will be stretched thin as they are forced to patrol the polar icecaps that are melting and bringing in near-peer competitors such as Russia into the area of operations. Russia wants to dominate the Arctic. This will create a new territory that can lead to accidents or miscalculations and spark an international incident.

Another country concerned with sea level rises is the United Kingdom. The British military is going through a critical time. It is cutting resources, personnel levels, and weapons systems. Britain has to figure out what the future of its military will be. Will it focus on island defense and defense against climate change, or will it seek to become a more active NATO player to balance against Russia? The Middle East looks like it will be ruled out for further deployments. The British do not really have an expeditionary force or the political will it takes to employ and deploy troops in a conflict zone in another region.

Other U.S. allies are already suffering from the effects of climate change. Bush fires have ravaged Australia with incredibly hot temperatures that have scorched farmland and killed people and livestock. The Australian military also has difficult choices to make. It lives in a dangerous neighborhood with a powerful China continuously flexing its muscles while military budgets are constrained.

Canada is deploying its own forces to help countries deal with climate change. New Zealand is a nation that must divert resources to mitigate the effects of climate change. Africa is in the most danger. Certain economies in African states are agriculturally-focused and floods and droughts brought on by a changing climate are a risk. African governments are already challenged by public health emergencies such as HIV-AIDS and Covid-19, not to mention other communicable diseases that require resources that would normally go to militaries. Fragile and failing states in Africa, such as the Central African Republic and the Democratic Republic of Congo, will become more of a problem in the future.

While military personnel will need new specialized training to deal with and react to climate change, they will also be enhanced by gene editing, robotics, cyborg implants, exoskeletons, and improvements to biotechnology. Exoskeletons have their pluses and minuses. They can give soldiers more speed, strength, and size, but they have disadvantages when it comes to donning the suit and fitting different soldiers' body types. There would also be a period of inertia from moving from a standing position to a motion that goes full-speed.

CRISPR gene editing consists of "molecular scissors" that can breed a super soldier. China is reportedly already doing this. There are obvious ethical ramifications of this therapy. Humans must give consent, but China is an authoritarian and hierarchical culture, especially in the military, and soldiers can simply be ordered to accept the therapy. Meanwhile, CRISPR tool kits are easy to purchase on the open market. These kits can eventually take the best genes from people who are bigger, faster, and stronger, or who have excellent military skills and replicate those attributes in another person.

Cyborg implants or a chip inserted into a human can connect a soldier to a central processing unit. This is life enhancement therapy that would allow soldiers to be monitored for vital signs and enable doctors to react quickly to wounds suffered on the battlefield. The cyborg implants could also work in tandem with an exoskeleton to achieve better command and control over soldiers. This would enable soldiers to have better situational awareness for improved intelligence, surveillance, and reconnaissance at the individual level.

In order to integrate these and other future weapons systems to the U.S. military in a more seamless fashion, it is necessary to merge research and development centers into military bases. This can lead to advances in technologies such as hypersonic missiles. Hypersonics are bursting onto the defense scene. The arms race is on as Russia and China are developing their own hypersonic weapons programs. Combat is evolving into a stand-off missile fight. This is affecting the strategy and techniques of forces such as the U.S. Marine Corps since missiles are replacing the need for a direct kinetic attack using humans.

Air defense artillery will soon be dominated by lasers that can shoot down enemy aircraft or drones. These will be mounted on vehicles and ships. Electromagnetic rail guns can also defend against enemy aircraft, cruise missiles, and ballistic missiles. Rail guns fire a 45-pound projectile at speeds up to 5,000 miles per hour. This is a kinetic round that does not use an explosion with gun powder. Parts of these kinds of weapons systems could potentially be created with 3D printing. These new technologies will be enabled with 5G networks.

Quantum computing is the next technology that will re-shape the battlefield. It will control drone swarms, improve cryptography and encryption, and enhance radar and sonar. Drone-on-drone warfare is coming to the battlefield as well. Drones are becoming smaller. They are now able to fit in the palm of the hand. Unmanned ships are becoming more prevalent. This includes undersea unmanned vehicles.

Unmanned vehicles can be controlled by the human mind or connected to the Internet of military things, which can lead to a greater propensity of a cyber intrusion. Cyber warfare will become more difficult to define and this creates hazards on the propensity of striking back after a cyber event. Cyber war will also enter outer space. The new U.S. Space Force is ready for this state of affairs, or so they claim. Countries will attempt to jam each other's satellites. Perfect storm cyber-attacks will become a fact of life. This will trickle down to the individual soldier as cyber analysts will look to new tools such as virtual reality headsets to create an immersive environment that is better able to react against incoming cyber-attacks.

Russia is dominating the cyber realm and it will also seek to dominate information warfare. Information operations come second nature to the Kremlin and its intelligence organs. Bots and human trolls, a Russian specialty, will continue to be a major part of the information operations domain. China also uses information warfare against Taiwan and Hong Kong to ensure that neither of these provinces achieve a complete and enduring independence. Deep fakes are becoming a bigger aspect of information operations, along with media manipulation of the news of the day.

In conclusion, I hope that this book has answered numerous questions about the future of warfare. It has updated the sociology of war literature – research that has not seen new material in over ten years. I targeted three audiences – the academic, the military practitioner or expert, and the general interest reader who loves envisioning the future. Sociologist Max Weber's views on warfare and the military are exceptionally important in order to understand the future that I envision. And Weber is quoted throughout the book.

Understanding the sociology of war led me to share the advent of mega-trends in urbanization, corruption, migration, and food insecurity. Covid-19 has given rise to the importance of biodefense during pandemics. Over 500,000 people have died due to the disease in the United States alone as of this writing in the Spring of 2021.

The future of warfare, in the end, is human. Humans make accidents, they create awe-inspiring technology, and they can revolutionize the battlefield. But the human fallibility is what drives the ethics and sociology of warfare, and by studying the years ahead and the way forward, we are now better attuned to what humans can accomplish in the brave new future of international security.